THE CITY OF WOODS AND FIELDS

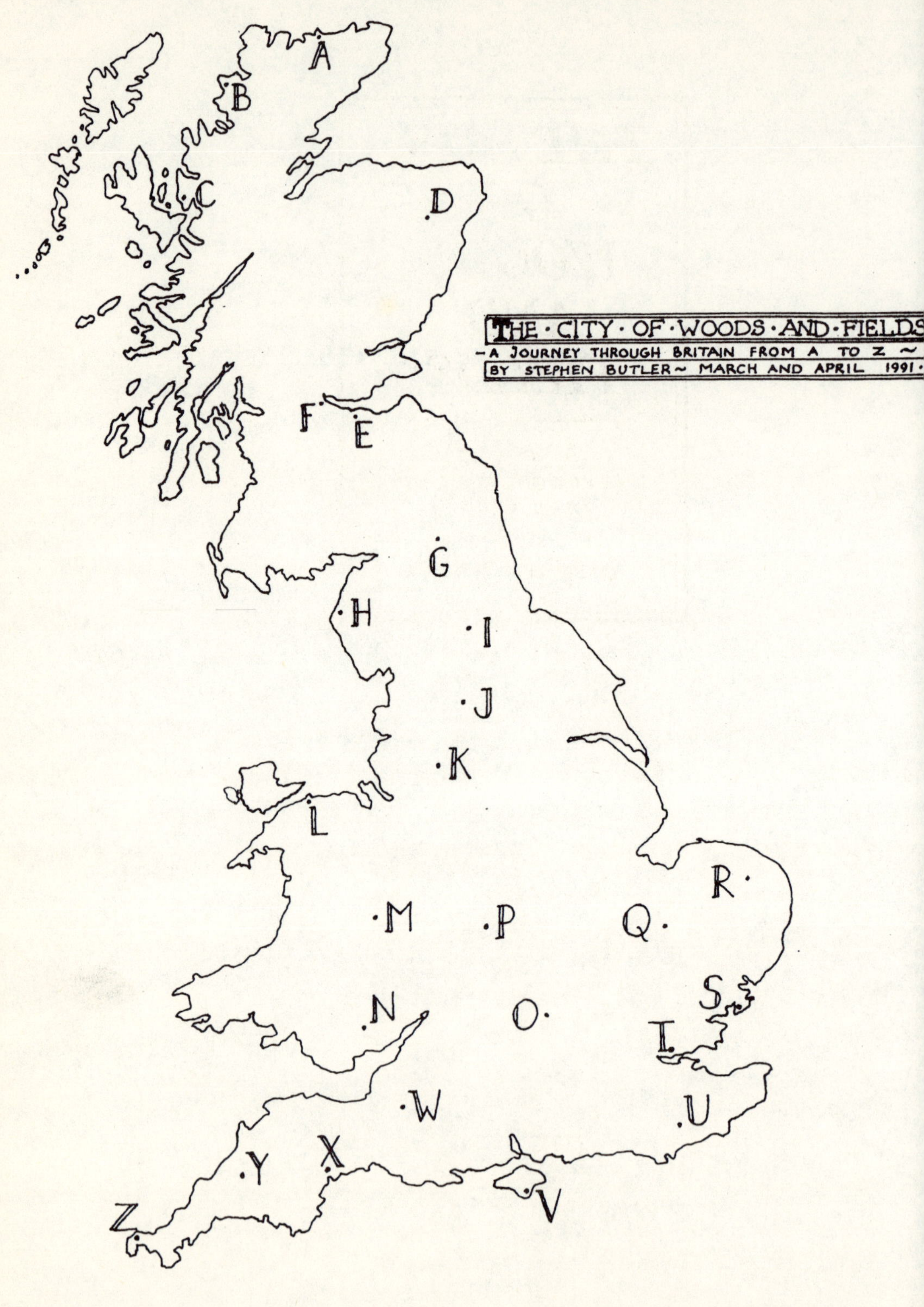

THE · CITY · OF · WOODS · AND · FIELDS
~ A JOURNEY THROUGH BRITAIN FROM A TO Z ~
BY STEPHEN BUTLER ~ MARCH AND APRIL 1991 ·
A
B
C
D
E
F
G
H
I
J
K
L
M
N
O
P
Q
R
S
T
U
V
W
X
Y
Z

THE CITY OF WOODS AND FIELDS

~

*A Journey through Britain from **A** to **Z***

Stephen Butler

MAINSTREAM
PUBLISHING

EDINBURGH AND LONDON

First published in Great Britain 1992 by
MAINSTREAM PUBLISHING COMPANY (EDINBURGH) LTD
7 Albany Street
Edinburgh EH1 3UG

ISBN 1 85158 354 8 (cloth)

A catalogue record for this book is available from the British Library

Typeset in 10/11.5pt Ehrhardt by Intype, London
Printed in Great Britain by Billing & Sons, Worcester

For Kate

Travel broadens the mind 'til you can't get your head out-of-doors.

Elvis Costello

Many thanks are due to the following people:

For permitting: Tim Waterstone
For fixing: Andrew Jaffrey Smith
For encouraging: Douglas McCreath
For agreeing: Bill Campbell
For long-suffering: Natalie Caira, Alan Clifford and Richard Barker
For repairing: Jim Wood
For lending: Fionna Doney, Ron Hill, Katrine MacPhail, Jane and David Fleming
For accommodating: Steve Bromley, Sarah Shalgosky, Sarah Knights, Tony Barnett, Julia and Geoff King and David Butler
For understanding: Kate Powis

CONTENTS

PROLOGUE

I am glad I resisted the temptation to set off on my journey in the depths of midwinter. Our inability to cope with even a few centimetres of snow is something we Britons are almost proud of. Roads and railways grind to a halt. People rub their hands together gleefully at the first sight of a snowflake and look forward to a morning in bed. Snow-tyres and chains, ubiquitous throughout northern Europe, are almost unknown here. British drivers, convinced that they are the finest in the world – let's face it, everybody else is *foreign* – but in fact arrogant and overconfident, refuse to adjust their speed or distance just because Michael Fish has been blethering on about a bit of ice. I recently read a newspaper report of a man stopped by police on a motorway because he was leaning out of the side window whilst driving in a blizzard. It was an old car, he explained, and the windscreen heater and wipers weren't worth repairing.

Blodwen, who usually plods along as if her tyres were liberally coated with superglue, becomes positively skittish on icy roads, wiggling her bottom as if in the finals of *Come Dancing*. Luckily it is almost impossible to travel at a dangerous speed in a Morris Minor which has passed 198,000 miles, or possibly 298,000 – I'm not sure.

So I creep through the slush at 35 miles per hour, doing my best to prevent others from overtaking me – for their own safety, of course. Unfortunately, this has a negative effect on my fellow-commuters, whose frustration at being 'stuck' behind a J-registered vehicle is such that they will take almost suicidal risks in order to get past and continue – at 38 or even 39 miles per hour – with a view through the windscreen uncluttered by relics of Britain's once-proud motor industry. Having narrowly cheated death, they have the added satisfaction of reaching their destination at least three seconds before I do. No, winter in Britain is no time to be out on the roads, particularly if you plan, as I do, to cover the length of the country from north to south. It's not the rain or the snow or the cold that frighten me. It's my fellow humans.

A Morris teaches you the Christian virtues. It forces you to turn the other cheek, for if someone carves you up you cannot respond aggressively except by hitting the horn (which only functions during MOT tests in Blodwen's case). You ease up and let them pull in just before they meet the oncoming truck. Getting into a Morris is like putting on a cassock; as we know, in Britain that means that you are to be treated with contempt.

My original plan was to depart in the spring of 1990. My employer had generously agreed to two weeks' paid leave of absence, with the other two weeks taken off my holiday allowance. A month or so before the departure date the manager of the shop where I work announced that she was leaving. I applied for and got her job, but could hardly justify departing for a month immediately afterwards. So I decided to go in the autumn. Unfortunately, the Powers-that-Be decreed that the branch would be audited during the month I had chosen. Another apologetic letter departed to the publishers. By now I know better than to make any firm promises. I did toy with the idea of a heroic journey through the vicissitudes of a British winter, but the car, sensing this madness, displayed a vast range of psychosomatic symptoms and I abandoned the plan. During the past three months Blodwen has had new rockers, a de-coke, a new rear suspension spring, a new mainbeam light, a new exhaust, a new dynamo, a new windscreen washer pump, and a new battery. Before I set off she will need another headlight bulb, a new indicator unit, two new tyres, new pistons and rings and a replacement gearbox. Perhaps, after all, it is fortunate that I was delayed. I plan to leave at the end of March, not a season renowned for its balmy sunshine but giving me at least a 50–50 chance of survival should Blodwen give up the ghost between, say, Achiltibuie and Ullapool. Somewhere along the way, the mileometer will pass 99999.9 again and perhaps Blodwen will respond to this landmark by rediscovering her lost youth. Maybe I'll give the old girl a lick of paint to boost her psychologically. Or maybe I'll just hoover the carpet.

Comparisons are odious, say the British – a statement of the most staggering hypocrisy in the most class-conscious society in the world. In endeavouring to write a British travelogue, one is inevitably confronted by the awful knowledge that so much has been written so well and from so many perspectives over the past 500 years. Johnson and Boswell, Priestley, James, Defoe, Morton, Chesterton, Cobbett, Fiennes, Carlyle – how will I ever fit all those ghosts into the back of a Morris van? To say nothing of the still-lively bulk of Messrs Theroux, Raban, Murphy, Wallington and his dog . . . The answer, I decided early on, is to pretend ignorance of this magnificent heritage (though in most cases I don't have to pretend), find my own angle, resolutely stick to reading novels in the period leading up to my departure and pray that I don't reiterate in feebler, less lucid prose the observations of these illustrious predecessors. Of one thing I am confident, however; if ever there was a country which, however often it is crossed, however tellingly described and thoroughly probed, will always yield up further surprises, bizarre or beautiful, then that country is Britain. Not simply because, as has often been remarked, Britain has an astonishingly varied geography for its size, but because we British are so downright weird.

As for the angle, having realised that I wanted to write a travel book about Britain, and having astonished myself by making the opportunity to do so, I was thrown into a state of panic as to how to go about it. Circumnavigation has been done so often that the edges of the island are wearing smooth in places. There is a deep groove from Land's End to John O'Groats called the Charity Rut. The pavements of our major cities are littered with Bainbridges, Priestleys and Betjemens. The entire country is sinking under the weight of home thoughts which arrive continuously from abroad. There is no aspect of our national culture or character which has not been held up for ridicule by one American or another. The vast weight of writings about British rural life from Scilly to Shetland forms a deep mouldering mulch in the basements of public libraries throughout the land. Given only one month in which to add my ha'porth to this treasury I could not hope to be thorough. I would have little time to pause and summon adjectives when confronted by awe-inspiring vistas, or to question Britons probingly about their cultural underwear. Provided Blodwen did not let me down, I would be here and gone with barely time to make mental polaroids of what I saw. I needed a way of making the journey interesting in itself – not so much an angle as a gimmick.

I already knew that the journey would be for charity. Partly, this was simply expedient; a Good Cause is necessary when pleading with your boss for time off on full pay. Waterstone's Booksellers had recently been involved, naturally enough, with fundraising for the British Dyslexia Association, so there was no difficulty there. (Incidentally the BDA is based very aptly in Reading.) One problem remained: how to make the journey a fitting way to raise money for that particular cause.

Light bulb overhead: 26 letters in the alphabet; 26 different places in a month, each beginning with a different letter in the correct sequence. This (I hoped) would also allow me a few days leeway for rest and repairs. Even better: do not choose the destinations in advance. Start at somewhere beginning with 'A', open the atlas at random, pick a 'B' and set off . . . right through the alphabet and right down the country. Brilliant. But wait – was this possible? Somewhat guiltily I opened the road atlas and selected one of the many places beginning with 'A' which are conveniently scattered across northern Scotland (since I live in Scotland it seemed sensible to begin there – besides there are 'Z'-places in Cornwall but none up here). Plenty of 'B's within striking distance. Lots of 'C's, 'D's and 'E's . . . it would work, though I'd have to be careful with 'J', 'O' and . . . well, with 'X' I'd just have to cheat. Not wishing to spoil the prospect of adventure further, I closed the atlas.

Then a terrible thought struck me. What if, on arriving at (for instance) my 'M' (chosen that morning in 'L'), I found as I climbed stiffly from behind the wheel onto a deserted, rainy street that there was absolutely nothing to write about? I envisaged a rainy Sunday in, say, Lincolnshire; around five in the evening there is not a soul in sight. The pubs and shops are closed, the Primitive Methodist Chapel is locked and decaying. Beyond the line of pebble-dashed semis the beet-fields stretch like . . . like Lincolnshire. Only the flickering of television screens behind Dralon curtains betrays that the place is inhabited. What then?

I would have three options. First, I could knock on somebody's door. 'Hello, I'm travelling through Britain for charity in a 1971 Morris Minor van . . .' Slam! Secondly, I could hunker down in the van and write deathless prose about a rainy Sunday night in a Lincolnshire village where everyone is watching *Strike it Lucky*. About 12 words should suffice. Or thirdly . . . tentatively, I opened the atlas again. I found Lincolnshire, and somewhere beginning with 'M'. Then I breathed a sigh of relief, and lit a cigarette with shaking hands. There were at least four other places within 20 miles beginning with that letter. I could simply drive off and pretend I had never been there. I could cheat. Later I realised that if I were to look for something in each place beginning with the same letter – Litter in Letchworth, for example – this might artificially generate something to say about even the most tedious place, and so remove the need to cheat. This resolution was never very strongly adhered to, however, and became more of a distraction than an analytical device.

I spend hours looking at maps. To me they are magical objects, mysterious and powerful. To sit and read a map of somewhere that I have never been is an intense and particular pleasure, very different from the utilitarian function of a map in the field, relating this clump of trees to that green mark on the paper. Reading a map is like reading a work of fiction; I agree with A. Wainwright, the Sage of the Fells, who remarked that on the whole he would much rather read a map than a novel. Indeed, I have known novels with much less content than a good Ordnance Survey sheet – 151 for instance, or 137. I await the day when *Ipswich and the Naze* is shortlisted for the Booker Prize. Maps are poetic, precise, romantic, sexy. Their coded description of the world is a wonderful shorthand distillation of a topographical epic, as if *War and Peace* had been reduced to a series of *haikus*.

As a child I spent many hours making maps of imaginary countries:

treasure islands surrounded by salivating sharks; conurbations full of airports, launchpads and tortuous interchanges; wilderlands roamed by orcs, dragons and trolls, dark with forests and spiked by awesome mountains. At school, in Geography, I produced state-of-the-art maps of peanut cultivation in the southern USA and population density in the Seine Valley using a pencil honed to lethal sharpness. To read a map is to travel in imagined but not imaginary space. It is like taking part in one of those multiple-choice adventure games – the terrain is defined but the choice of direction is yours. You travel mentally not only in space but in time, for maps whether old or new are historical documents. They contain the marks of mankind's triumphs and tribulations, advances, conquests, vanities, retreats, defeats. When I first came to Scotland I found to my delight that I was living on the absolute northern frontier of the Roman Empire; a line, now more clearly visible on a map than on the ground, held by the Emperor Septimus Severus for a mere seven years. This deliciously exaggerated the already strong sensation that any Englishman has in Scotland of standing on the edge of the known world.

I said 'mankind' earlier advisedly for maps seem to be of greater interest to men than to women. My wife finds them dull or unintelligible or both; so do many women I know. It has been men, I suppose, who for the most part have made marks on the land, made maps necessary. Maps are of the male world. Men love to have maps, especially in that masculine preserve, the car. Cars are totems of power, and maps are the circuit diagrams of the male machine.

Britain's roads are so well-signposted for the most part that it baffles me why anybody should actually need to consult a road atlas, except for entertainment, more than once or twice a year. For daydreaming, or for the site of a particular battle, certainly... but to get from Cockfosters to Cheam? Come off it. The best journeys are made up as you go along; not knowing where you are precisely forces you to notice things and turns the most tedious suburban journey into an adventure. By all means take a map, but don't look at it until you are actually lost. Aren't the most boring people the ones who will harangue you endlessly about whether it is quicker to leave the motorway at Junction 14 and take the bypass or carry on until Junction 15 and cut back through the industrial estate? Who cares how quick it is? It is better to travel hopefully than to overtake.

If I have time on my hands I very often open an atlas at random, and more often than not an atlas of the British Isles. Apart from the endless fascination of topography and history there are simpler pleasures to be had, not least the naming of places. Take, for instance, East Anglia. Full of lovely, resonant names: Bradfield Combust, Bruisyard, Stoke by Clare, Pixey Green. Pink Green is a classic. There are historical titbits to be gleaned: Norse names like Thwaite, Norman names like Walsham-le-Willows, Anglo-Saxon ones like Wetheringsett. Self-explanatory names: Red

House, Great Green. Peculiar and baffling names such as Rishangles or Occold. Quaint names (Combs, Upend), magical names (Drinkstone, Fingal Street – what was he doing so far from his cave?) and hilarious names (Dallinghoo, Wissett, Creeting, Copdock). Turning the pages, who on earth lives at Timble? As the eye roams across South Wales amongst the Porthhyrhyds and Cwmbachs, how delightful to come upon a village called Red Roses. What happens, if anything, in Reiff? (Look it up and you'll see why I ask.) Is Cold Norton cold? What does Eccup mean? Is Bugthorpe plagued by insects? Surely the inhabitants of Nidd must have a sense of humour, though perhaps not as well-developed as those of Frisby-on-the-Wreake, or Scrooby. Why is Whale 30 miles from the sea? How do you pronounce Ae? And what kind of a name for a place, for God's sake, is Fodderletter?

The great appeal of this plan is that it artificially extends the dimensions of this tight little island into something resembling the size of Asia. We live, after all, cheek-by-jowl on a piece of flotsam which can be traversed with the aid of a Ford Sierra and a thermos of black coffee in under 24 hours. Quicker still if you take that short-cut outside Wantage past the sewage works and then second left beyond the vicarage. My journey is designed to chop this pitifully small remnant of a once-great empire into microcosmic pieces. Despite its alphabetical logic, it will be a random journey, which will, I hope, inject a sense of the pioneering spirit as I trundle past the gasworks, even if by some chance my journey takes me somewhere which is already so well-known that its inhabitants paper their bedrooms with copies of last year's tourist guide. So I won't worry too much. There's nobody the British like to read about so much as themselves; how else would our appalling local newspapers make any money? In any case, I'm the sort of person who stops, does a three-point turn, and goes back to look *behind* the gasworks.

LEAVING

A razor-sharp wind cut across the flood-plain of the Tay. The stars were very bright, dimmed only in the north-east by the reddish glow of Dundee and in the north-west by that of Perth. In the harsh light of the fluorescent lamp in Jimmy Wood's workshop we reminisced about epic drives and heroic breakdowns we had known while he fitted a new water-pump, the last of a series of new intestinal gadgets installed by virtue of necessity or precaution beneath Blodwen's bonnet over the past few weeks. Chief amongst these had been a new set of pistons; Jimmy had saved the old ones in order to show me the deep grooves etched in them where the engine had once seized up. The archaeology of the Morris Minor. Blodwen had been drinking oil like a jackaroo drinks lager; I had two spare gallons in the back to take with me.

It was 11.30 by the time Jimmy closed the bonnet and said, 'Well, whatever trouble ye have on your travels I don't think they'll be mechanical.' My feet and fingers were numb. Surely I was mad to be setting off the next day, 28 March, in brass monkey weather? I handed over to Jimmy a sizeable proportion of my total expenses for the trip; far more than I had anticipated, despite his ridiculously generous rates. The bond of Morris Minor owners, present and former, is a strong and sentimental one, as I was to discover. 'When I think of the number of these I've fitted over the years. . .' Jimmy would say, holding up some indecipherable component with a sigh, like a father putting Elastoplast on the grazed knee of a wayward child.

My fear of hypothermia was not allayed by the fact that the four-mile drive home was insufficient to warm the engine and thus, via the heater, the lower portions at least of the driver. I crawled into bed after midnight and lay awake thinking about all the things which could go wrong. A Morris Minor has about 2,000 different components. It took me a while to get to sleep.

The next morning only the weather seemed encouraging, bright and warm despite the assurances of the BBC that it was in fact raining hard. In the usual way of departure days, the morning was spent bad-temperedly searching for small but vital things which were there yesterday, getting in the way of the innocent pursuits of wife and children and periodically locking myself in my study, chain-smoking and staring glumly at the road atlas. Gradually the car filled up with equipment: sleeping bags, blankets, a borrowed tent, cooking utensils, spare components, tools, cameras, binoculars, a plastic crate of books both informative and entertaining, water bottles, food, boots, old newspapers (for the floor – the windscreen leaks), and reams of writing paper and a tinful of writing implements. Finally a vast suitcase containing nearly every item of clothing that I possess, and a small tape recorder housed in the glove compartment on which I intended to convey, in seamless prose, my instant impressions of This Great Country Of Ours.

By lunchtime I was nervous and nauseous and my palms were sweating; never mind that I would be back in a few days on my way south. (The one concession in my determinedly random schedule was to be at home for my daughter's fourth birthday.) This was it. I had to resist the urge to drive half a mile round the back of the hill and spend a month camping and making it all up.

'Is this you away, then?' the neighbours kept asking on their way past to the shops.

'This is it,' I replied, and they would smile indulgently at the off-white, rust-specked car with the suspiciously squashy-looking tyres. I felt as mad as their expressions told me I must be.

Leaving was as awkward as I expected. Georgia was engrossed in *Sesame Street* and said 'Bye Dad' without glancing away from the screen. Maeve, 16 months, tried to pull my nose off, presumably as a keepsake. Kate kissed me and told me to drive carefully and went inside without waiting to see me off. The mileometer read 99100.9. I drove into Perth keeping under 50 miles per hour on Jimmy's advice because the pistons needed wearing in for the first couple of hundred miles. I stopped at Halfords ostensibly to buy a couple of spare bits and pieces but mostly just to delay the serious business a little longer. I contemplated a tin of radiator sealant for about five minutes, wondering if £2.99 was a worthwhile investment, but the radiator was barely a year old. Halfords also stock the really important things; I bought a Twix and a carton of Ribena and then, taking the bull by the horns, I hit the most dangerous road in Scotland, the A9 north to Inverness.

16

As with many dangerous roads, the problem is not the topography but the people who use it; after only five miles I was almost killed by an idiot in a Fiesta who hadn't realised that the dual carriageway had run out a mile back. But the traffic was light and the sky was cloudless and the flat fields north of Perth were tilled to the colour of *café-au-lait*. A steady 50 mph gave me ample opportunity to concentrate my hypochondriac tendencies on Blodwen's engine. What was that odd rattle? Surely she didn't squeak like that yesterday? Was it just the slight gradient or was there a Serious Loss of Power? These concerns reciprocally manifested themselves in sudden muscular aches and stabbing pains in my neck and back; a truly symbiotic relationship.

Lack of sleep the previous night had left me fazed and jittery; the tensions of the morning had ganged up and were munching at my frontal lobes. Past Pitlochry, second only to Aviemore in the Ugliest Town in the Highlands stakes – a town so full of wool shops that it appears to be not so much built as knitted. From Dunkeld, just south of the Jumper Capital, the road smashes through lovely rocky scenery; the police attribute many of the fatalities on this road to motorists gawping at the view. The Pass of Killie-crankie, now about as romantic as the Bedford bypass, leads into Glen Garry, and the road climbs steadily for 15 miles to the Pass of Drumochter between seriously big mountains with unpronounceable names. Streaks of snow appeared on the tawny hillsides and screes on either side; here and there long plumes of blue-grey smoke mingled with the golden afternoon haze as the grouse moors were burnt off in preparation for the coming new growth. The steady roar of the engine and the warm afternoon sun made me gradually less nervous and more drowsy. Now and then a big Volvo or Mercedes overloaded with children and retrievers would glide past on their way to a second home, and more rarely Blodwen would summon up the energy to pass a tanker or a tractor toiling up the interminable incline. But for the most part I had the opportunity to shake off my blues and little by little begin to look forward to the coming journey with equanimity and then the adrenalin rush of anticipation and joy. I was away! The world, as Arthur Daley would say, was my lobster.

I also began to think seriously about what I was doing, and to make verbal notes as I went along. One soon runs out of adjectives for the colour of Scottish mountains, however, and I realised when I found myself describing a conifer plantation that only a certain amount of detail would be advisable.

At the top of the Pass of Drumochter I stopped in a lay-by to stretch my legs and roll a cigarette; I had deliberately bought rolling tobacco to reduce my consumption on the road since I have not yet mastered the art of manufacturing cigarettes whilst in motion. A cursory inspection of the car revealed water dripping from the grille; closer study showed that this emanated from a hairline crack amongst the mummified moths on the radiator. Immediately I was in an utter panic; the road was empty as far as the eye could see, I was 2,000 feet up and the only sounds were of running water, some in a burn below the road and some onto my shoes from the car. I cursed myself for ignoring the can of sealant which had virtually pleaded with me to be bought in Perth, but removal of the cap revealed only the slightest proportion of water gone, and I eased down Glen Truim to Newtonmore, my mind flashing vivid pictures of the tiny fissure rapidly becoming something the size of Robert the Bruce's cave. I bought a can of sealant in a spick and span Esso station, read the instructions about 13 times and was reassured to see that the drip had stopped. In fact, now I came to think of it, it had stopped by the time I opened the bonnet and put the sealant in.

Onwards without incident, save a couple of near-death experiences with boy racers, towards Inverness. I was having trouble coming to terms with what I was doing; this rapid journey up the A9 was not really part of the journey proper, merely the quickest way of getting to my first destination, Armadale in Sutherland. Yet I felt very ambivalent about shooting through this great central fastness of the Grampians – which for many people *is* Scotland, a kind of spiritual summary in rock and heather – and glimpses of lovely fast shallow rivers – Tay, Tummel, Garry, Findhorn – did not lessen the feeling that I was missing something of quintessential importance. I tried to console myself with mental assurances that in the first place these mountains were so well-known as to be almost worn out with boots and tyres, and secondly that one of the points of the exercise was to look for the less famous, even the banal, in an attempt to redress the bias of tourism and armchair travel towards the stereotypes of lovely topography. But I found it difficult to convince myself of this, and the snowfields of the high Cairngorms turning pink and orange in the late afternoon sun to the east seemed to confirm the pointlessness of my ambition. As it turned out, these concerns – the difficulty of ignoring the beautiful, the feeling that I was bypassing all that was significant and meaningful in the landscape – were to become one of the overriding themes of the journey as a whole, a kind of personal battle against the ideologies of modern tourism complicated by the fact that I was experiencing Britain in the most conventional way of the modern tourist – from behind the wheel of a car – and by the realisation that my expectations and enjoyment of the country were almost insurmountably conventional too.

So I concentrated hard on the fact that much Scottish upland scenery is about as attractive as the outskirts of Calais on a wet Sunday, and a good deal less varied, and that the mountainsides were crammed with people so unimaginative that they thought climbing a sheer rock face in the middle of nowhere a really interesting thing to do, and that in any case the whole area was an artificially-sustained environment designed solely so that people with more money than sense could spend their time slaughtering dumb animals for fun.

By the time I came down the steep hillside over the lovely Moray Firth, and crossed the delicate suspension bridge by Inverness to the Black Isle (not an island at all, but a promontory of wooded farmland), I was determined to find something appealing in the rows of modern grey pebble-dashed houses of North Kessock, the commuter development which lies at the north foot of the bridge. Alas, North Kessock is undeniably one of the crassest and most tedious collections of breezeblock ever assembled. Like many such places, it has been built so that people can enjoy a view, but to enjoy the view of the firth and the rolling hills one has to forget that one is in North Kessock.

A shallow, muddy little estuary, the Beauly Firth, runs into the Moray Firth at the narrow neck of the Great Glen here, and since it was by now evening rather than afternoon I decided that this might as well be my first night's destination. Along the little single-track road on the north shore a campsite was marked on my map; I nosed the car along in second gear, almost completely blinded by the low sun shining directly into my eyes and exaggerated by the gleaming mud and water. I turned into the campsite and a man came out of the caravan which served as an office.

'Hello, I'm looking for a tent-pitch, please.'

'We're not open for tents.'

I stared around the large and completely empty field before us. Somehow I could not quite grasp what he meant; here was a place where you pay a small fee, take your tent out of your car, and put it up somewhere in a totally empty field of about five acres. How could the place 'not be open' for tents? Now, if this had been a hotel or a guest-house and the owner had said, 'I'm sorry, we do not have any rooms available,' I could have coped – dust-sheets still spread, no hot water, beds not aired; fine. What did this man have to do before he was 'open for tents'? Comb the grass? Buy a wallet to put my five-pound note in? Shave?

'I don't need to hire a tent, I just want somewhere to put mine up.'

'We're not open for tents.'

'I see,' I said slowly, 'It's just that the sign saying CAMPING confused me. Well, thanks anyway.'

All along the shoreline in the lay-bys and passing places were large yellow signs: POLICE NOTICE/ NO CAMPING/ NO OVERNIGHT PARKING. Bugger that, I thought, and mentally prepared a little speech: 'Well, officer, I have a long way to go and I felt very tired so I felt it would not be safe to continue until I had had a rest. No – what signs? The sun was in my eyes.'

I found a grassy bank under a gnarled and lichen-covered little oak just above the beach of big round shingle stones, plastic fishing nets, broken glass, rusted cans and nervous oyster-catchers. I had a little Camping Gaz stove with me, and brewed tea and cooked a can of beans and sausages. I sat on the wave-cut edge of the bank with my feet on the beach and watched the sun set as I ate. They say that food cooked out of doors tastes better; this must be true as I managed to eat the entire contents of the tin. The sky was cloudless and angelically blue; the hills turned to silhouettes. It began to get cold. I smoked a carefully-crafted postprandial roll-up and hauled the borrowed tent out of the van.

Despite the apparently endless stream of guy-ropes and pegs which fell from the bag when I shook it out, I managed to construct something which closely resembled a tent without much difficulty, an inconsiderately placed gorse bush notwithstanding. I then repaired to the front seat of the van and sat writing up my observations from the tape recorder first by the fading sunlight and then, shivering and cramped, by torchlight. By the time I had finished it was completely dark. Occasionally a car would come along the lane; one had parked in the next lay-by and I could dimly hear voices and the hiss of cans of drink being opened. A man walking his dog came up the road and peered at the van and the bright orange tent and said nothing, but on his way back ten minutes later ventured that it was a braw evening. Lovely, I agreed, whereupon he added that there might well be a touch o' frost bimmorning. Since the air temperature was already about minus six, this country wisdom failed to impress me.

I crawled into the tent and after the usual yogic contortions of undressing and sorting out mats and sleeping-bags, lay down and closed my eyes. It was 9.30. By 10.30 I was still awake. Apart from vehicles in the lane, some of which slowed down or stopped presumably to stare at the van and the tent, the car radio was on in the next lay-by, a number of trains had left Inverness station and grumbled away into the mountains and the constant traffic on the A9 sent a continuous low booming rumble echoing around the surrounding hills. The number of oyster-catchers, redshank and other weirdly-piping birds along the shore seemed to have assumed a record-breaking level, competing for the airwaves with at least three owls, something small and scurrying in the gorse bush and the beating of my own heart, which could probably have been heard in Aberdeen. So it was with some surprise that I found myself waking from a dream about swimming, having slept almost a whole hour. The dream seemed to have been prompted by the sound of the lapping waves on the shingle, which from inside the tent sounded about six inches away. I clambered out; a full moon fell on my campsite like a searchlight. The waters of the firth were a reassuring 20 yards away. The traffic over the bridge had quietened to the level of an Iron Maiden concert two miles distant; the birds had either flown away or, I hoped, drowned; the car had gone from the next lay-by. The tent was stiff with frost. I slithered back inside and slept for seven hours.

ARMADALE

Atomic power and alpines

By the time I had folded up the contents of the tent and stuffed the still-frosted acre of canvas back into its bag my fingers were completely numb. I walked around eating a bowl of muesli and drinking a cup of tea to keep my circulation going and, having washed up and locked the van, set off along the lane for a morning constitutional. By then it was seven o'clock; the dawn chorus had woken me soon after five, and I had lain awake listening to the chuckle of shelduck and the gradually increasing noise of the road and railway, reluctant to leave my cocoon. I was determined to ensure that I got sufficient exercise each day and the simplest way of doing this seemed to walk for an hour before I did anything else, not taking notes or thinking about the trip. Like most such resolutions, it didn't survive long.

The early morning is always the best time of day for a country walk and this was no exception; only two vehicles came down the lane, their drivers nodding cautiously at me as I stood back to let them pass. On one side the half-full firth had a mobile fringe of small waders, shelduck, curlew and rooks. The landward side was marked by a drystone wall covered in grey lichen which bordered a gently-rising series of tilled fields and pastures backed by woodland and long stands of mature Scots pine. One of the dead branches of an oak transformed itself into a buzzard and flapped heavily away. Rabbits scattered like starlets disturbed in their dressing room by Errol Flynn. I was curious about what appeared to be a stick standing upright in the middle of the road; 50 yards away I decided that it couldn't be a stick unless it was wedged in a hole in the tarmac; 20 yards closer I decided that it was a stick after all; I was within ten yards when the stoat gave up trying to hypnotise me, got off its hind legs and bolted into the undergrowth.

The rising sun revealed high snow-covered mountains to the west which must have been shrouded in haze the evening before: Beinn a' Bha'ach Ard and Carn Ban in the Erchless Forest the colour of tinned salmon. I turned back having reached the ruined tower of Redcastle and photographed a very dead sheep. By the time I returned to the car the frost had melted and the day seemed set fair. I drove into Muir of Ord to buy milk and gas cylinders at a wonderful shop, a warren-like combination of stationer's, baker's, ironmonger's, newsagent's, grocer's, delicatessen and gift shop staffed by a squadron of garrulous wifies, and then went to the petrol station, to perform my ablutions in the filthiest lavatory this side of Istanbul. By now faintly worried about getting behind schedule I bypassed Dingwall and pressed on up the Cromarty Firth to Alness and Invergordon. Here the flat, sandy fields are given a surreal backdrop by oilrigs moored inshore for repair, looming over the long lines of Scots pine and wobbling in the heated air. The light has the fluorescent, almost shadowless quality that one only finds on the eastern seaboard, bouncing and refracting off the pallid brown sea and the beige dust of the fields, and the effect is as if one has stepped into a Salvador Dalí dreamscape.

Progress on the cratered and meandering road around the coast of Easter Ross was slow; there seemed to be roadworks every two hundred yards, and where there were no roadworks there were tractors or ambling cattle, so it was lunchtime by the time I reached Bonar Bridge, where the road forks right for Thurso and Wick, and left for the bleak moorland of the far North. I swung left and parked in a lay-by which advertised itself as a 'viewpoint'. The view consisted of a large expanse of long, dead grass, two portakabins, a line of pylons, a conifer plantation, a wrecked car and a vast and hideous Victorian Gothic pile on a distant hill. Closer to hand amongst the scree of litter were the twin delights one always hopes to see when eating a picnic lunch, the Used Sanitary Towel and the Contraceptive Sheath hanging triumphantly from a flowering gorse branch. The other occupant of the lay-by was a farmer bent under the bonnet of a Daihatsu jeep so rusty that its original colour was indeterminable. I offered to sell him a used Morris Minor van; like many others he wished that he had never sold the one he had owned. Eventually the jeep coughed into life ('Three bloody hours I've been here') and I was left alone with my cheese and onion crisps and the inevitable NO OVERNIGHT PARKING sign. Why the hell not? What possible harm could it do to fall asleep in this insalubrious lay-by?

A high veil of cloud turned the sun white, then hid it, and the wind picked up. By the time I reached the shallow, stony River Shin it was a chilly gale. Lairg is the last village of any size on this road for 40 miles; beyond it the land is an almost flat wilderness of grim and unvarying moor.

The tiny road lies across it like a tape-measure on a brown carpet and the wind becomes the dominant element, attempting to carve your face in the way that it has carved the scattered rocks and, one feels, scoured away all surface features. This hellish landscape is unrelieved except by immense plantations of small conifers, fenced off like nuclear arms dumps and so thickly planted that the passage of anything larger than a fox through them would be impossible. For a great distance they stand on both sides of the road, a black 15-foot chasm through which one passes like a pinball in a groove. In contrast to a mature conifer plantation, silent and cathedral-like if ecologically unsound, these wretched and apparently pointless monocultures on the Sutherland road make even the dourest telegraph-pole farm seem like tropical rainforest. When one emerges once more the limitless expanse of bog and rock seems as inviting as the beach at Cannes. You suddenly notice the subtlety of the colouring of this undulating ground: fawn, mustard, bitter chocolate, pine green, with here and there an iron-coloured lochan.

About 15 miles north of Lairg is a lonely pub, the Crask Inn, with one attendant cottage. Local wisdom has it that it never closes and I suppose there cannot be a remoter hostelry anywhere in Britain. It stands a mile or so from the watershed; I had been driving up the valley of the little River Tirry, crossing and recrossing its pebbly bed, and climbing imperceptibly for many miles. Now the water by the road flowed north instead of south, and just as subtly the road descends Strath Vagastie towards the tiny settlement of Altnaharra. I stopped at about the highest point, and fought with the wind to open the door. No trees, no buildings, no fences, no bushes, no birds or animals, no sound or movement but the wind. Apart from the strip of tarmac it seemed that mankind had never touched the place. I was quickly disillusioned of this false impression, however, by the arrival of a gigantic quarry truck which was too wide to pass. I hastily climbed in and set off as fast as I dared on the buckled surface, suspension groaning like a ship's timbers. The truck driver bullied me along, three feet from my rear, until I took advantage of a passing place to stop again, for something extraordinary had happened to the landscape. It had sprouted a mountain. This was Ben Klibreck, the first of the vast, isolated peaks of the far Northwest. Eight miles long and over 3,000 feet high, Klibreck appears in this desolation like the Lonely Mountain in *The Hobbit*. Although I had often seen images of these peaks on television – Foinaven, Arkle, Canisp, Quinag – this had failed to give an accurate impression of their weird majesty. Although none approach the height of the biggest of the Grampians, their self-containment makes them far more spectacular, and their complex local geology gives each a wholly individual character. Klibreck from the south-west looks as steep and smooth as a limpet on a rock. As the road skirts it and one sees the length of its northern side, the mouldering carcass of a dinosaur comes to mind, sinking over millenia into the surrounding swamp. Now, to the north-west, the peak of Ben Hee appeared as well, a huge beehive.

The road descended more steeply. Smoke drifted across the flanks of Ben Klibreck. I could make out tiny figures up on the mountainside, here beating the smouldering ground, there setting a flaming branch to a fresh swathe of heather the colour of beer. At Altnaharra I turned right along the B873 – the single track on which I had been travelling counted as an A-road, so I masochistically decided to experience the next grade down. This route follows the shore of Loch Naver, and when I say follows I mean just that – it copies faithfully every arabesque of a shoreline which could have been designed by the scribe of the Book of Kells. On the left hand side of the road, which is barely six feet wide, is wet bog scattered with huge boulders the size of houses and small ones like wolf's teeth; on the right, the unfenced drop is just sufficiently high to guarantee that you and your vehicle will be smashed to pieces. The loch is seven miles in length and the road along it perhaps 12 or 13 ornate arm-wrenching, gear-gnashing miles. Thereafter it runs fairly straight down Strath Naver, and the country-side gradually becomes less rocky and more green. This valley, 20 miles in length, contains a dozen or so houses; it was the scene of one of the most brutal episodes of the Highland Clearances, an eyewitness recording that on one night he counted more than 250 croft houses set alight. Such is the price of private fishing; there were gentlemen in waders and Barbour jackets all along the River Naver.

Emerging at the coast near Bettyhill the sky had turned the colour of cinders, and the road afforded glimpses of pale sand beaches between headland cliffs of almost slaty darkness. Even on this relatively calm day the smell of salt spray was strong, yet the sea appeared as unruffled as a sheet of zinc. Bettyhill has a museum of the Strathnaver clearances and a famous Nature Reserve but I was by now too impatient to stop and look around. Seven miles to the east I came to a sign pointing left marked ARMADALE and turned off onto the verge by a cattle-grid at the junction. My small feeling of triumph at reaching here was quickly overwhelmed by the realisation that this was the beginning, not the end.

Armadale lies on the seaward side of the main road, along a single track. The Armadale burn has created a shallow, wide valley of greenery below low moorland hills. The upper end of the valley shows signs of once having been crofted but is now a single farm, with a big farmhouse on the main road. I got out into the wind and drizzle and walked into the village. Old cottages and new houses and bungalows straggled at random along the street, some close together and some separated by a couple of hundred yards. What few low trees and bushes there are, and the telegraph poles and streetlights (yes, they have streetlights) lean drunkenly; everywhere the dry-stone walls are tumbledown and crazy, partially replaced by fenceposts and wire. Old machinery, abandoned cars, tractors, piles of building materials and planks litter the landscape. Here things are simply left where they finally conk out. Sheep wander apparently at liberty in the street, fields and gardens, as do chickens; the smell of the air is wonderful, an equal mix of sea, sheep and peat smoke. I walked right through the village and did not see a soul.

At the seaward end the track forks amongst a denser collection of cottages on more steeply-sloping ground. In this nucleus the ground is a kind of visual cacophany of stone. The dry-stone walls are apparently constructed from rounded, unshaped beachstones; inevitably most have fallen into disrepair and have been clumsily rebuilt or reinforced by wood and wire, but the effect is of a field of stones which by some fantastic accident of nature has been arranged into complex quasi-geometrical shapes. The older houses seem to grow out of this like natural outcrops, each with its lean-to of boulders and corrugated metal, while the new places sit uncomfortably amongst the rubble like a child's building bricks scattered on a gravel path. It is no longer practical to keep up the walls of the little fields; maintaining them must have been an unending, backbreaking labour. They have splayed and disintegrated, and more often than not the new fences lie two or three feet inside or outside the old field-line, for a fallen wall occupies a wide strip of ground. Even within the confines of a tiny village like Armadale there must be many miles of wall. They are an eloquent symbol of the sheer grinding difficulty of living off this land, and they were so finely constructed that they will still dominate the land long after this first generation of wood and wire has rotted and rusted away.

I carried on beyond the last house until, abruptly, unmarked, the road ended an arm's length from the clifftop. A hundred feet below in a narrow cove a couple of small fishing boats were hauled up on the shingle. From here it was possible to see that despite the apparent easiness of the sea the feet of the cliffs were seething and boiling with spray. The most precarious of paths picked its way down to the cove: at the top were a couple of breeze-block sheds and a tank of DERV, a collection of rusted winches and anchors and a copse of poles from which fishing-nets were hung out in the mizzle.

So my first impression of Armadale was of a place which seemed more than half abandoned, a place in which the natural processes of entropy and decay were speeded up like a time-lapse film, and where the parallel phenomena of growth and construction were stunted and muddled by the overweening salt wind. The chilly gloom of the afternoon and the apparent desertion of the village added to this dispiriting – if romantic – atmosphere. Walking back, I met on the road an ancient woman wrapped in a gigantic windcheater – somehow it seemed inevitable that the first person I met would be old – and I asked her whether anybody in the village did bed-and-breakfast. She replied that 'her at the big house' sometimes did but she wasn't sure if she had opened for the season yet. I thought, they have

25

a *season* here? The woman's accent was a combination of Scandinavian vowels and a sing-song Welsh inflexion, with the consonants all sounded by the front of the mouth, not at all like the guttural Highland speech. She walked slowly towards the cliffs, bent double in the wind, her coat flapping as if at any moment she might be lifted clear into the sea.

I was glad to regain the relative comfort of the driving seat, brew myself a cup of tea and try to warm my fingers around it. The wind had left me feeling as if I had been mugged. I was filled with admiration not only for the people who had lived here in the past, but for those who evidently still made a living from the thin soil and the grim sea. I could barely imagine what kept them here; no doubt many more had left than returned. Yet I think that if I came from such a place, a place not so much built as continually fought for, I would find it difficult to abandon so long a struggle, written as it is in lines of stone.

I drove the short distance to the big farmhouse, but the woman there did not have a room ready. She suggested I went to Melvich along the coast. So I drove east, but had not gone far when I passed a sign pointing down the road to Strathy Point: 'B&B 1½ MILES LEFT AT PHONE BOX.' This I could not resist: Strathy Point is one of the most northerly headlands of the coast, sticking out into the Atlantic like a crone's finger. A gorse fire was burning by the road a little way along; a family stood on its windward side and watched apparently with equanimity. I bounced and rattled out over the moor, passing no more than a couple of houses and a few ruined crofts. By the telephone box stood a brand-new pebble-dashed bungalow, into which I was warmly welcomed by Pat Macaskill.

I had come through a succession of weird landscapes that day, yet somehow this was the strangest moment of all, to enter a warm, modern house with brand-new furniture and deep carpets and gleaming paintwork. Well, I thought, what did you expect, a cauldron on the fire and bearskins on the earthen floor? I sat and warmed up in the spotless kitchen surrounded by fridge-freezer, colour television and microwave and stared out of the double-glazed window at a landscape which looked to me like the surface of Uranus. Pat's husband Donald worked as a joiner at Dounreay, the nuclear reprocessing plant a few miles along the coast. Pat herself was from Caithness, but Donald had been born and brought up in the house which stood on the opposite side of the road, now derelict. The cottage they had first lived in was behind the new house. It had been condemned and they had received a grant to build a new place with Donald doing most of the work himself. The wind keened in the eaves, but the snug kitchen and the motionless curtains bore testimony to his craftsmanship.

I explained my journey and talked with Pat about life there whilst playing with Donald Junior, aged three, under the watchful gaze of Michael, three and a half months, from his baby-rocker by the Aga. To the obvious subject of atomic power (Dounreay employs a high percentage of the local population), Pat added that of alpines. It was odd to realise that even here in this bare and inhospitable land, the inhabitants are as keen on gardening as anywhere in this famously horticultural island, although soil and climate severely limit the choice of plants, not to mention winter nights which last from three in the afternoon until ten in the morning. A few days previously Mrs Macaskill had been to a film show in Melvich given by a local garden centre, about alpines; Strathy Point is also the home of one of the rarest of British plants, the alpine *primula scotia*, which flourishes only here and in the Orkneys. Gardening and DIY: the recreations of millions of households from Lerwick to Land's End. The Macaskills' bungalow, with its neat garden borders, matching bathroom suite and PVC double glazing could have been in Cheam or Chepstow or Church Stoke; the main difference is that for the Macaskills the round trip to B&Q in Inverness is 120 miles.

Donald Senior came in and we sat down to tea. I asked how local people had reacted to Dounreay at first and whether they had come to accept it. Much had been made in the early days, apparently, of a prophecy by the Brahan Seer, Scotland's Nostradamus, that all the land north of the Great Glen would one day be consumed in fire and brimstone and, detached from the rest of Britain, crumble away into the ocean. Once the plant had become a reality and the focus of the local economy, most of the brouhaha had died down; only now, with the foreseeable cancellation of Britain's nuclear programme and the consequent shedding of employees at Dounreay had the place once again become a subject of anxiety. There were promises of funding for new industries; all along the coast, including Armadale, I had seen large signs in the fields announcing that 'This land has been selected for industrial development' and that 'enquiries should be directed to the Highland Development Agency'. Without exception the signs were weather-beaten, their letters peeling away and I had seen no new factories or even building sites. Now, too, people were talking more openly about the practice in the early days of the nuclear plant of simply dumping waste untreated into the sea, a practice which caused much more vociferous concern in Orkney a few miles north, than it did amongst the people who had come to rely on Dounreay for their livelihoods. I did not care to interrogate Donald too deeply on the subject which he discussed with apparent uncon-cern, and we did not talk about the new reports of a leukemia 'hot-spot' around the plant. There were several copies of the Dounreay in-house newspaper in the kitchen which were full of bright, cheerful stories about plant workers surpassing safety standards, achieving targets, and doing good works amongst the local communities. Nowhere was there any suggestion, except by very distant implication, that nuclear power was a controversial issue and of dubious commercial value. 'Dounreay Workers Help Rebuild Church Organ' – that was about the level of it.

I stared out at the line of cliffs and the dark sea, and at the distant constellation of lights which marked the reprocessing facility. I grew up four miles from a nuclear power station myself, and there was an undercurrent of rumour about the high incidence of cancer, and about mysterious roadblocks and alarms in the night, but in general I never gave the twin squat lumps on the horizon a second thought. I went out for a brief walk in the dusk, and called Kate from the phonebox. Apart from the lights of Dounreay there was nothing to be seen; it was too misty to see Orkney. Poor Orkney, I thought; Sullom Voe to the north of them, Dounreay to the south, and the devil of a mess in the middle.

In bed I read some of the *Dounreay News*. The run-down of the British Industry has forced them to send out missions to tout for business abroad. There was more about the attempts of the Highland Development Agency to diversify the local economy, but who, I wondered, would choose to relocate on this desolate coast? Somehow I couldn't imagine a factory at Armadale making Kawasakis or Zanussi tumble-dryers. Perhaps local initiatives would regenerate the district. Gardening seemed popular: maybe they could produce gnomes with a half-life of 100,000 years?

In the morning both Pat and Donald wished me luck and came to the door to wave me goodbye. I couldn't have wished for a more pleasant start to my journey and indeed nowhere else did I find such comfort or hospitality over the next month. I was their first guest of the season: Donald had only put the sign up the day before. I drove along the lane towards the lighthouse at the north end of the point, taking a few photographs. Here and there were shacks or weird amalgams of caravan and hut, but I couldn't decide whether they were inhabited or not. One had a huge whalebone attached to the wall.

I went back to Armadale. Again, as I walked up the street I had the impression of a deserted village, but gradually I noticed that everywhere in the fields round about, in the farmyards and up on the moors there were isolated figures at work, herding sheep, building fences, tinkering with machines, feeding chickens, hammering and sawing wood. These figures threw the landscape into a new perspective and instead of a line of buildings along the street, the settlement now seemed to sprawl across the valley. I saw for the first time that the long slope of the valley-side was still laid out in the strip fields of the crofts. I felt like an intruder, an idler in this place where people had always worked harder than I had ever done. I met no one on the road; a few distant figures turned to watch me momentarily. The camera strung around my neck made me self-conscious. Two small girls were playing with a pony in a small enclosure by one of the houses. Something about them told me that they too were visitors here. Why should I have concluded, on the evidence of pink shellsuits and new wellington boots, that they were not natives? I suppose I presumed that local children would wear sweaters and anoraks and have muddy, not shiny boots. Grandpa came out of the cottage and took a photograph of them, so I was right. I wondered where they came from and what they made of the place. For all

I know they were from Melvich, or Bettyhill. All through this trip I fought to stop myself drawing similar pat conclusions about people I saw, but everywhere I went people conformed alarmingly to my expectations of how they would look, speak and behave.

The wind had swung from east to north and the sea sent in lines of four-foot breakers to crumple on the long white crescent of the beach beyond the village in Armadale Bay. The roar of the sea pervaded everything, and out on Strathy Point I could see volcanoes of spume rising 40 or 50 feet above the rocks. The morning was drawing on and it would soon be time for me to leave. I had reached the clifftop once again without meeting anybody. I did not dare knock on any doors just to get a bit of conversation, nor did I want to march into the fields and disturb people at their work. So I decided I would simply have to take a few photographs and hope to justify my brief and superficial observations. It was only then that I discovered the reason for Armadale's apparently haphazard layout; it is almost impossible to get a decent view of the village except, perhaps, from high on a nearby hillside, for all the older houses are built in tucks and wrinkles in the land. One doesn't notice this from the road; the place simply looks chaotic, but there is a logic, based on the practicalities of shelter and warmth, in the placement of every building. And this, too, is why the new houses look so unsettled: having insulation and double-glazing they do not need to hunker down in a gully or behind a bank, and they stare into the howling wind with blank, dumb faces.

Back in the car I pulled out the road atlas to look for my letter B, but before I could select one I had to make a broader decision. There are so few roads in the north of Scotland, that whether I turned east or west at this point was of major importance. If I turned west the road was infinitely more tortuous, and the opportunities to leave it and cut inland very few, but after a couple of days I would have the chance to move east without too long a drive – or so I thought. I was also aware that compared to the west, the far north-east is almost unknown, mostly because it is scenically unromantic, and this appealed to me strongly. It was quite some time before I closed the atlas, crunched into first gear, and swung west towards Cape Wrath. In retrospect I think that in spite of my good intentions the lure of spectacular scenery was the over-riding factor. There are many places beginning with B on the north-west coast; one which looked eminently reachable that day had a wonderfully grim-sounding name: Baddidarach.

BADDIDARACH

Bad weather, bad vibes, bad dreams

I had only come about 12 miles from Armadale when I pulled off the road in front of the only building in sight, a deserted farmhouse, in order to dry out. I had left in a penetrating Scotch mist which seemed to be equal parts fresh and salt water. Now, suddenly, the skies had cleared completely and the sunshine had transformed the sodden brown moor into an Indian shawl. The light was dazzling, as the rain and the stiff breeze had cleared the air of dust, and I walked down a rough track to a small lochan a couple of hundred yards from the road; I was dry by the time I reached it. In the distance a veil of cloud was rising rapidly from a mountain I knew from the map to be Ben Loyal, which being only 2,500 feet in height I was not expecting much of. In a kind of meteorological strip-tease Mother Nature put me right, first revealing lower flanks which seemed to be completely vertical, then a fantastically jagged crown, and finally a peak in the shape of a claw or an eagle's beak. If you were to paint this mountain as an illustration for a children's fairy-tale it would be rejected as being way over-the-top. Closer to hand, it was easy to see why the house was now derelict: there didn't seem to be enough vegetation for a vole to survive on, let alone a flock of sheep.

The road had dipped inland but rejoins the coast at Coldbackie Bay, a circlet of white sand beneath the cliffs fringing a turquoise sea. Where the tide had brought in darker material, sand or weed, it had formed immense marbled patterns on the beach and beneath the clear shallows. The effect was exotic, and a large party of tourists from Ulster had left their coach perched precariously on the cliff road and were in danger of falling en masse several hundred feet as they tried to photograph it.

Tongue is doubly sheltered, crammed into a steep little valley which itself nestles on one side of the Kyle of Tongue, a large fjord-like inlet. It had trees, which looked weird after 80 miles where nothing grew taller than one's shin. I stopped for petrol, hand-pumped from an ancient machine by a bearded young Englishman; we talked about our common experience of being Englishmen abroad until without warning the petrol tank overflowed and filled my shoes. I speculated about the possibility of being the first Human Torch to travel from Scotland to Cornwall. He was very apologetic; usually, it seems, a pronounced gurgle gives ample warning of full capacity being approached. The pump, which had a handle like a railway points switch, only measured in gallons, while the price list was in litres. After three or four attempts to work out the cost on a pocket calculator we struck a bargain and I departed, to find that around the next corner was a new self-service station. Still, I am all in favour of picturesque low-tech, especially when one receives free foot-deodorant into the bargain.

From Tongue the road runs across the Kyle on a causeway and onto the promontory called A'Moine. Ben Hope, to the south, looked as steep as Ben Loyal but is hunched and rounded where the other is gap-toothed and sharp. Their loneliness makes you appreciate these mountains like gigantic sculptures, though Ben Hope brought to mind a more prosaic simile; it is as if some cosmic elephant has emptied its bowels on to the moors. Strangely enough this train of thought seemed to be confirmed a couple of miles further on; one of the signs which warns you that there may be cattle on the road had been deftly transformed into an elephant by some wag. It was the best kind of graffiti, entertaining without destroying the original message.

From the Kyle of Tongue to Eddrachillis Bay 20 miles south of Cape Wrath the landscape changes bewilderingly every two miles or so in a kind of geological *tour de force*. Here the motorist is at a severe disadvantage, for so complex are these changes, and so rapid, that the fraction of attention you can afford to divert from the demanding road is barely enough to take in the briefest impression of each chapter of this stone epic. First, Loch Eriboll, where the only sign of modernity is the geometric pattern of salmon cages on the surface of the water, a vast sea loch with the 2,600 foot slope of Cranstackie at its southern end. The loch shores are almost pretty, green and scattered with small boulders as if by over-enthusiastic Zen gardeners, but the highest slopes have a sort of Wagnerian brutality. The scale and simplicity of the place are astounding; the car creeps around it, mile after mile, like a thunderbug trekking round the bathtub. At Laid on the western shore, a long straggle of crofts; the stone from which the dry-stone walls and the buildings are constructed is almost white, and despite the immense number and density of the field walls there are still a million times more stones lying loose on the ground, so that the world appears to be nothing but stones, and there are more stones than you thought there could be in the world.

As the road proceeds, so the rocks change and the soil and vegetation dependent upon the rocks change with them; now the walls are pale grey, now brown, now slate-blue; and because they break differently the walls are looser or denser, and because the walls dominate the landscape the changes are both subtle and complete.

Loch Eriboll on this cloudless, diamond-clear day left me dumbstruck. It is not the kind of place which makes it onto calendars or postcards, not the kind of grand, complex, romantic scenery that typifies Argyll or Perth-shire. Nor does it have the awful doomy presence of Glencoe, all crag and wounded rock. Its grandeur is a majestic combination of scale and simplicity. When I first came in sight of it my jaw not only dropped open, but I laughed out loud with delight.

Towards Durness the stone symphony moves into a quieter passage, with wide green swathes and only the occasional blast of naked rock. Durness itself is a positive metropolis, spread loosely over the neck of Faraid Head, clean and bright and prosperous-looking. I stopped there for cheese and oatcakes and again the shopkeeper was English. But I did not wait and eat in Durness, though as usual there were a lot of people parked carefully so that the view was completely obscured, sitting on aluminium folding chairs and enjoying the vista of the petrol station and public conveniences. I wanted to digest my thoroughly Highland lunch whilst contemplating at least a few hundred acres of moor, and preferably a sizeable mountain. Eriboll had made me hungry for *big scenery*. I was not to be disappointed. The road climbs gently but unflaggingly for many miles along the Kyle of Durness and over the southern neck of Cape Wrath towards Loch Inchard. There is only one building on it, Gualin House. Northwestwards the Cape itself is of scoured hills; south-eastward are the peaks of Beinn Spionnaidh and Cranstackie. It is an indication of the tortuousness of this coast that 15 miles beyond Durness you are only about five miles as the crow flies from the head of Loch Eriboll, some 35 miles distant by road. The vast glaciated valley of Strath Dionard opens to the south-east with Cranstackie looming over it to one side. On the other side is Foinaven. A monster rising in one continuous slope from 500 to almost 3,000 feet, as sharp as the Matterhorn and with flanks of bare rock shimmering with thousands of streams, Foinaven was just what I wanted for lunch. Beneath these two peaks at the bottom of the strath a tiny white cottage threw the dimensions of what I was seeing into stark perspective. Fair weather cumulus threw cloud-shadows which crept across the vast slopes altering colour and distance. The wind was a distant choir holding a single interminable chord. Nothing moved except water and shadow.

After a long time a faint buzz became audible. Many minutes later a motorcycle came into sight way down the road towards Durness. A while later it passed and gradually the noise faded; one could plot the turns in the road ahead from the hiccup of each gear change. Strangely enough, this interruption added to my sense of isolation rather than spoiling it. When it had gone the faint sound of the wind seemed even more strange, inseparable from what I was seeing, as if it were the song of the land itself. It seemed impossible that one could see so much and hear so little. The periodic grinding of my molars on oatcake sounded like the Battle of the Somme.

The road falls more steeply than it climbed. A haze was beginning to dim the distances. Beyond Foinaven, Arkle was so different that it seemed extraordinary that they were in the same country, let alone neighbours. Whereas Foinaven is grey and sharp, Arkle is a titanic hump of dark rock like a burnt loaf. Even on this bright afternoon it was the most frightening mountain I had ever seen, rising sheer from the plain and apparently wider at the top than at the bottom.

The geological freakery goes on. The basic ingredients of rock and moor are mixed and remixed with bewildering rapidity. Here, a smooth baize with half-sunk rounded boulders; now a rock pavement strewn with stones and pocked with gravel-filled holes; a field of heather with tall sharp menhirs like snapped-off tree trunks; a fantastic landscape of tiny egg-shaped stones delicately balanced on football-sized boulders themselves perched on big round mother rocks, the whole so finely poised that one feels that if one coughs, everything will fall apart.

After leaving Cape Wrath the road crosses Ceatramh Garbh, which translates from Gaelic as 'The flat bit where nothing will grow'. Glaciers have chewed off the top of the ground leaving nothing but flat rock and small lochans. Now and then a more hardy variety of stone rises ten or twenty feet from the flayed surface like a kind of wart; at Laxford Bridge the road is cut through such a dome in a canyon. But despite this almost total nudity, a subtle but complete change has occurred: the light is softer, the rocks are more rounded and covered in lichen, and what little greenery there is is *really* green; this is the west coast, tempered by the Gulf Stream and drenched with its attendant rain. Nowhere is this coast, along its thousands of miles of indentation, as bleak as that of the far north; even just below the Cape everything has softened compared to places like Loch Eriboll and Strathy Point. I felt as if I had emerged out of the wilderness into Canaan, except that Canaan probably had fewer caravan sites.

The road, after a hundred miles of single track, becomes a modern two-lane blacktop hacked through the bluffs and headlands, furnished with such fripperies as crash-barriers and warning signs. Blodwen touched 50 mph for the first time in nearly three days. We rolled down to Kylestrome through scenery which could have been in Scilly or Brittany, the generic type produced by the juxtaposition of pink granite and Atlantic Ocean:

rocky low promontories running out like breakwaters and scattered with big round boulders, twisting little sea-lochs full of wrack and islets and dotted with white houses; here and there a tiny sand or pebble beach and a few lonesome pines. After the rawness of the past few days it looked as artificial as a studio set for *Whisky Galore*. The good road means, of course, that this is holiday country, crowded in summer and fairly busy even now. It is extraordinary how the few miles of road which connect the west to the north coasts seem as great a barrier as the sea, though no doubt in five or ten years time the road will be improved and the north side opened up to the dubious delights of full-blooded tourism. As it is, I knew I had left one of the very few parts of the mainland that one can seriously call remote; on the west side only a couple of the greatest promontories, Ardnamurchan and, above all, the trackless Knoydart peninsula, approach its isolation. Of course, 'remote' is a relative term, as the Macaskills' forays to the DIY superstore demonstrate. Compared to the fastness of the interior, where a farm might be a two-hour drive off the nearest road by four-wheel-drive jeep, or even only accessible by boat, I had been nowhere remotely remote. But there is a difference between north and west which results from, and is as subtle as, the changes in climate and topography and light. There is a shift in the economy, and this changes everything.

Above Loch a'Chairn Bhain on the steep descent to Kylestrome I stopped at a 'viewpoint', in other words by a large lay-by with a picnic table and a sign saying 'No Overnight Parking'. From the picnic table one can enjoy a tremendous view of the bin and whatever cars happen to be there. But by climbing a mere 20 feet of sheer rock wall one can enjoy the massive valley of the triple loch, a'Chairn Bhain, Glendhu and Glencoul and the full glory of Quinag, a basalt peak of splendid ruggedness. If truth be told the best viewpoint would be half a mile further down the road, but at this point you are struggling to keep the gearbox from exploding through the floor of the car in third at around 55 mph, sparks flying off the brakes and prayers being offered to St Nobby, the patron saint of very long slopes. Once again the walker has the advantage over the motorist, particularly if he has legs like Diego Maradona's and is similarly fortified with cocaine. Up the pass between Quinag and Glas Bheinn and down again to Skiag Bridge, where I turned right along Loch Assynt towards Lochinver, and my destination, Baddidarach.

Assynt is lovely, scattered with little pine-crowned islets like a Chinese scroll. All along the fast modern road on the south side of Quinag minibuses were parked, presumably waiting for those idiots who had climbed the damned thing. Scottish weather is treacherous, Scottish mountain weather notoriously so, and now the haze had thickened up sufficiently to reduce the peaks of Suilven and Canisp, only five miles to the south, to tantalising outlines, blue on blue, and a sickly orange-white veil of high cloud had crept off the sea, turning what had been a cooling breeze into a cold gale.

Rain was evidently not far off. I'm not saying that those people were idiots because they had ignored the weather forecast. Indeed they had probably timed their climbs to perfection to take advantage of a glorious morning and afternoon. I'm saying that anyone who wishes to climb 2,700 feet of jagged rock in whatever conditions instead of sitting down with a good book, a crate of Newcastle Brown Ale and 20 Marlboro has got to be seriously disturbed and quite possibly a dangerous sociopath. If God had meant us to climb mountains he would have given us crampons instead of vertigo.

On either side of the new Lochinver road, the old track is visible from time to time, twisting like a rattlesnake and crumbling away into the bogs and pools. Assynt drains down the ink-blue Inver through a forest of Private Fishing signs. The village of Lochinver is a single curved street of white terraced shops and houses along the shore, leading to a decrepit fishing dock. The loch was grey and choppy in the now very unpromising light, and I was very tired after a drive of 130 miles on tortuous roads, many of which would shame Afghanistan. I drove dutifully along the mile of minute road which led to Baddidarach to find only a grim housing estate and a scattering of caravans and holiday chalets on the headland, with posher or twee-er houses occupying the best nooks and crannies in a landscape which is 50 per cent nook and 50 per cent cranny.

Perhaps it was the effect of arriving somewhere so banal after two days in the most fantastic surroundings or maybe I was just very tired and, for the first time, a little homesick, but I disliked Baddidarach on sight. I tried to tell myself that the very banality of the place was interesting. I took a walk along the road, but grew even more depressed when I saw that the houses were built in a landscape which without them would have been magical – complex and delicate little bays and tumbling mossy rocks, water-falls and flowering shrubs.

Writing this, looking back, I really haven't the faintest idea why I decided against buying bed and breakfast that evening. Perhaps my cushy first night made me feel that it would be more virtuous not to – certainly the less I spent, the more would go to the British Dyslexia Association. But now I think I must simply have been too tired to make coherent judgments. I climbed back behind the wheel, every muscle protesting. My head was pounding and I was ravenously hungry, and for some reason I drove up a tiny switchback road that leads south out of Lochinver and runs through many miles of coastal wilderness to nowhere in particular. Ten minutes drive along this goat-track convinced me that I would find nowhere safe to park overnight; indeed the road was so narrow and steep that it took me as long again to find somewhere to turn the car round, and even that was a seven-point turn on a blind corner half-way up a one-in-four hill (in the process of which I almost sank the rear axle in a bog and then scraped the front numberplate on a rock). Only when I had completed this extravagant manoeuvre did I realise that I had been holding up a Range Rover coming down the hill and a BMW coming up, both crammed with people who looked as if they owned the bog I had despoiled with my Michelins and would sue me for the scratch on their pet rock. Symbiosis again: to match my embarrassment Blodwen refused to get into first gear and I had to kangaroo-hop away in second. So by the time I found myself once more cruising the main drag at Lochinver (and believe me, drag is the word) I was a desperate man. The sea-front consisted almost entirely of bed-and-breakfast places, give or take the odd craft shop, and I was sorely tempted. Then I remembered the old road which meandered across the new one along the Inver from Loch Assynt: I thought it might be possible to get on to it here and there. So it proved, although in the gathering dusk I failed to notice a drop of what seemed like two feet between the new road and the old. The engineers had thoughtfully left a 20-foot bank behind which Blodwen could creep, out of sight of the traffic.

I switched off the engine and to unwind put the radio on, catching the end of the weather forecast: '. . . rain will get into western Scotland by nightfall . . .' Immediately the first drops pattered on to the roof. The forecast was followed by a programme of Scottish Country Dancing. This was all I needed: driving rain, a view of desolate brown bog rapidly fading into desolate black bog, the prospect of a night spent curled up into a space too small even for a starved Jack Russell and the kind of music which drove Scotsmen to seek their fortunes in the leprous swamps of Africa rather than ever hear an accordion again. I twiddled the tuning knob but some geographical irony dictated that Dougie McMinge and His Kilted Kretins was all I could get – apart from something which sounded like six Frenchmen arguing in an amusement arcade – so I left it on to drown out the dreary drum-roll of raindrops while I heated up a tin of Cassoulet beans with the stove balanced precariously on a briefcase and Roget's Thesaurus.

A raven flapped off a rocky perch as I was trying to digest these jaw-numbing pulses, rose briefly into the teeth of what had become a ferocious gale, thought better of it and returned, presumably resigned to a quiet night in. Since it was obvious that it was going to rain very hard for a long time I hoped that the ominous appearance of this feathered fiend did not mean that what was left of the old road would finally be washed away that night. Now it was almost dark; the music had given way to an interminable discussion of the possibility that the referee of the game between Skye and Kingussie in the Highland Shinty League was born out of wedlock. There was nothing for it but to go to sleep.

Those of you who have never spent a night in the back of a Morris Minor van on a moor in Sutherland in March have not lived; those who have, have not slept. The preliminaries are easy. You remove your shoes and socks, leaving them by the pedals, but a little to the left due to the water which leaks from the windscreen, down through the glove compartment to the floor. Having removed said socks you naturally want to get as far away from them as possible, so you push yourself up until you are sitting atop the back of your seat, bent double by the roof, and then you fall backwards like Jacques Cousteau leaving a dinghy. You are now in Position B, flat on your back with one foot through the window in the rain and the other trapped between the driver's and passenger's seats, and the saucepan of cold water you forgot you had left on the back seat creating an interesting sensation in the higher buttock area. Position C is similar, except that the feet are reversed, and the saucepan you have pulled from beneath you is now inverted in the groin. Undeterred, the seasoned Morris inhabitant now removes his jeans, scattering small change over a wide area and, remembering that in order to get into the sleeping bag it is first necessary to unroll it, climbs crab-wise into the front seat once more, attaining Position D, in which the head is in the vicinity of the accelerator, and the socks in the vicinity of the mouth. In once more achieving a traditional upright posture it is necessary to remember that the proximity of the gear lever to the now-vulnerable Y-fronts can lead the unwary to maim themselves, whilst care should be taken not to catch the handbrake with the left shin as a) this damages the shin, and b) it sets the vehicle in motion. At this point the amateur may choose to sleep in the driving position or set fire to the car and walk to an hotel, but if the latter option is preferred, remember to retrieve your trousers first. The professional, however, pulls the sleeping bag from under the cans of oil, suitcase, crate of spare vehicle parts and spare wheel and, removing any rusted components which may have worked their way inside it during the day's journey, unrolls it along the back seat whilst kneeling in the front with his underpants at half-mast and his bottom pressed against the windscreen. Do not be deterred by the fact that the bag is three feet longer than the seat, or, indeed, that you are. Wedge the pillow, if you have one, in the gap between the end of the seat and the side of the van; it is of no use since it quickly sinks out of reach but at least it is not in the way. Finally, regain the back seat using the Cousteau Flop as above and insert at least some of the torso into the bag. Remove glasses, ring and watch and balance them on top of the back seat, along with your vital night-time supplies: torch, cigarettes and radio. If these are still in the glove compartment the whole process must be repeated. Finally, by a series of violent physical jerks draw the sleeping-bag up to the level of your neck whilst in the foetal position, close your eyes and breathe deeply to promote relaxation. Since you have now achieved a position unknown even to the most venerable yogis, a state of unrivalled mental clarity is quickly achieved, and it becomes obvious that in the first place you are dying of thirst and the water bottle is on the floor behind the pile of cooking equipment beyond the passenger seat, and in the second place it is still pouring with rain, the wind has begun to actually rock the vehicle from side to side, it is pitch dark and you are desperate for a pee.

You may think that I exaggerate, but this is fairly close to the awful truth. When I had finally got reasonably comfortable (in other words found a position where I wasn't in actual pain) I lay awake for what seemed like hours. The sound of the steady, gentle rain on the metal of the car was strangely soothing and the occasional light-show of passing cars was only faintly disturbing. The wind grew stronger; a tin can rattled along the road. No, not a tin can, a motocycle engine; the police had spotted me. The patrolman rapped on the window; I woke with a start to find the rain pelting down so hard on the roof that the noise was like the inside of a ball-bearing factory. I lay awake, smoking the occasional cigarette for the next four hours – when I had been awakened by the phantom lawman it was only 11 o'clock. Periodically the rain would slacken off and I would settle down and try to blot out the faint scratching, but my hearing had become fantastically acute and I learned to recognise the faintest change in the whisper which heralded an imminent furious downpour. Once or twice I dozed off. I have the most obvious dreams and the return of a heavy squall would produce an image of a ghostly white horse – my brain saying, 'this is a nightmare'. Apart from the lack of sleep, I realised that this was the night when the clocks were put forward and I was an hour closer to tomorrow. Two cars passed between two and three o'clock – who? why? – and when I finally fell asleep again I dreamed that I was demanding free cigars in a hamburger joint. Not so obvious, I grant you.

Morning came in shades of grey, but the heavy rain had gone and the wind with it. The cloudbase was no more than 100 feet above the car and visibility was only a quarter of a mile or so, leaving Suilven and Canisp hidden. I forced myself out of the sleeping bag and began the astronaut-like tasks of dressing, cooking, cleaning and packing in a tiny space. The surrounding bog was now brim-full and the River Inver had risen to the lip of the bank. I drove back down to Lochinver, where a choppy grey sea made grabs at gulls flapping to no avail, completely stationary against the wind off the loch.

I crossed the road to the public lavatory, and Lochinver immediately went up a couple of points in my estimation. When was the last time you were in a public convenience which had lavatory paper, towels and locks on the doors? Where the seat was dry and the air fresh with the tang of salt spray? A trifle chilly on the nethers but heartily to be recommended to the needy.

Being the Sabbath, the place was absolutely lifeless. I was not convinced that Baddidarach had any more to offer but felt nevertheless that I must do my duty, so I walked along the headland in the freezing drizzle and poked about desultorily for half an hour. Again I was struck by the almost faerie landscape, but more forcibly by the huge amount of litter and rubbish lying around: old crab-pots and nets, tyres, deflated rubber dinghies, a smashed caravan, ends of rope, lost toys, and a kaleidoscope of indestructible plastic of dubious origin along the high-tide mark. What might have been a pretty, park-like place was messy, dank and uninviting. A few irises pushing up between the bits of rubbish. To cap it all, some wag had placed a traffic cone atop the highest rock. That's entertainment.

As I turned back the drizzle stopped. I paused a while on the old bridge where the Inver shoots into the sea down a series of rapids; across the way an old graveyard was laid out in a long strip along the shore, a pleasant Scottish habit, near the squat Free Church, which is rather good in a righteously grim way. Toytown Gothic. Scottish church architecture is occasionally sublime but usually ridiculous. The Minister was the Rev. S. Tamata. That cheered me up no end. The weather, though, stayed gloomy, blocking my view of Ben More Assynt as I came back eastward along the loch, past the ruined castle on its promontory, and headed south. At Elphin, in the middle of an otherwise deserted stretch of moorland, there was a tearoom. It had only been open for three days this season. The cockney couple who run it have been there for 15 years, though. Goodness knows what they do in the winter. I ate an excellent venison roll, bought another for my lunch and drank a coffee to the strains of taped muzak which was so worn that it provided a background noise akin to a ship's engines heard from the upper deck. While I was eating the sun came out. There was piping hot water in the gents and I imagine the owners must have thought I was suffering from a serious internal complaint, so long did I spend at my ablutions. Back at the table I studied a poster advertising cruises to the 'lovely Summer Isles with their famous tearoom' and others for craft shops, studios, and a gallery selling 'contemporary landscape painting'. I was back in civilisation with a vengeance.

Out of Sutherland and into Ross and Cromarty and, simultaneously, into the Inverpolly National Nature Reserve, in which no Nature was visible except a row of gnarled trees. The road surface, however, provided ample entertainment. Ullapool, the first sizeable town I had come to since Muir of Ord, is a peculiar amalgam of resort and serious port in the shelter of the long and narrow Loch Broom. It is laid out on a grid pattern and the back streets of white houses, greenswards and neat hedges have a very un-Scottish look, as if Felixstowe had been transported to the Highlands. Out in the loch a couple of hefty trawlers were laid up, rusting in a slow race between the sea and the economic upturn. At the quay, however, was a big Russian trawler, the *Vasily Golovkin*, and it seemed as if the whole town had turned out to greet her. They call them the Klondykers . . . a Russian crew has been known to empty the shops of goods in a matter of hours, and presumably a brisk trade goes on also in vodka, genuine antique samovars, caviar, KGB surplus underwear and exit visas.

Despite the fact that it was Easter Sunday, there seemed to be little religious activity in any of the churches. As I walked around the town I noticed the hierarchy of sects had allotted themselves a corresponding variety of buildings: Church of Scotland (big church), Free Kirk (little church), Pentecostals (chapel), Episcopalians (converted semi) and Catholics (ex-corner shop).

Since much too much of this narrative seems to be taken up with the splendours of public conveniences, I ought to mention that Ullapool has one of the most magnificent. It is a two-storey job, with the Ladies upstairs and the Gents below. The male floor has about thirty cubicles and forty urinals with basins in proportion. It also has a road map of the British Isles on the wall for you to contemplate as you commune with nature. I suppose this is a subtle MI5 aid to Soviet fishermen wishing to defect, though someone I spoke to thought it was more likely to encourage Ullapudlians to head for Murmansk.

Coming south along Loch Broom I passed a picnic area thoughtfully provided by the Forestry Commission so that those who cannot bear lovely marine scenery can find solace amongst cloned conifers, where I noticed a man staring intently at the car, sitting on the picnic table nearest the road on an embankment about ten feet above me. I wasn't travelling fast so as I approached he had plenty of time to study me and I him. He was a fat man in owlish thick glasses and a brown cardigan. His head turned very gradually as I came towards him, but the incredibly glum expression on his face did not alter. I waved cheerily when quite close, hoping to inspire some reaction, but not an eyelid did he flicker. I bet he was Austrian.

Up and up we climbed in a huge hairpin towards An Teallach, through the Dundonnell Forest. Like most Scottish 'forests' it is a treeless waste, 'forest' originally meaning 'hunting ground'. There were plenty of cars parked along the road, despite the low cloud which here shrouded the peaks, so there were presumably many hardy souls enjoying the mud and bits of stone and damp. The road almost touched the snowline before descending very rapidly between huge grey cliffs until we were once again in the chocolate-box countryside – mature Scots pine and mossy boulders – of the coast at Camusnagaul on Little Loch Broom.

At Gruinard Bay, a spectacular expanse of pale sand between rocky headlands and, out at sea, the scattered Summer Isles, the same party of Ulster tourists as at Coldbackie had once again abandoned their coach and were rushing lemming-like toward the clifftop clutching their Instamatics. Aultbea, on Loch Ewe, was full of garish signs for this and that café or holiday park, but at the south end, Poolewe was contrastingly neat and prim. As one crosses the next promontory there is a sudden and brief view inland up Loch Maree which tantalises but can only be reached after a long loop through Gairloch, a straggle of houses on a flat, narrow coastal strip beneath gloomy knuckles of rock. There I gave a lift to a New Zealander spending his holidays walking the Scottish Highlands, his first visit after five years in a London bank. I'm almost sure, however, that he wanted to steal my road atlas – he had no idea where he was. Only after he had got out and saw that I was resolutely staring at the book in his hand did he put it back on the seat.

Loch Maree seemed to me the quintessence of the cream of the loveliest Highland scenery. Elegantly long and narrow, dominated by high peaks, dotted with wooden islets, it is the kind of place that the BBC chooses when they want to film a particularly naff folk group grinding out reels and dirges. Cue helicopter shot and slow-motion osprey grabbing a fresh salmon hors d'oeuvre. Shoot the sunset through vaseline and fade to graphics in Celtic script; you know the sort of thing. Luckily Loch Maree is beautiful enough to survive even an imagination as cynical as mine.

The road opened up again and worried about the weather and the time, I belted down to Kinlochewe, where it began to rain steadily. On the off-chance that it was only a shower I spent longer in the village shop than I should have, but it was a big shed-like place which not only sold papers and cigarettes but antiques and bric-a-brac. Needless to say it was run by English people and, so far as I could tell, the 25 or so customers were also English. The car park was stuffed with brand-new mobile homes and Volvos and kagooled 40-somethings milled around peering at old furniture while their loutish offspring sniggered at the X-rated videos the place rented out.

I fled down Glen Torridon, famously the wettest place in a wet country. True to form, it bucketed, and I caught only glimpses of this narrow and precipitous pass. What little of it was visible consisted of vertical rock and falling water in equal proportion. The road is a writhing tricksy thing; it was like being inside a washing-machine. Despite the rain, Loch Torridon was breathtaking, with a shore as strange and delicate as a Zen painting. Very sheltered, very mild, very wet, Torridon is a kind of high-humidity Shangri-la secreted away in the complexities of the Wester Ross coast. It is the kind of place that despite all evidence to the contrary makes you feel that you are the first to discover it. The chief bit of evidence was another stretch of straight, wide road, but this is purely designed to soften up the exhausted motorist for the sucker punch: the coast road to Applecross.

CAMUSTERRACH

Chapels, crab-pots and cascades

If you have never been to Applecross, get out your road atlas and have a look at the road which runs along the north side of the promontory from Shieldaig to Fearnmore. You will see that it is extremely convoluted. Well, those convolutions have convolutions and there are convolutions on the convolutions of the convolutions. Also, the road rises and falls like a Big Dipper. Although only ten miles as the hoodie flies, this stretch is probably twice that distance, but it does have the compensation of being perhaps the single most beautiful length of coastline anywhere in Britain. It combines delicacy and ferocity, verdant growth and picturesque settlement, set off by the placid, sheltered loch and a backdrop of the high uninhabited mountains of Wester Ross. Although the road was apparently designed by St Vitus, the surface is good and the whole thing is more fun than fright, despite some dizzying drops and a notable lack of metal barrier between you and Davy Jones's Locker.

When one passes Fearnmore, however, and rounds the headland of Rubha na Fearn, the character of the route changes utterly, running almost dead straight and level for ten miles southwards across a vast slope which appears to emerge from the sea and continue at precisely the same angle upwards for 2,000 feet. Across the Inner Sound, on this dreary afternoon, the islands of Rona, Raasay, Scalpay and Skye hung on the horizon like broken pieces of slate. No trees grow on this immense brown incline and periodically the road crosses a stream which is almost a waterfall, frothing white and tawny like a torrent of brown ale.

Applecross village lies in a square bay nicked out of this straight line as if by a ticket-punch, a green, gentle surprise completely enclosed by high mountains. It was half-past five when I turned off the engine and sat for a moment watching the procession of enormous breakers running in ranks like infantry to die on the wide shingle. It was immediately apparent that this was a special place, somewhere with an atmosphere, a smell, a light all its own. Arriving for the first time you feel that in an intangible way you have come home. In the rapidly fading light and rain as heavy and straight as stair-rods it seemed to say, never mind about what happens elsewhere – here everything is as it should be.

This very Celtic spell, melancholy and serene, was rudely shattered, I'm sorry to report, by the sign posted on the door of the public lavatory. You will by now be convinced that I spent an enormous portion of this trip in some kind of perverse exploration of the civic plumbing of Britain; not so, I promise. I am no Lucinda Lambton, although on this occasion I did have to venture into her domain, since the notice on the Gents read 'This toilet is out of order and there is no money to fix it. Please complain to the Tourist Board'. Consider it done. Emerging from the Ladies, I had to mutter apologies to a procession of matronly women who had appeared from the deserted street during my ensconcement; doubtless some kind of moral Neighbourhood Watch.

My already high opinion of Applecross was bolstered by the discovery that the first house I came to did Bed and Breakfast – after driving 150 miles on spaghetti-like roads I did not fancy a long search in the gloom. The door was answered by a shaven-headed piratical Yorkshireman; yes, they had a room. I paid 75 pence extra for a hot bath, money well-spent simply for the entertainment afforded by the plumbing system. The bath was a big Edwardian tub of about 4,500 tonnes – possibly once used as a ferry. Turning on the taps produced a distant bellowing, followed a few minutes later by a stream of hot water ejected from the faucet with the force of a Saturn Five at lift-off. This lasted about a second; the water, the colour of Castlemaine XXXX, then dried up completely, and another distant roar announced the departure of a further pint from somewhere near the centre of the earth. Meanwhile the cold tap shuddered and clanged, disgorging a steady gallon an hour. It was as if the whole system was being controlled by handpump in the basement by a 96-year-old retainer. Nevertheless, it was worth the wait.

By the time I emerged spotless and radiantly beautiful a tantalising scent was drifting up the stairs; in my room I found a menu on the dressing-table. An evening meal cost extra, and since the room, though by no means expensive, had set me back a little more than I had expected, I had decided to eat a cold supper of cheese, biscuits, fruit and chocolate brought in from the van. Reader, of all the horrendous sacrifices I made on this trip this was the greatest. Place yourself, if you will, in my shoes for a moment (the Odour-eaters are quite new). You have driven an immense distance on appalling roads. You spent the previous night in a tin box bent double and deafened by a raging storm. The previous evening's fare consisted of a tin of beans; this morning's muesli has been supplemented only by two venison rolls and a Twix. You find yourself in an enchanting domain and in a house of character. The knots and kinks in your shoulders and neck have been soothed away by the administration of hot Australian beer. You have on fresh underwear and socks (and other items). Your stomach is emptier than Wembley Stadium during a friendly between England and Lichtenstein. And then, in explanation of the nasal treat wafting from below, you read:

> Garlic Mussels
> Leek Broth
> Apricot Lamb with Almond Rice, Carrots
> with Honey and Glazed Broccoli
> Pear and Walnut Flan.

In a display of self-control which would have impressed St Cuthbert, who survived for 40 years by eating cormorant feathers, my own menu was:

> Beef crisps
> Co-op Cheese Spread
> Two Oatcakes
> Four squares Cadbury Fruit and Nut
> Jaffa *au naturel*

washed down with a refreshing draught of Carbonated Highland Spring.

In the sitting-room downstairs I found the landlord, Mr Warrington, and two elderly ladies. He asked where I had come from that day; when I replied 'Lochinver', he remarked with true Yorkshire forthrightness that I'd 'not seen much then'. Since I had come through some of the most amazing scenery I had ever seen this puzzled me for a moment, but I was already falling into the trap of imagining that traversing a long distance in a car amounts to seeing a lot. He knew that the opposite is the truth. So I explained what I was doing, and was encouraged by a 'What a good idea!' from one of the ladies, and 'What's that he said?' from the other. The explanation was repeated at a full bellow by her companion.

'What a good idea!' said the deaf one.

'She's very bad today,' explained her friend unnecessarily. 'It's the damp.'

We talked about various charitable enterprises; the landlord's shaven barnet had been his contribution to the local effort for Comic Relief. £137 had been raised in Applecross – I should imagine this represents at least £2 per head. Then we swapped 'Dyslexics I Have Known' stories. The two ladies had a Hinge and Brackett-style relationship, with an added dash of surrealism due to hearing problems.

'Wasn't it Nigel who was dyslexic, dear?'

'No, no, Lionel was awfully bright. Went to Cambridge.'

'Not Lionel – Nigel. It's the damp.'

'Which lamp? It was Nigel, dear. Went to that special school. Did awfully well.'

'Yes. There's a special place run by an awfully nice man quite near us. What's his name, dear?'

'What was the name of that clever man who started that school?'

And so on. They were the archetypal English Ladies, straight out of E. M. Forster, all tweeds and sensible shoes. They had been caravanning once or twice every year in Scotland since 'long before it became fashionable'. Now this was beyond them, they drove a small car from guesthouse to hotel. They were full of stories. In passing they would mention that they had changed a wheel on a one-in-four slope in driving snow, or that the brakes had failed half way down the Pass of Brander. They weren't boasting; this was all part of the fun. I felt my own journey pale into insignificance. They mourned the passing of the days when one could simply pull off the road and park your caravan on any available piece of flat land, since today there are threatening police warnings and, in some cases, deliberately placed boulders to prevent such impulsiveness. On one occasion they had found a perfect site, unhitched the caravan and driven to the nearest village for supplies. On their return they found to their dismay a second caravan alongside their own. (This dismay is a thoroughly British reaction: the Germans, the French or the Greeks would never understand it.) So they hitched up the caravan and prepared to depart. Out of the second caravan came a (quote) Little Welshman. Are you going?, he asked. Yes, they were. He begged them to stay; he had been so relieved to find some company in that remote spot. Why? Because he was frightened. Overawed by the landscape; it was all too much.

I couldn't work out whether this story was supposed to illustrate some inherent weakness in the Welsh character, or the potency of Scottish scenery, or whether the ladies had forgotten to mention that poor Taffy was also being chased by a psychotic axe-murderer, but this bizarre reminiscence brought back another. Once again isolation seems important, and I think the stories were meant to illustrate the virtual impossibility of achieving it even in the 'old days'. On this occasion our heroines were on Cape Wrath in December – I told you they were tough. They had pulled off the road some way from the Cape Wrath Hotel – somewhere, in fact, near the spot where I had eaten my Foinaven lunch two days before. This, however, was in the mid–1950s, when caravanning on Cape Wrath in December was not the Brownies' jamboree it has since become. It was getting late; they decided to turn in for the night. Outside a howling gale was blowing, as one might expect. Just as they were getting into bed came a knock on the door. They hesitated; it might be (I inferred) the Welshman's axe-wielding friend; on the other hand it might be some poor motorist foolish enough to be driving across Cape Wrath in December without a caravan who had run into the Monarch of the Glen and gone through the windscreen. So with trembling hand they opened the door. It was a Pakistani trying to sell them things out of a suitcase. It took them 'simply ages' to get rid of him.

The conversation turned to what I might find beginning with 'C'. Down the coast from Applecross are three villages beginning with that letter, all minute; it didn't seem to matter much which I chose. Mr Warrington mentioned that there was also an inlet called Coillegillie where there was a coral beach. So, feeling that I had struck lucky, I climbed up to my attic room to write up the day's notes and eventually to sleep. At 8.30 p.m. the rain stopped suddenly, and the sound of the sea a few yards behind the house whispered through the skylight.

In the morning, however, the stair-rods were back. Apparently the rain had only stopped for about half-an-hour and it had been raining at Applecross more or less solidly for three days. After breakfast I said my goodbyes and hefted my suitcase, camera-case, briefcase and laundrybag into Blodwen's leaky rear, which I had parked towards the sea in an effort to prevent the engine getting damp. Alas, three layers of clingfilm and an oilskin tent would not have prevented some penetration of her innards that night. She hiccupped and jolted along the tiny road which hugs the foot of the cliffs south from the village. Great torrents of water were falling from this precipice onto the road, which was almost completely awash. So unhappy was Blodwen that I decided that the first village I came to, Camusterrach, would have to do, coral beach or no. I needed time to attend to her insides before another long drive, so I got out into the rain and looked.

Camusterrach lies on a tiny inlet, protected by a tiny jetty, behind which was moored one tiny fishing boat in front of a row of tiny cottages. Behind the cottages are new houses, perhaps built by the council, but no lights were showing in either cottages or houses despite the gloom, and although as I arrived there was one man and his collie on the street, they immediately got into a pickup and departed. I wandered from the jetty (crab-pots, a broken-down tractor, oildrums) up the street, to the chapel and across the very swollen stream and down the other side of the little bay, where there is a single row of white cottages backed against the cliff, a petrol-pump, a white-painted church of Scotland and some sheep. I returned to the jetty and tried to take a couple of photographs in the lee of a shed and holding up an umbrella against the rain; the waterfalls down the cliffs opposite were spectacular. While I was wrestling with this impossible task the Two Ladies drove up, parked for about three seconds, and departed, presumably in search of solitude. After all, the last thing one wants to see when arriving in a bijou little Gaelic fishing village is a Saxon lout chasing an umbrella through a flock of sheep. It simply ruins the effect.

The three miles back to Applecross were if anything worse than ever;

several times the engine stalled altogether. I began to suspect that damp was not the only problem. Back in the village I was faced with a dilemma. There are two roads out; one is the long coast road around which I had come the night before. The other is the Pass of the Cattle, beneath the peak of Sgurr a'Ghaorachain. Mr Warrington had told me, rather gloatingly I thought, as I examined it on an Ordnance Survey map on the living room wall that morning, that it was the second highest pass in the British Isles. But this shortcut is a single-track road, rising to over 2,000 feet, full of hairpin bends and 12 miles long and without a straight or level yard along the way. Indeed its steepness is legendary.

I put up the bonnet and tried to remove the spark-plugs; not one of them would budge. So I sprayed the engine with liberal quantities of water repellant and sat revving the engine for ten minutes to dry it out. By the end of this period Blodwen seemed in perfect health, idling sweetly. I decided to risk the pass.

The cloudbase that morning was no more than 200 feet. The road is marked 'Unsuitable for caravans and heavy vehicles' and there is also a moveable sign saying whether the road is open or closed during severe (i.e. normal) weather. Immediately after the turn, the road begins to climb at about one in five. Any sane person in a Morris would have taken the other road, though it is three times as long. However, I was running out of petrol – since I had forgotten that it was Bank Holiday Monday and had omitted to top up the day before. I guessed that the nearest station would be in Lochcarron, 20 miles away via the pass; I kicked myself for not knocking on the cottage door next to the petrol pump in Camusterrach. I poured in the spare gallon and hit the trail with gritted teeth. When we were 100 yards along and 70 feet up, the engine cut out. By extreme pressure on the footbrake I managed to keep the van stationary for about one second. Then we rolled back. Visibility through the rear doors of a Morris van is minimal and to compensate for a blind spot which encompasses almost the entire road I have two side mirrors and two internal mirrors. Unfortunately, on a severe slope these become redundant. I have never worked out why this should be, but there it is; I suppose the car is at a completely different angle to the road surface due to the pressure on the rear suspension. To make matters worse the weather had steamed up all the windows anyway. I found myself travelling backwards, unable to see what I was moving towards, on a very steep, very narrow road bounded by stone walls. Did I panic? Of course not; I pulled on the handbrake. Downward acceleration continued almost unabated. Did I panic? You bet your socks. I stomped on the footbrake and tried to get into first gear: crunch, clang, grind. Nothing doing. In order to shift the gear lever I had of course to let go of the handbrake, which had had some slight effect since we picked up speed nicely. I tried the ignition: no dice. By this time the dry-stone wall to the left was very close to the nearside of the van. Invoking several reasons why

I should be permitted to live a while longer, I swerved back into the middle of the road and tried second gear, again to no avail. So I simply kept both brakes on as hard as possible and waited for the end of the hill. We glided to a halt across the coast road to the astonishment of a man in a Landrover who pulled up a couple of feet from the passenger door. I gestured sheepishly at the engine; his eyes took in Blodwen's unlikely lines and his expression suggested a man humouring a half-wit playing with a Kalashnikov. Once more I tried the ignition and of course she fired first time. Suddenly the flat coast road snaking into the mist along the immense mountainside looked really inviting.

It was one of the longest hours of my life, nursing the engine and making frantic gear changes in order to stay off the brakes and save petrol, fighting the wind all along the seaward stretch and, on the horrendous bends and climbs of the Torridon side, trying to keep my eyes off the petrol gauge which had sunk past the 'E' level. I passed only one other car the whole way. At the Lochcarron turning I seriously considered a ten-mile walk up to Torridon village with the petrol can, since the next inhabited place southwards, Ardarroch, was still 13 miles away. But I couldn't remember seeing a petrol station in Torridon anyway, so I decided to drive as far as I could – at least I'd be going in the right direction.

But Blodwen was just kidding; we made it to Ardarroch where the Kishorn Post Office is also a petrol station. Despite the Bank Holiday, it was open. The owners were, of course, English. Are there any Scots at all left on the west coast? Leaning insouciantly on the doorpost watching the rain and my arrival with his usual scowl was Alan Warrington, who had come over the pass.

I muttered something vague about Blodwen's engine but his expression told me I'd be better to keep my mouth shut. His look said 'Southern. Soft. No Bottle'.

All down the Ardarroch road and on to Lochcarron the road was flooded, sometimes five or six inches under water, while the valley-floors were lakes and the hillsides invisible under curtains of foam. I stopped by the loch and looked across to the cliffs on the other side; dozens of pencil-thin waterfalls plummeted to the bottom, where the railway to the Kyle of Lochalsh weaves along the shore. I had come from somewhere which felt incredibly remote to within sight of the most celebrated stretch of the West Coast, the road and railway to Skye. It was already well after midday. I felt I had seen enough of the west; from here southwards it becomes more and more populous and commercialised. So, at least, I told myself, conveniently forgetting the fastnesses of Knoydart and Ardnamurchan and Morvern. Besides, I was sick of the rain, and I had run out of adjectives for rock and water and steepness and beauty. East I went, feeling a hundred years old. Parked on the little road just outside Lochcarron were four big trailers marked

'AID FOR ROMANIA'. Here they looked impressive; in Romania they must look pitifully small.

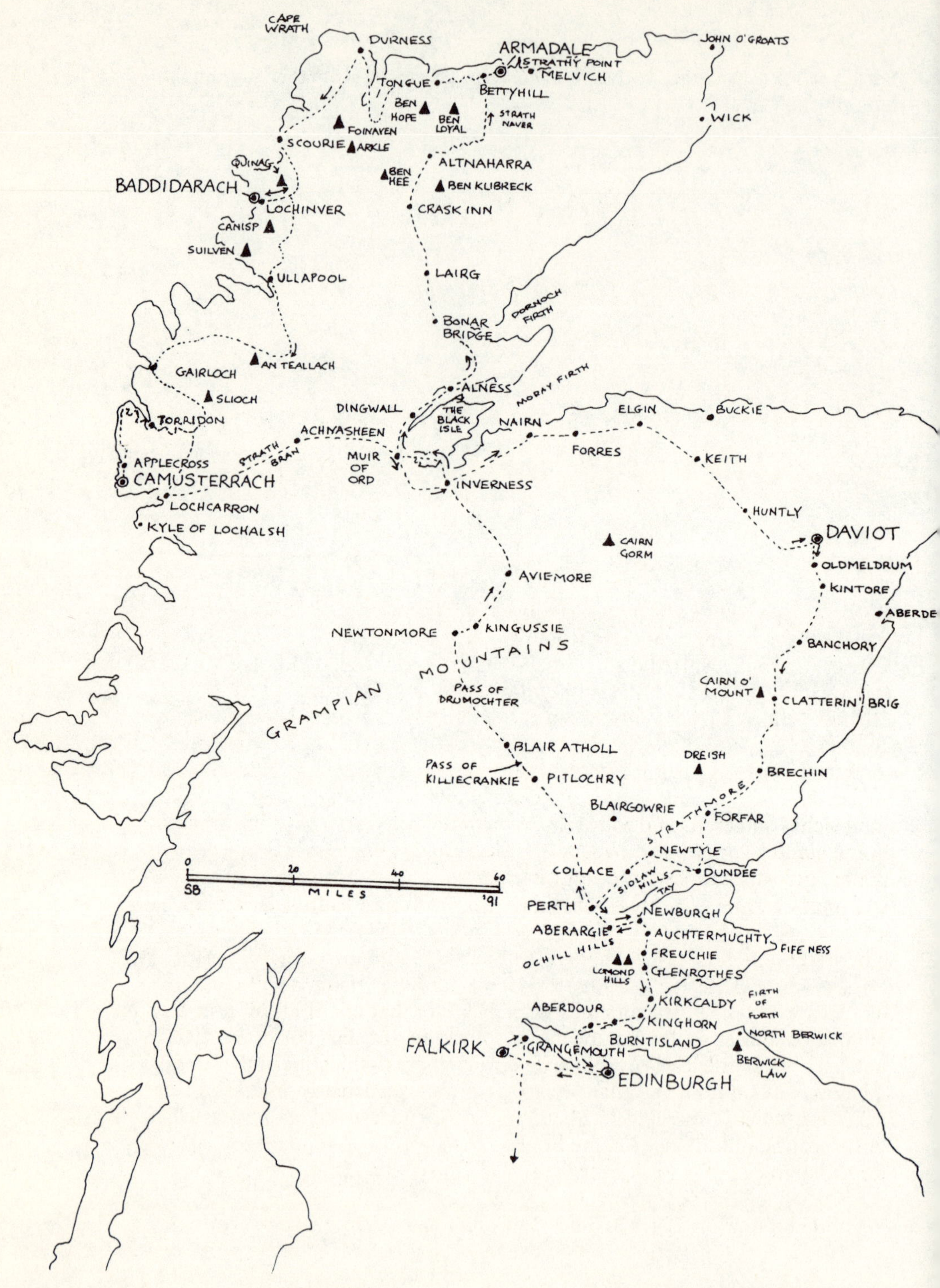

CAPE WRATH
DURNESS
JOHN O'GROATS
ARMADALE
STRATHY POINT
MELVICH
TONGUE
BETTYHILL
WICK
BEN HOPE
BEN LOYAL
STRATH NAVER
FOINAVEN
SCOURIE
ARKLE
QUINAG
ALTNAHARRA
BADDIDARACH
BEN HEE
BEN KLIBRECK
LOCHINVER
CRASK INN
CANISP
SUILVEN
LAIRG
ULLAPOOL
BONAR BRIDGE
DORNOCH FIRTH
AN TEALLACH
GAIRLOCH
ALNESS
SLIOCH
DINGWALL
THE BLACK ISLE
MORAY FIRTH
NAIRN
ELGIN
BUCKIE
TORRIDON
ACHNASHEEN
MUIR OF ORD
FORRES
KEITH
STRATH BRAN
APPLECROSS
INVERNESS
CAMUSTERRACH
LOCHCARRON
HUNTLY
KYLE OF LOCHALSH
CAIRN GORM
DAVIOT
OLDMELDRUM
KINTORE
ABERDE
AVIEMORE
BANCHORY
NEWTONMORE
KINGUSSIE
GRAMPIAN MOUNTAINS
PASS OF DRUMOCHTER
CAIRN O' MOUNT
CLATTERIN' BRIG
BLAIR ATHOLL
DREISH
PASS OF KILLIECRANKIE
PITLOCHRY
BRECHIN
BLAIRGOWRIE
STRATHMORE
FORFAR
0
20
40
60
SB
MILES
'91
NEWTYLE
COLLACE
SIDLAW HILLS
DUNDEE
PERTH
TAY
NEWBURGH
ABERARGIE
AUCHTERMUCHTY
FIFE NESS
OCHILL HILLS
FREUCHIE
LOMOND HILLS
GLENROTHES
ABERDOUR
KIRKCALDY
FIRTH OF FORTH
KINGHORN
FALKIRK
GRANGEMOUTH
BURNTISLAND
NORTH BERWICK
EDINBURGH
BERWICK LAW

1 APRIL

DAVIOT

Development

So it was that by late afternoon I found myself back in Muir of Ord, having traversed the length of Wester Ross up Glencarron and Strathbran and, at Garve, descended into the sheltered, gentle scenery which tells you that at last you are out of reach of the chilly damp fingers of the Atlantic. For 50 miles the road toils through these long upland passes between open swathes of moorland, playing tag with the railway line and the fast shallow mountain rivers. The little villages along the route, Balnacra, Achnasheen, Achanalt, Lochluichart, survive it seems only because they supply tea and sandwiches and crafts and souvenirs to the holidaymakers who pour through in the summer. Except perhaps to the dedicated walker and the sportsman the countryside can have little to offer.

Twenty-five miles up the road from Lochcarron the sun was shining in a cloudless sky, but heavy rain was still falling, blown inland on the gale. There were rainbows everywhere. It was like being trapped inside a stained-glass window. At Garve the road at last was dry. The land is still cluttered by the wrecked cars, tractors and farm gadgetry that one finds all over the Highlands but it is by no means as bleak as the far north; in fact I noticed several little Swiss-cabin style developments, which mean that this is Timeshare Country. In other words, it is not particularly interesting or beautiful but it is possible to photograph it in such a way as to persuade unsuspecting suburbanites in the South to part with large amounts of money for the privilege of a week every year in a flimsy hut with a view of several acres of agricultural scrap metal.

Gradually the broken machines vanish as the land becomes more precious; by Strathpeffer the scenery is a mix of ploughed and pasture fields, well-wooded and gently rolling under a huge sky. At Marybank I stopped to examine a silo disguised by a concrete shell with battlements. A ginger-haired man chopping logs at the roadside told me that it was a common practice hereabouts to disguise silos in this way. I couldn't decide whether the effect was successful or just kitsch. Sometimes a shiny metal silo can enliven a view.

I gave a lift to a student from Muir of Ord to Inverness. Coincidentally his mother was the district nurse at Applecross, which summoned up a picture of the poor woman toiling up Sgurr a'Ghaorachain on a pushbike like Nerys Hughes. As we came along the south side of the Moray Firth he told me that in the summer, schools of dolphins are to be seen there, while in spring and autumn migrating ospreys are common. On this bright and breezy afternoon the firth was alive with sailboats. He was at Aberdeen University; there is a strong tendency among Scottish students to attend the university nearest their home, unlike the English who generally want to get as far out of parental sight as possible. I dropped him in downtown Inverness at about four o'clock. Even after only a few days it was weird and a little unnerving to be back amongst multistorey carparks, office blocks and supermarkets, and driving in heavy traffic. The city looked fine, with its great curve of buildings along the Ness; wide streets and clean lines, with a kind of Scandinavian pallor. But I had a long way still to go, and I wove my way along the ring-road and out towards Nairn with few regrets.

Once you are out of the city, the fields become immense and the land almost flat. The poor soil would naturally support only heathland and the lovely big pines which still stand in long ranks on every horizon, but the whole area is now under the plough. No hedges break up these immense isotropic farms; dry-stone walls of great length delicately criss-cross the land. Near Culloden I nearly crashed into a car turning right across the dual carriageway; as I overtook I knew exactly what the driver would look like: a stout woman of about 55 wearing enormously thick winged spectacles. Sure enough, there she was. This odd prescience recurred several times along my journey, notably in Yorkshire, but that is another story. I contented myself with yelling a torrent of well-chosen Anglo-Saxon obscenities, which of course no one could hear but myself. Somehow it seemed inevitable that at Culloden of all places there should be a sign advertising a pottery and wholefood restaurant.

Just outside Nairn there was a fine demonstration of the drawbacks of attempting high-intensity farming in such a landscape – the soil was blowing thickly across the road like a steady pink smoke. It was dense enough to force people to put their headlights on, and it was blowing directly into a neat estate of bungalows on the outskirts of the town. Nairn itself was a dreadful bottleneck, and looked fusty and frowsty – shortbread country. I pulled off the road into the drive of a private hospital; being a Bank Holiday, nobody in the Private Sector would be ill. As I sat rolling a cigarette a man came down the opposite side of the street staring intently at the car, or me, or both. Now I am quite used to people staring at Blodwen; she is unusual. But something about this man caught my attention. Certainly there was nothing remarkable about him: greying, in his 50s, a little overweight, wearing glasses and carrying a plastic carrier bag. He walked evenly, did not appear to be drunk, and his clothes implied that he was not sleeping rough. Yet he gave off the unsettling vibes of one about to accost you for the price of a cuppa and treat you to a tour of the Supplement to the Oxford English Dictionary if you refuse.

In between glances down to check that the tobacco was still in the cigarette paper and not in my lap, I watched him – not once did he lower his gaze. By now it must have been obvious that I was staring back, but he continued unabashed, his face set in a frown, his head gradually turning as he came abreast of and then passed the van. I began to pray that he would walk smack into the next lamp-post, but he seemed to have supernatural peripheral vision. When finally he could screw his head around no further he actually began to walk backwards so that he could keep me in sight. At last an intervening hedge took him out of view. By then I was completely unnerved. Something about the man had given me the strong impression that he was about to rip me limb from limb.

There seemed to be a plethora of strange men about that afternoon. A little later, on the road to Forres, a figure in a yellow kagool was striding along the busy, dead straight carriageway at a great pace, despite a severe limp. The traffic was heavy and Blodwen was moaning along in second and third gear, so I had time to notice that the man, who was sweating profusely and had a deep scowl on his face, was carrying a Bible. A strange weather-proofed prophet of the North-east.

Just after the turn for Burghead we came through a wood, and something about it struck me as odd, until I realised that it was largely deciduous – beech, birch and oak. After days of pine and spruce these trees, even in incipient bud, seemed weirdly exotic.

Elgin was busy. I stopped to buy a canned drink and walk up and down the main street, dominated by a lovely neoclassical City Hall, severe and clean, as if Wren had teamed up with Albert Speer. In front of it is a wonderful Great War memorial in the art-nouveau influenced style they called New Sculpture, lithe and romantic. Nobody passing gave it a glance.

The place has the air of a sleepy country town dolled up in Italianate togs for a low-budget version of the *Decline and Fall of the Roman Empire.* Its status as a city endowed with a prim little cathedral is overstated by the vast neoclassical buildings donated by the first Lord Elgin. His own massive columnar memorial exaggerates this uneasy mix. Still, the place seems to have much more in the way of shops and clubs and cinemas than many towns twice the size. Here for the first time I saw the classic North-eastern face, so sharp that it looks as if it has developed in a wind-tunnel, which I suppose it has. Imagine Bruce Forsyth with a small chin – not a pleasant exercise I grant you – and you have it. This face is everywhere in Buckie, Peterhead and Aberdeen.

Lhanbryde and Mosstodloch are road-villages very typical of eastern Scotland, straggling and dour and now encircled by Legoland bungaloid development. Fochabers, on the Spey, is grander, presumably due to the huge Baxters canned food factory which employs a large chunk of the populace. In the grounds of a hotel here, a life-size model stag had had its antlers vandalised. They hung down over its eyes like wet hair. On the way out the garden centre was flying a row of Union Jacks – something I have never seen before in Scotland.

The apparent flatness of the land is deceptive – it consists of huge long low hills, and in any view there is a great deal of 'dead ground' lying out of sight. Gradually the inclines get steeper as you traverse the furthest outskirts of the Grampian massif. Ben Rinnes, a big, isolated outlier, and the Ladder Hills dominate the southern skyline from the highest points on the road. For the most part, however, you are surrounded by clean-lined, pine-serrated hills faceted by the immense pale grey dry-stone walls – dykes, as they say here. It seems, oddly, a much bigger landscape than anywhere in the West, with more distant horizons and a sky which seems far more complicated. It is at the same time civilised and harsh, and very beautiful.

Alas, the same cannot be said for Keith, described a few days previously by the MC of the country dancing radio show as 'the bonny toon o' Keith'. I think he must have meant Keith, Wisconsin. It is a gloomy little town, on the tourist map as part of the junket known as the 'Whisky Trail', on which large numbers of people under the pretence of an interest in the means of production get completely incapable and sleep it off in the coach. Huge bonding sheds line the railway sidings making modern whisky production seem as unromantic as that of detergent (though doubtless more profitable). Looking at these dull slab-like buildings, I wondered that the stuff doesn't actually taste like detergent.

Despite the lovely openness of the land many of the farms have a pinched, boondocks look to them at odds with the pristine look of the fields. The farmsteads, built of massive granite setts, don't have the crazy untidiness of the west and north but they do have an unimproved, decaying look, as if all the money is going into the soil and none into the buildings. I passed a bus. It was the first one I had seen in four days. So much for the market force.

Huntly seemed to consist almost entirely of an industrial estate, the first sign of the economic impact of the oil boom on the North-east. Most of the rest of it was a big grim housing scheme, with the tiny old part of town harbouring the traditional craft centre and tea room. With this sign of the times came the first echo of the oldest recorded Scottish culture, one of the rash of placenames beginning with 'Pit-' which covers the North-east, supposedly marking Pictish settlements; this one was Pitmackie. Another uneasy marriage of old and new stood to the left of the road near Wells of Ythan – Logie House, a ruined shell in a lovely park. Behind its elegant, brittle walls the new owners have built a vast American-style ranch-effect dwelling. Such subtlety.

The land had flattened out a little, and the high hills with their stony granite summits had been left behind. A few miles short of Inverurie I turned left onto the first country road I had been on that day, which had been a mad dash in a more or less straight line on the trunk route. My first view of the village of Daviot was of a huddle of new grey bungalows in a hedgeless expanse of cereal and rape fields. It looked utterly undistinguished. I drove slowly through it, noting the location of the pub for future reference, and climbed up the gentle hill to the north to where a Stone Circle was marked on my map. I found it at the back of the Scout Camp.

It was a clear evening, windy, with long lines of slate-grey cloud majestically exaggerating the wide horizon westward toward the hills. The stone circle was a neat, intimate place with a series of informative plaques explaining its construction and origins which did not wholly spoil its melancholy and enigmatic atmosphere. Even more melancholy and atmospheric, however, was the Scout Camp; there's nothing so spooky as an empty barracks or an empty school, and this had something of both. In a grove of thin coppiced trees was a Nissen hut and a curious extension which I thought looked rather like an old railway carriage. This was because it was an old railway carriage, which had been rendered with cement, presumably to disguise the fact that it was an old railway carriage. A couple of windows were broken and there were signs that someone had been having a rare old time burning the odd mattress. It was the kind of place where you expect at any moment to see a face appear at one of the long line of empty windows, but you only expect it because you are frightened that it may actually happen and the wind is rustling the dead leaves and the lapwings are keening in the next field and after all, who but a psycho would try to set fire to Boy Scouts' mattresses?

So, whistling loudly, I went back to the van having decided that both neolithic astrochronometer and paramilitary youth camp were unsuitable places for a gentleman of refined sensibilities to kip for the night, and proceeded up the hill, only to find that beyond the Scout Camp lay the cemetery, a spick and span acre of regimented stones boxed in by a trim beech hedge. Being a fan of cemeteries, I took a quick look round and it struck me that the modern burial ground was a good deal stranger than the sacrificial circle which had been unearthed next to the standing stones down the hill. We seem to be a great deal more caught up in death than our wolfskin-clad forebears, who not only suffered from all the horrific diseases we are proud to have conquered but were also at the mercy of drought, famine, wild animals and the thirst for blood of their priests, to say nothing of the next tribe coveting their crop of millet. What a fuss we make of it compared to a race among whom only a king warranted a few lines scratched on a boulder. Would the Picts have understood the concept of a 'Dear Nan and Mum' memorialised in white marble for the next thousand years or more, covered with green glass chips and protected from who-knows-what by iron chains? As our standard of living has risen, and the length of our days increased, so our standard of dying has risen and the trappings of death have become a parody of the trappings of life; we keep up with the deceased Joneses.

Opposite the cemetery was a little reservoir surrounded by a high wire fence, barely bigger than a swimming pool and smelling about as drinkable. It was sheltered by a line of beeches and there was a grassy patch behind a bank where the Water Authority vans could turn – an ideal parking-and-sleeping place, out of the wind and hidden from the lane. A good deal of litter bore testimony to its popularity as a boozing-and-snogging area, but tonight would be too cold for such romantic shenanigans. I cooked and ate a meal, listening to the radio, singing along at the top of my voice to 'Solsbury Hill'. I washed up, then sat and wrote notes until dusk, when I locked the car and headed down to the Smiddy Bar. Despite having driven 190 miles that day I felt fine – something to do with the long, bright evening and the austere beauty of the land.

There were only five people in the bar, plus the barman. I ordered a pint and sat writing up memoranda of the day's drive before they were washed away by time and alcohol. The bar was typically Scottish: lit with fluorescent lights, lino on the floor, plain modern furniture – the bare necessities. The television was on with the sound turned off and a tape was playing a 'Tribute to Elvis' concert by an impersonator. Nobody gave me a second glance, though they'd given me a careful first one. Eventually I struck up a conversation with the barman, whose name was Bill. A former Youth Worker, he had only been in charge for a few weeks. His former calling gave him the advantage of knowing which of the local kids were too young to drink. The previous tenants had 'let the place go' – drinks slopped on the bar, short measures, short change and surly service, if any. Bill quietly outlined his plans for the place, namely a four-point strategy based on cleanliness, friendly service, politeness and good beer. The last of these was the key one; most of the incomers to the village were English. Used to the very different English tradition of carpets, soft lighting, fruit machines, a jukebox, and good bar food, they had stayed away in droves from what was basically a concrete box for drinking in. But the curse of Scottish hostelries, bitter (known as 'heavy' in Scotland) served at lager temperature, had probably put them off most. Bill had been given a list of 'approved' beers by the

56

brewery who owned the bar. He read them out to the assembled throng, now eight strong including myself, and each brand was given careful consideration, meeting either groans or non-commital grunts. Bill put away the list, looking a little resigned. His main problem was storage; the popularity of draught lager meant that it was almost impossible to keep bitter at the correct temperature in the same cellar.

Of the multitude of revellers, only three were Scots, and none of those three was originally from the village, though one was from Buckie. Of the others, two were from Yorkshire, one from Lancashire and one was a French-Canadian. I didn't count. Bill the barman was from Wick, and a couple from Perthshire came in a little later. Oil was what had brought them to Aberdeenshire, and high prices in Aberdeen were what had brought them to Daviot. The Perthshire couple had been in the village 11 years and according to them, it had changed beyond recognition during that period. From my own perambulations I would say that 80 per cent of the buildings were less than a decade old.

Four items decorated the beige, bleak walls of the bar: three mirrors with pictures of James Dean, Elvis Presley and Marilyn Monroe printed on them, and a menu. This was it:

> Beefburger and Bun
> Hot Dog
> Stovies
> Lasagne
> Haggis, Neeps and Tatties
> Cottage Pie
> Chicken Curry
> Spaghetti Bolognaise

I didn't mention to Bill that I thought perhaps it might benefit the pub to overhaul this cholesterol-packed list. The Scots are fiercely proud of their dreadful diet and one of the national papers recently ran a campaign to save their massive consumption of mince from interfering Sassenachs and Eurocrats.

For some reason various ludicrous stories about animals were aired. I told them about a bloke in my old local in Essex who had been known to sink 18 straight whiskies at lunchtime and then drive home with his dog in his lap. This was topped by a Daviotian who recalled a cat which insisted on driving everywhere with its owner, not only travelling on the driver's lap but standing on its hind legs and looking out of the windscreen while resting its paws on the horn, a habit which led the motorist to disconnect the mechanism and thus fail his MOT.

I said my goodnights and they wished me luck. I walked back up the hill through velvety darkness, moonless and windless. In the van I brewed tea and listened to the radio, watching the tangerine glow of Aberdeen on the clouds. Then I went through the ructions of getting into bed. Somehow it seemed a lot easier after three pints of Guinness.

In the morning the gale had returned, but it did not discourage the birds: the combined racket of robin, chaffinch, thrush, skylark, curlew and rooks – hundreds of rooks – woke me at five. I dozed until six, dreaming that a group of men were coming along the lane. 'Look, Dad,' said one of them, 'there *is* someone in there.' I tried to sit up and wave, but could not open my eyes or mouth, rising from the back seat like a zombie. I reached out to tap the window and woke. It struck me as very stupid to dream that the youth had an English accent, until I remembered where I was. A man driving a tractor came along the lane, peering curiously over the hedge at me. Five minutes later he came back the other way and peered again, and five minutes after that once more. This time I waved, but got no reaction, possibly because I was getting dressed at the time and my trousers were not immediately apparent.

By nine I was back down in the village. It was deserted, except for an old man hoeing his garden and a fat golden retriever lying on someone's drive. The 'white settlers', as Bill had called the English incomers, commuted *en masse* to Aberdeen. The village had a couple of hundred houses and a church, the bar and a derelict shop. On the outskirts, along a private land and hidden behind trees, was a large building which might have once been a Victorian baronial house, but which had notice boards of the kind you see outside hospitals. I took it for either an isolation hospital or a mental institution. I spent three-quarters of an hour wandering the few streets – not a curtain twitched. Apart from two cars nothing moved but the golden retriever, which yawned and shifted to its other side.

Walking through Daviot I felt like Clint Eastwood walking into town, with the cowed populace shivering indoors and the bad guys waiting in the Last Chance Saloon. It is as quiet now as it was 5,000 years ago, but for the wrong reasons. It is no longer a village at all, merely somewhere to sleep. I doubt that many more attend the other traditional focus of community, the kirk, than drink in the Smiddy Bar. With no shop, no park and, as far as I could see, no school, there is a coldness about it, an atmosphere of introversion. The boxy, grey, neat little bungalows with their manicured lawns seem no more real than model houses in a toy village. Without the oil boom Daviot might still be alive; tumbledown, isolated, depressed but sentient. Instead it has grown and died.

Away to the west an extraordinary hill glowers over the plain. It is steep, almost pyramidal, and has a rocky summit which looks for all the world like a fortified watchtower. Like something from *The Lord of the Rings*, it seems to stare down balefully, adding to the uneasy quiet of the village, which crouches low in the fields as if to avoid its gaze. Next to the church is a fine house, presumably the manse, which has a shield of mature beeches,

58

but even these seem to cringe. I was not sorry to leave; I felt I might go mad if I stayed under that hill for too long.

I walked up to the stone circle; on the way the man in the tractor passed again. Perhaps he had lost a field somewhere. At any rate, this time he waved at me, so I knew I still had my trousers on. I read the information plaques – the circle dates from between 4000 and 5000 BC, and the burial site next to it had contained around 30 cremations. The circle seemed to be for measuring the phases of the moon. At its centre a single body was buried: a man clutching a stone pendant. On one of the stones were 12 Pictish cup-marks; these are indentations, the size of coffee-mugs, of doubtful symbolism. I could only find two. As far as anyone can tell, the burial in the ring, the burials next door and the cup-marks are more likely than not unconnected with each other or with the original function of the ring itself. So much for archaeology. But by now the sun was shining, taking the edge of the freezing wind, and the circle in its swathe of rabbit-cropped bright green grass had the pleasant atmosphere of garden sculpture. Beyond, on a hill a few miles away across the plain, a television mast echoed the tall stones. I lingered a long time, touching the rocks and trying to guess why they had been put there, half-way down the hill rather than at the top only a few hundred feet away. Less far to walk, I suppose. Normally you feel instinctively that a prehistoric monument is in the right place; it makes sense of the land, or vice versa. This is not so at Daviot, which makes it stranger than usual. I wonder if it worked; maybe they realised but couldn't be bothered to take it all down and start again, bumped off their astronomer, buried him in the middle and used it for keeping chickens in.

As I drove out of the village the man in the tractor passed again; that tractor seemed to be doing more miles than I was.

Here and there in the Aberdeenshire countryside there remains a tract of land where the dry-stone dykes have not been grubbed up to form gigantic open spaces, but cluster instead in a difficult little twist of valley or in the narrow space between forking roads. In such places one gets an impression of what the entire landscape must have been like a couple of decades ago: a mad Mondrian-like geometric quilt, with each tiny rectangle a subtly different shade of green, or, if bare, pink.

It was almost spring – primroses were flowering along the road, rooks were quarreling and showing off in the stiff breeze. I went down to Inverurie, another boom-town with a big unsightly industrial estate and lots of new car showrooms encircling a prim core of granite villas. On the wide main street were five pedestrians. In case the visitor should be in any doubt as to the source of the town's new wealth, and be wondering where the population have gone, there is a boutique called 'Rig Out'.

Across the Don on the main road you pass signs to two Scandinavian settlements, Thainstone and Clovenstone, adding to the Tolkienish atmosphere. I turned off towards Dunecht. New houses and bungalows were everywhere. Anyone with a serious desire to be rich should consider becoming a builder in Aberdeenshire. Strangely, there were also a good many plundered railway carriages and trucks being inhabited by both humans and chickens, though one hopes not together. Thirty years ago they must have blessed Dr Beeching for solving the housing crisis. Echt was completely deserted. Stopping at the crossroads I could see at least a straight mile of the village street but there was not a soul in sight. Across the way, a lovely chapel stands, dated 1804, a simple box with gigantic perpendicular windows, so that there seems to be more glass than wall – totally un-Scottish.

I was nearing the easternmost arm of the Grampians and snowy peaks were now visible ahead. The beechy countryside gave way once again to poor, sandy, pine-lined fields, and at the foot of the hills lay Banchory, very much a highland town despite its lowland location. Dark and baronial in style, tightly grouped and almost without new development, it is full of the kind of 'Ladies Fashions' which consist largely of pleats. It was much more like Pitlochry or Crieff than anything else I had seen in the North-east, where the towns are pale and straggle in long lines along the roads. Over the Dee and into the hills, the road ascends in steep steps, levelling out periodically into mezzanines of pasture or mature pine forest before kicking upwards again. Eventually you emerge on to high moorland, completely treeless, and with no more than two inches variation in the height of the heather as far as the eye can see. It feels like the top, but the road continues upward more gently for a mile or so. I pulled over into a lay-by for a drink; the wind screamed around the car, but the sky was cloudless. Uniform blue above, uniform brown below; the simplest place. While I was resting – it's a toughish road up from Banchory – a tiny M-registered Daf pottered past, heading up. The unsung heroism of everyday life.

Descending from the summit is easy – having paused to admire the tremendous view of the Howe of the Mearns and all the coast for 40 miles backed by the twinkling sea, the car simply falls off the hill. For more than a mile the road descends at between 14 and 16 degrees, with hairpins and no respite. I came down in first gear and by the time I reached the bottom I had cramp in the leg which I'd jammed on the footbrake.

I drove through Clatterin' Brig and into Strathmore, the great vale. Was it my imagination, or do the buildings on this leeward side stand up more from the fields? The trees, too, seem taller and more muscular. Fettercairn, the first substantial village, seemed to confirm this new freedom from gravity with a little Victorian spire and a curious arched gateway across the road, a feature echoed more grandly in Edzell, where a big Gothic arch straddles the end of a main road of almost ceremonial grandeur, lined by prosperous-looking hotels. Beyond it, on a two-mile straight, the wind made a concerted effort to finish the trip by blowing me sideways into the conifers; whenever it swirled behind the van I could feel it pushing Blodwen forward like a turbocharger. On the big dual-carriageway A94, completely exposed to the wind, the lorries lurched drunkenly from side to side as they tore down towards Dundee. Most were still travelling well over 60 mph, with some going closer to 80, barely under control and scattering saloons like sharks among mackerel. I had planned to get quite a way south on this road; I was glad to get off at the first opportunity and wiggle across country through Brechin and Aberlemno.

I stopped for lunch on a hillside overlooking a great swathe of Strathmore, with the line of hills beyond running straight as an arrow from Cairn o' Mount (which I'd fallen off earlier that morning) in the north-east to Blackcraig Hill in the south-west above Blairgowrie. I picked off the summits on the map: Hill of Wirren, Sturdy Hill, Hill of Garbet, Auld Darkney, Hill of Couternach, Cat Law, Drumderg. Behind, the snowy summits above Glen Clova and Glen Prosen could just be glimpsed, rising steadily toward the 3,000-foot Driesh and Mayar. While I was eating, a hare came out of a gate a hundred yards up the road and sprinted down the hill for a quarter of a mile until the next gap in the wall, where he turned in with a skid of his back legs sending a little cloud of dust away on the wind. Someone should have told him March was over.

Despite the intrusive main road on the valley floor, Strathmore is to my mind one of the great sights of Scotland. Indeed, the east of Scotland as a whole has much lovely and varied scenery – high hills, bare rock outcrops, sinuous moorland summits, bogs, pastures, forest and woodland and long lines of Scots pine like alien calligraphy across the skyline. In England it would be famous; in Scotland it suffers in comparison to the spectacular highlands and islands. Tourists do come, but for the whisky and the castles and the fishing and the golf. Perhaps it is because it is intensively farmed that it is somehow felt to be less valuable than the wildernesses of the North and West. Yet of all the industrial farmland of Britain this is probably the most lovely. Not all is rural idyll, however, as Forfar painfully proves. Despite a good crude medieval church tower and a pretty spire or two, Forfar makes no bones about its industrial importance. I took a wrong turn in the dour outskirts and found myself once more on the dual carriageway at the mercy of speeding artics. By the time I could get off that road, I was out of Strathmore on the southern side of the Sidlaw Hills, looking over the unbonny suburbs of Dundee.

Dundee itself is an extraordinary place. It has perhaps the finest setting of any British city, spread over steep hills above the Tay, here comparatively narrow at two miles wide. Spanned by the delicate Victorian railway bridge and the ruler-like modern road bridge, the Tay is forced out through this narrow neck, producing some ferocious tides. Those unfortunate enough to fall or desperate enough to jump from the bridges are rarely found. When the old Tay Bridge collapsed in a storm in 1873, the train crossing it at the time was never recovered; some of the carriages washed up in Norway. Although the river can be glimpsed (to the delight of estate agents) from many parts of the city, a major road, much industrial wasteland and the old dockyards mean that Dundonians are curiously cut off from it. Instead of redeveloping the waterfront for leisure, as has been done so successfully in Liverpool, Hull, Bristol and London, the City Council in their wisdom are building gigantic retail warehouses and supermarkets along the shore.

Scotland's third city has a spirit all its own, a fierce pride in its sheer dismal awfulness. For though from afar, Dundee looks like Naples by day and Manhattan by night, inside it has few redeeming features. Never particularly wealthy, usually grindingly poor, throughout history it had a reputation for violence, squalor and ugliness, meanness and introversion. 'Buildings', wrote Thomas Hood in 1815, 'crammed into corners that cannot be found . . . as though so ill-built . . . that the town were ashamed they should ever be seen'. The hopelessly bad poet William McGonagall, who elsewhere might have been merely teased, left the city in disgust having been pelted with stones on the streets. And in the 1930s, as the Dundonian James Cameron remembered, Dundee was a place of 'singular desolation . . . that from the beginning of time had reconciled itself to an intrinsic ugliness . . . black and terrible, [it had a] brutal melancholy, a facade of unparalleled charmlessness, an absence of grace so total that it was almost a thing of wonder'.*

Not much has changed. The smoke has cleared, but apart from the vast empty jute mills, the city centre is remarkable chiefly for its almost total lack of decent buildings compared to most cities half the size. A couple of pompous banks, a grim academy in straitlaced neoclassical black Doric, a cathedral no more exciting than the average parish church; there are really only two good structures in the entire place: the City Museum and Art Gallery, a little gem of Victorian Gothic, and the offices of D. C. Thomson, the newspaper and comic publishers, a splendid block which looks as if it has been transported from the Chicago of the '20s. Most of the new development is awful; some is disastrous. The endless estates which encircle the city remind one strongly of the worst excesses of Eastern Europe, and the climate strongly amplifies this impression. But Dundee has something of which it can be truly proud: Dundonians.

Unintelligible, brusque, garrulous and supposedly aggressive, Dundonians sustain a reputation beside which the worst excesses of the Gorbals or Leith pale into respectability. It is of course ill-deserved for the most part, but the visitor to Dundee today cannot fail to be convinced that the city's history is writ large in the physiology of its inhabitants. Dundee was the first place I ever visited in Scotland; I remember being forcefully struck,

* *Point of Departure*, 1967

62

even in the depths of the recession of the early 1980s, at how poor its inhabitants looked. Pale, stunted, undernourished-looking, Dundonians looked to me, freshly arrived from the soft South, like extras from *Little Dorrit*. It wasn't that everyone was poor – far from it – simply that there were more evidently poor people than I had ever seen in one place. Pallid families with bony children decked out in the cheapest market-stall clothing. Comparatively young men and women who had clearly had rickets as children. People with tubercular coughs (TB is on the increase again). Young women with no teeth. People wearing shoes which were barely more than scraps of plastic. And too frequently the evidence of chronic economic failure and discrimination: men ravaged by alcohol and women displaying cuts and bruises like tribal scars. The effect was powerful enough to colour my first impressions deeply. Today, perhaps through familiarity, it seems better.

No doubt Dundee is little worse than Liverpool (the city it perhaps most closely resembles) or Newcastle or Glasgow or Swansea. The difference seems to be that unlike all these places, Dundee has never been grand; its wealth from jute and shipping (and latterly oil) has somehow slipped through its fingers. Despite everything it is a likeable place; the unremitting cheerlessness of the streets is almost saintly, as if it carries on its shoulders an unselfishly large chunk of past and present social evils. And just as the citizens of those other great cities have their own easily patronised but nevertheless vital spirit (Scouse cheek, Geordie generosity, Glaswegian sentimental pride), so Dundonians have a wry, undefeated, pawky quick humour. They have tongues like knives. For me the spirit of Dundee was encapsulated by the great Dundee United team of the mid-'80s: a bunch of raggedy, scrawny, mercurial kids who looked as though they were kicking an empty can of Irn-Bru around the close, and took Europe by storm.

For a couple of hours I picked my way along the Sidlaws, first around Auchterhouse above Dundee, then back over on the Strathmore side above Coupar Angus on a tiny little road which runs absolutely straight along the hillside and could well be Roman in origin. The Sidlaws are a strange dinky range, geologically part of the volcanic Ochil system, but now cut off from them by the Tay and the Earn. Like the Ochils they begin quietly at their northern extremity with steep rolling hills only a couple of hundred feet high, now mostly under the plough except where the slope is too steep or the soil too stony. They rise steadily to the south, gradually becoming more verdant and increasingly harbouring little wooded glens and dens until above the confluence of the Tay and the Earn, they reach over 700 feet. Here, Kinnoull Hill has been sliced open by the river leaving a massive vertical cliff known locally as Suicide Point. Across Strathearn the Ochils pick up the torch and continue southwards until above Stirling they are serious mountains well over 2,000 feet in height. Again, in the South this system, which contains some beautiful scenery, would merit the kind of attention given to the Cotswolds or the Chilterns; here it is almost unre-marked. Indeed, if you confess an admiration for them in a country ever more obsessed with scaling Corbetts and Monros you risk at least ridicule and at worst, serious slurs on your manhood.

Between the Sidlaws and the Tay lies the flood-plain known as the Carse of Gowrie. This and the 'Braes of the Carse' – the sunny south-facing escarpment of the hills – have become prime real estate for the commuters to Dundee and Perth. Strangely, however, the north side is very sparsely settled despite wonderful views over Strathmore and the mountains, until just short of Perth, where a rash of 'designer' dwellings (no architects seem to have been involved) invade the slopes of Kinnoull Hill, and a quarter of a million will buy you a view to rival any in Scotland and several acres of crazy paving.

I pottered along to the tiny village of Collace, which marked 800 miles since my journey's beginning only 120 hours previously. The day was still dazzlingly bright and windy, and the pale denuded northern side of the hills, here and there punctuated by a verdant den or a stand of decrepit pines, had a faintly surreal atmosphere, like a Paul Nash landscape. Collace sits under Dunsinane Hill, from where the vegetation set out to seal Macbeth's fate, and the highest point hereabouts is King's Seat, thought by some to refer to King Arthur (Arthurstone is a hamlet not far away). Finally the road skirts the last of the Sidlaws at Balbeggie from where you can see westwards to Ben Vorlich and Ben More 40 miles away, and drops down to Scone, Scotland's most emotive historic site. I hope that if one day Scotland secedes, its government will do something about Scone. The site is now occupied by a gloomy Victorian Gothic palace, which is open to those who wish to be channelled through a collection of antiques of varying merit into a giftshop. Outside in the grounds the former site of the Coronation Stone, arguably the most significant symbol of nationhood the Scots have, is indicated by a pokerwork wooden sign of the kind which might indicate the way to the Gents' in a Swiss chalet village. Rarely can a place of such actual importance and potential magic have been rendered so banal. I felt as if, on entering Westminster Abbey, I had been confronted by a Kentucky Fried Chicken stall.

Perth is often said to be to Scotland what Cheltenham is to England, by which we are meant to gather that it is a well-heeled, comfortably conservative town which gives itself airs. Certainly Dundonians tend to hold this view, which is voiced with increasing vehemence now that Dundonian soccer is on the slide and St Johnstone are on the rise. In fact, Perth has little of Cheltenham's classy architecture and still less of its wealth; Hunter's Crescent, an estate on the north-east side, is as miserable a slum as one could find in Europe, or was, until the council decided to turn it into a housing co-op and rename it 'Freshfields' or something equally idiotic. In essence Perth today is a small county town blessed with pleasant location and easy access to all four of Scotland's largest cities, as well as the mountains, the West Coast and the North Sea – it has a small but busy port. Given these geographical advantages it is extraordinary that the city has remained as underdeveloped as it has; apart from the headquarters of two large companies dealing in whisky and insurance (which surely gang thegither!) it is primarily a shopping town. Its history is really one of long decline; its grid-plan streets are held to indicate that it was intended as the model capital of the newly-united Scots and Picts, though others argue that its origins are earlier, and the streets indicate a late Romano-British settlement attached to the nearby fort of Bertha (Abertay = Bertha = Perth). It is held that Kenneth Macalpine, the first King of all Scotland, would not have chosen a grid-plan, since no towns had been laid out thus in Britain for 400 years. To which the sensible reply would seem to be, if the man was bright enough to unite the Scots and the Picts he could have realised the advantages of straight streets.

In any case, Perth was superseded by Dunfermline and then Edinburgh and still has a faintly aggrieved air about the whole business. There are some pleasant streets but apart from St John's Kirk, where in 1559 John Knox delivered one of his more volcanic outbursts, the only really interesting building is the amazing City Hall, a neoclassical slab decorated in the worst possible taste by the addition of four gigantic cherubs with their fat bums perched uneasily on the parapet. They look as if they must have been left over from another building three times the size. Otherwise, though graced by two enormous parks, a couple of attractive Georgian terraces, and the lovely old Perth bridge, the city has nothing left of any early grandeur. Perthians (or Johnstonians) are held elsewhere (again, particularly in Dundee) to be surly and cold and snobbish; they supposedly think of Dundonians as louts and Fifers as yokels. As an Englishman I had better reserve judgment, except perhaps to venture that any city which can elect as MP Sir Nicholas Fairbairn cannot be all that worried about the opinions of others. So I found myself cruising back along the winding road from Aberargie to Abernethy and over the border into Fife. From the top of the rise at the west end of Newburgh the Firth of Tay spread out eastwards between the hills in the late afternoon sun, spanned distantly by the fragile Tay Bridge like a piece of brown twine stretched over a blue silk scarf. It was hard, confronted with such a glorious view as I am every day, to ignore the sensation that I had come home for good and resist the urge to kick off my shoes and relax. I had completed a gigantic figure-of-eight which had taken me through so much astonishing scenery so quickly that I felt I could never do even these opening four letters justice – as I haven't. But I had to keep myself psyched up – I had barely begun and the wild uncivilised wastes of England beckoned, to say nothing of Wales. I had to break the journey and fly down to London for an interview, so Edinburgh would perforce be my letter E. In any case it was time I tackled somewhere big.

But that would be after a day's rest and all the comforts of home. I turned off the engine and went indoors, feeling as if I'd been away for a month already.

EDINBURGH

An evening's entertainment

This pause in the itinerary gave me a chance to reflect on how things were developing. The most striking thing about it, which seemed at the time to be mildly disastrous, was that I had come into contact with relatively few people. The pressure of my schedule meant that nearly all my time was taken up with driving, writing or sleeping. A few sentences with shopkeepers and garage attendants were all I had managed except when staying in a guesthouse or visiting a pub. I had a continuing sensation that I was missing much that was important. I had with me a number of guidebooks but had referred to them no more than once or twice, from a fear that if I opened them I would discover exactly what it was that I had missed and become demoralised. I told myself that the terms of reference of the trip were open and that I should have no preconceptions about what to look for and what I 'ought' to find. After all, spending eight hours a day behind the wheel of a small car does put severe limits on the ability to gather material.

Of course, it was ridiculous to expect that the journey would provide any great insights into either my own character or that of Britain and the British. Even a work which claims to do so, such as Paul Theroux's *The Kingdom by the Sea* proves on close inspection to be largely solitary observation coloured by prejudices and preconceptions, despite the writer's more relaxed timetable and sociable mode of transport. I reminded myself that the main point of my journey was to raise money for charity, not to solve the Matter of Britain. Whatever the outcome, however introverted and sociopathic I became spending four weeks in mobile solitary confinement, my first obligation was to *finish the trip*. I had to keep this in the forefront of my mind; the necessity to *get there* had to be the impulse, not my desire to see as much as possible. Forget Theroux, I thought. Try Hunter S. Thompson, even if the Howe of Fife does not closely resemble the Mojave Desert.

Auchtermuchty – the Las Vegas of Scotland? Hardly. I suspect that many people think that it's a joke place, a sort of Scottish Much-Binding-in-the-Marsh. It's a pretty, close-built village with a reputation for being a rough-house on Saturday nights, perhaps a legacy of a more industrial past. It lies exactly on the divide between the Ochils and the flat central plain or Howe. As you come into the village you are driving through steep winding little valleys, densely wooded, damp and mossy, and as you leave you enter dead flat sandy fields bordered with pines and which have been much dug for gravel and sand. Ahead, the enormous brooding shape of Easter Lomond, the basalt core of an extinct volcano, towers over the plain. That day was one of sudden heavy squalls and bursts of brilliant sunlight, setting the whole landscape flickering and drawing veils of diaphanous material across the hills. Through the hamlets Charlottetown and Giffordtown in blinding light, to reach Freuchie (pronounced Frookie) in near-darkness and torrential rain. Apart from once winning the national village cricket tournament, Freuchie's chief claim to fame is that it was a sin-bin for courtiers at James V's favourite house, Falkland Palace, a few miles west. Those unfortunate enough to incur the monarch's wrath were in the habit of moving to Freuchie for a month or two until the fuss had died down, hence a local expression 'Away with you to Freuchie and eat mice', meaning 'I told you so, now eat humble pie or I'll smash your face in'. Nobody says it anymore, not surprisingly.

Many of these Fife villages – Freuchie, Falkland, Kinross, Milnathort, Strathmiglo, Gateside and 'Muchty – now have substantial English communities: immigrants working in the new high-tech industries of Glenrothes and the Forth valley have bought up large chunks of these attractive places, forcing up prices. I once spent an entire evening in a Falkland pub and heard only one Scottish accent – the barmaid's. This is probably fine with the rest of the Scots, who regard Fife in general as the Chinese regard Outer Mongolia. For the English, of course, Fife corresponds to their ideals – bijou cottages in lovely countryside at dirt-cheap prices near a motorway – closely enough to convince them that they would rather be living in Scotland than in the Cotswolds or the Surrey hills.

Glenrothes is a new town, an exercise in post-war modernist utopianism, airy and clean. Like all new towns it was designed for the car; it is impossible to walk any distance in it without being run over or having to fight your way through gigantic shrubs on concrete islands. It is not bad in a very dated kind of way, probably because it has not grown apace and therefore has not deteriorated from overpopulation, traffic jams and vandalism.

I pulled off the road, partly to let a pack of vast lorries get by and partly because the windscreen wipers kept giving up. From my vantage point to the south of Glenrothes it was possible to see what the planners had intended, and also, perhaps, to see what went wrong. The British have always hated the idea of social planning, unlike the French, who think their equivalents of Milton Keynes are wonderful. Lately this antipathy has been rationalised by such luminaries as the Prince of Wales; these post-war developments, it seems, have no 'sense of community', are inorganic, sterile. Ironically enough, this is precisely the opposite of their intention, and indeed nearly all new towns are laid out in order to foster a sense of community; people live together either in high-rise blocks or on estates, work together in the factory or office zones, and shop together in the precincts. They go to the same cinemas, theatres and sports grounds and their children all go to the comprehensive. Their impulse was socialist and democratic, if paternalistic. Why then are they considered such a failure? Why is Milton Keynes a joke? There are two answers. The most important one is that many are not failures at all; Glenrothes for example is highly successful. The great antipathy to the New Towns comes from the English middle and upper classes, who perceive the inhabitants of the New Towns to be lower-middle and working class. Since many are 'overspill' towns, there is some truth in this. New Townies often rent or buy at subsidised rates; they rely on cars and buses and tend to 'value' new things rather than old.

This runs against the ideology of the middle and upper classes: their impulse is antisocial; for them the ideal way to live is in an isolated cottage with a garden or in an antique town house with 'character'. They feel guilty about over-reliance on their cars and have no wish to shop in centres or precincts, because they feel that convenience means lack of quality. Their entire life's effort is geared to demonstrating their self-reliance, and their homes are their castles, fortresses of privet and roses. They never use buses (New Town transport *par excellence*) and will get their children privately educated if they can. Modernism appals them – it is both communistic and foreign. The French, who invented modernism and have always been more sympathetic to both strong leadership and social democracy, regard their town planning as triumphant evidence of their egalitarianism; in Britain the words 'Town Planning' have the same effect on people as 'Militant' and 'Social Worker'.

So the New Towns are partially successful in that they work for the people who live in them but they don't attract all the people for whom they were intended. Why is Town Planning so derided in Britain? After all, the last thing you want is a factory on your doorstep. The middle classes do not want to live anywhere even vaguely associated with manufacturing. It is this prejudice which has resulted in the great English institution of the unplanned yet thoroughly inorganic suburb of identical semi-detached villas. Places such as Surbiton and Sutton Coldfield demonstrate the almost masochistic lengths we will go to in order to try and square this circle. They are in effect unplanned New Towns with none of the conveniences or planned facilities necessary to a real community, and their style is a pathetic apeing of the rurality they have destroyed, but they are utterly uniform – far more so than any New Town. They are the ghettoes of the middle class, trapped by the ideology of their social superiors, by the economic constraints of their employment and by an almost pathological disgust at evidence of manufacturing work. New Towns are anathema to these people not because they have failed to foster a sense of community but precisely because they *do* foster a sense of community. For a nation which will always take the last spare seat on the bus if it means conversation can be avoided, this is unforgivable – they might have to *talk to each other*. Worse, they are being forced to do so.

If you ever want evidence that an organic town may not be all that Prince Charles makes it out to be, go to Kirkcaldy. The first of a string of ex-coal, ex-heavy industry, ex-everything towns strung along the Fife coast of the Firth of Forth like rotting onions, Kirkcaldy can be imagined as Dudley-by-the-Sea. Factories, mostly old and many abandoned, are jumbled together with houses, mean little rows of shops, garages, tyre centres and used car lots, all covered with a patina of old soot and new rust. To be fair to our future king, he objects as strongly to urban decay as he does to the legacy of Le Corbusier; I don't know whether he has ever visited Kirkcaldy, though he may have stared at it from the train window on the way to Balmoral. He probably turned to Di and said, 'That can't be as bad as it looks.' But it is. It is one of the most ugly, scruffy, mean, gimcrack, raddled old dumps I've ever seen. Even the wide Firth does nothing to improve it; the front is a dreary two miles of rubble, mid-rise flats and abandoned factories. It probably has a wonderful sense of community, but then so did Colditz. I couldn't bear to stop in Kirkcaldy – I've been there before – but I did wander around Burntisland, a little further along the coast. More than half-resort, Burntisland is a good deal smaller and less jumbled than the home of Raith Rovers. I drove in down a wide, pleasant street of solid Victorian villas on one side and a park on the other, and at the end of the shopping street followed a sign advertising free parking for 650 cars. This I reduced to 649 – mine was the only vehicle on the six acres of tarmac. The carpark bordered a wide railway yard – presumably warehouses or factories had once stood there, because in Britain a carpark tends to be somewhere where something has been demolished but nothing can be found to replace it. I walked on to the tracks. Beyond them a truncated terrace of Victorian brick cottages stood on a low rocky outcrop, and beyond this the choppy Forth fronted the distant Lammermuir Hills. Huddled beneath an inland cliff covered with shrub, the place had an almost Blakeian sense of grandeur wood decay; in the strong slanting light under a slate-grey sky, the brown, steep little town, crumbling and sooty, retained a strong flavour

70

of the pride and solidity of its industrial heyday, but the deserted yards and cobbled streets by the docks lent a powerful sense of uncertainty. It was like a painting by De Chirico, enigmatic, expectant, paranoiac.

The rail yard was blowing away, literally, the salt spray of the Firth of Forth eating into the rails and turning them to flakes of red dust. Tall weeds and saplings grew between the sleepers. Even the litter was old – cans rusting into skeletal fragments, newspapers degenerating into wads of fibre. One dock has been modernised and remains open, but the fine old customs house opposite the gates, a really magnificent early-Victorian building, is in ruins. Next door another Victorian dockside building has become a block of flats. Burntisland seems to have a considerable population which has moved across the bridge from the capital; like many of these industrial southern Fife towns, it retains a pretty little core of medieval buildings, something which Kirkcaldy lacks. The town had a better class of housing than its bigger and more industrial neighbour and these are now attracting a new middle class, a process I have seen described as 'croissantification'. Further up the coast, in the ex-fishing villages of the East Neuk beyond the old coalfield, this process has reached absurd conclusions as the richest commuters from Edinburgh, Dundee and St Andrews, along with a considerable number of second-home seekers, hijacked the local housing market. Villages like Crail and Anstruther and Kilconquar are stuffed with Mercedes and BMWs, and tiny two-bedroomed cottages, which not so long ago were hovels with rafters hung with dried herrings, fetch laughably vast sums. The village shops sell oysters and quails' eggs.

The ugliness of industrial decay is gradually submerged by the ugliness of industrial success, and the great span of the bridge seems like a leap out of the past. Having toiled through narrow Victorian streets for the past hour the motorway comes as a shock, blasted through the rocky bluffs of the riverside and carrying you out over the river a couple of hundred feet above the huddled roofs of North Queensferry, so that you feel that you are flying rather than driving. To your left the inelegant cacophony of girders that is the Forth Rail Bridge seems a ludicrously elephantine means of transporting a tiny worm of train across the water.

Edinburgh, like a fussy old beldame, keeps her skirts clean; the road from the bridge traverses several miles of open farmland until you reach Cramond Bridge and the polite bungalows along the Queensferry Road, and before you know it you are climbing up through the New Town towards Princes Street. Even if you arrive by train you enter through a deep channel so that little can be seen until you climb out of Waverley Station into the great heart of Auld Reekie. It was late afternoon by now, and the clouds had blown away to leave a cerulean wash above the extraordinary skyline of the Old Town. The sun shone along rather than down upon the streets and the wind, Edinburgh's chief element, raced through the blocks like a maniac with a razor. I stood at the foot of Waverley Bridge looking up at the citadel and froze, not just because of the wind, but mentally because it seemed so foolish to attempt to say anything about the place.

> Edina! Scotia's darling seat!
> All hail thy palaces and tow'rs

. . . Burns at his worst, trying to be grand, but Edinburgh is the sort of place that makes any visitor feel like an unsophisticated lout. You have to get very close to discover that the city is a sham, and that beneath these fairytale towers and romantic long flights of steps leading up to the frowning castle walks a citizenry as ordinary as any, only a good deal more footsore and frozen to the marrow. As the English poet Thomas Gray put it more coolly than Rabbie, 'that most picturesque (at a distance) and nastiest (when near) of all Capital cities'.

Nevertheless, on such an evening Edinburgh is nothing if not seductive to look at. It seems to be a city in Cinemascope, with the immense length of Princes Street, the architectural fireworks of the gigantic hotels and the impossibly tall buildings on the Castle hill exaggerated by the deep canyon of the railway lines, the great bridges connecting the New and Old Towns and the grand pretension of the fake Hellenism beyond. It is a city of sweeping perspectives and vistas let down by a population which has refused to grow into a suitably heroic-looking race. Although ancient, it has a strangely quaint modernism; the sunken railway and station, the bridges in ornamented steel and iron rather than pre-stressed concrete, the (by British standards) impossibly civilised main street built only on one side and with a park along the other (imagine if they demolished one side of your High Street and grassed it over!), the Scott Monument like some Gothic attempt at space flight; it is as if you are watching a film of the 'City of the Future' made in 1880, except that instead of advanced toga-clad patricians the streets are full of ordinary folk and here and there wizened men in ludicrous tartan tam-o'-shanters with massive purple noses and beat-up shoes staggering from doorway to lampost and singing 'WHAAHeynagrafuchinbaashtardshdhfackinssschites . . .'

I made my way down the long ramp into Waverley Station. I had decided to try to look at the capital as a tourist might who had only a couple of hours to spare. And as any young tourist might, I decided to look for a publication called *The List*, Edinburgh's what's-on-for-the-young-sophisticate magazine, in order to get straight into the happening stuff. So, into the newsagent's on the station concourse where the first impression of the city is coloured by a ruckus going on in this establishment. The manager is attempting to eject a small, wizened man with a huge purple nose and a peculiar hat in psychedelic plaid who does not wish to leave, and who indeed may no longer have the motor skills with which to do so.

'I am sorry, sir. Please leave now.'

'Lishnyafushinbroonbashtarr . . . Gerchafackinschtinkinhaandshoffamah-coat.'

'I have called the Police. Please leave.'

'Polishisit?' The dwarfish one turns to address the tittering throng. 'UUthreatninmewithapoleeshnowisitt? Idinnagivafackinshite, yaBASH-TARD.'

. . . and so on. Eventually the man, who looks as though he may be infectious, reels a safe distance from the stand, still informing passers-by of the parental uncertainty attendant upon retailers. Then I approached the lady behind the till.

'Excuse me, please. Do you have *The List* ?'

Without replying, the woman stands up and suddenly screams at the top of her lungs, 'HEE ENA! WEEVNAEGO'A LUST HUVWEH?' (Excuse me, Ena, do we have a *List* at present?)

'AHDINNAE RECK'N. AH DOOT UT'LLBEYIN TAEMORROO HEN.' (Unfortunately not though we expect delivery in the morning.)

Oh well. There must after all be more newsagents in the city and one of them will have a *List*. After all, this is a capital city internationally famous for the Arts. It surely cannot be the case that the visitor will not be able to find out what is going on.

I trudged up the long ramp of the station, the low evening sun blinding me and reducing the people descending to wisps of ash, like satanic angels. I stood awhile at the top, examining the view along and up to the Castle, before turning right towards the road junction with Princes Street. A tiny sign catches the eye, pointing on to the roof of a submerged shopping mall in fake marble: 'TOURIST INFORMATION'. I mounted the few steps, to find a maze of walkways and flowerbeds, with here and there a bench set into the wall. On each bench was a small wizened man with a huge purple nose and a hat constructed by drug-frenzied Hebridean weavers. As I passed each one I was greeted by the same indecipherable question, 'Scuze me pal, canyespearissaborbferraecuppatee?'

Eventually I found the entrance to the Tourist Office which has a front entirely constructed of plate glass, enabling the visitor to see that it is wholly dark and deserted inside. However, near the door a couple of Japanese were doing something to a hi-tech machine rather like an automatic bank teller, let into the window. At first I suspected that in common with their compatriots everywhere they are merely trying to amass 30,000 points by knocking out little green invaders from Sirius, but a sign above the machine welcomed me to Edinburgh in several languages, and invited me to utilise this automatic 'touch-sensitive' equipment in order to find accommodation, transport, food, or, yes, entertainment while the Tourist Office is closed.

The Japanese, after prodding several buttons in a bemused way, muttered something which sounded like a Samurai curse and turned away. I stepped up to the machine and tentatively pressed the button which ought to have revealed facts relating to having a good time. The machine beeped but nothing else happened. The screen remained as the Japanese had left it, displaying the bus route from Corstorphine to Leith. I pressed the button again, and when that changed nothing, the next button. Whichever button I pressed, the machine was determined to get me on to a Number 32 bus. Finally, in an anarchistic, exasperated gesture under extreme duress, I pressed ten buttons at once. The screen darkened and flickered. There was a pause pregnant with microelectronic cogitation. At last the machine responded:

> We are sorry that this machine is out of order.
> The Tourist Office is normally open from 10 a.m. until 5 p.m.

> Will ye no' come back again?

Princes Street was deserted on this cold, windy March evening. Its immense length and apparent devotion to large retail establishments deterred me, and I started across Waverley Bridge towards the friendly-looking medieval clutter of the old city. At the far end of the bridge is a low building marked 'TICKETS, BOOKING CENTRE, CINEMAS, OPERA, THEATRE, ENTERTAINMENT' and other encouraging things. I went in – at least it was open. I found myself in an immense room at the far end of which was a small office desk where a middle-aged man sat. I approached the desk; the man glanced up from some paperwork.

'Excuse me. Do you have *The List*?'

'Sorry?'

'Do you have a copy of *The List*?'

'What list?'

I suppressed a sudden urgent desire to set fire to the man's tie. '*THE List*. It's a magazine of what's on in Edinburgh.'

'We don't sell magazines.'

'Oh. Thank you.'

By now I had used up an hour of the three and a half I had allowed as the time in which a capital city ought to be able to impress itself upon the visitor. Already footsore and hungry, and with the wind making my nose dribble, I continued up the winding street. I decided first of all to find sustenance, then continue my pursuit of spiritual refreshment. I expected the Old Town to be expensive, but was reassured by the fact that this street seemed to consist of 'alternative' shops selling cheap Third World imports, second-hand clothes, punk accessories and wholefoods. But a few more steps along the street revealed that all these establishments were closed and barred with metal shutters. In a couple of doorways there were some people, wrapped in a dozen layers of filthy clothing and in a comatose condition.

The Royal Mile: surely here at the very heart of Edinburgh's tourist trail I would find some form of life? Alas, the High Street was as deserted as the others, dotted with Japanese youths who, in the absence of anything else to do, were frantically taking photographs of each other. I passed a pub with a blackboard propped against the wall: 'LIVE ENTERTAINMENT EVERY NIGHT'. Well, at last! Along the bar three men, one wearing a blue pinstripe suit and reading a newspaper, one wearing a donkey-jacket and staring at a girlie calendar behind the bar, and one in a hat knitted from rainbow wool by a colourblind Peruvian shaman. The first two were silent; the third was singing 'WHAAheynagrafuchinbaashtarshdhfackinssschites . . .' He broke off and peered at me in the doorway. 'Zat yue Billy? Byzadrink pal . . .'

All the shops in the High Street were closed, despite the fact that the only people on the streets were tourists, and the shops only sell items of interest to tourists such as Edinburgh Rock, postcards whose humour is derived from speculation as to what is worn beneath the kilt (if anything), fluffy toys with tartan hats to indicate that they are completely pissed, and posters of Kylie Minogue and Jason Donovan. All I wanted now was a decent meal and then to sit down afterwards in a warm building and lose a couple of hours in the company of a few like-minded souls. This, I suppose, could be managed in any other British city; no one warned me that Edinburgh closes at five. The only eaterie on the street which might have been open was an international pizza outlet. No customers were visible, but four waitresses were sitting smoking and drinking cups of coffee. Against the evidence of my own eyes, I decided that Edinburgh must be able to offer better fare, and along the street I spotted a basement café with a menu posted on the railings outside. The menu was in French and the prices seemed to correspond to the monthly payments on a Volvo 740 but it was almost certainly going to be better than eating a circular piece of polystyrene smeared with lukewarm tomato purée. I descended the steps, but the door was locked. Next to the restaurant a narrow alleyway led to the top of one of the flights of steps which descended back down to Princes Street. On reaching the bottom about ten minutes later I found myself by the National Gallery of Art, which was, of course, closed, but opposite – yes! – a newsagent's which was open. I crossed the wide carriageway, avoiding a convoy of empty buses travelling at around mach one, and asked for *The List* inside. The Indian woman behind the counter shook her head silently. I turned, a broken man, eyeing the astonishing collection of porn on the shelf above.

From that point on I wandered the streets at random. The cold, uniform fronts of the New Town houses watched me pass with uncaring eyes. I capitulated and went into an international pizza outlet where I stood in the doorway listening to a tape of something which sounded like Lulu Sings Aïda (it was in fact Sarah Brightman Sings Lloyd Webber) next to a sign which said 'PLEASE WAIT HERE TO BE WELCOMED'. After ten minutes I had not yet been welcomed so I went in. The restaurant was decorated in a number of completely unrelated styles; most of it was 'farmhouse' brick and timber (except that the brick was printed and the timber was plastic), but the lighting was fake Tiffany, the fittings were fake Nautical Brass and the pictures on the wall were those airbrushed landscape posters where the name of the artist is printed three times bigger than the image. After about 20 minutes a waitress appeared and handed me a menu. Before I could ask for a coffee she was gone. Meanwhile the tape machine was playing a George Harrison song about Krishna, adding to the atmosphere of post-modern cultural mousse. Glumly I surveyed the few other patrons. The family in the booth to my left could not be anything except German: an immensely fat burgher, his thin smart wife and their flawlessly blonde daughter all scoffing a huge seafood pizza and drinking big glasses of lager. They ate, but did not speak. In the next booth two doleful Japanese, both watching the other eaters as they picked at salads and flinching whenever the waitresses came near. Beyond them a family of Italians; here the father was thin and smart and the mamma was fat with a torrent of curls kept raven black by some outlandish but obviously chemical process, eyebrows which would meet in the middle had they not been reduced to twin black crescents somewhere near her hairline, and a laugh which could slice salami at 30 paces. Their children wore the kind of clothes which subtly mix fluorescent turquoise and oil-fire orange and might be for skiing in. Behind me were two Edinburgh lassies, perhaps killing time between office and dates, talking nineteen to the dozen about various men they had been out with during the last lunar cycle, and the entertainment value afforded by the moon's gravitational pull upon the mysterious and unpredictably wacky world of ovulation.

Eventually I procured a coffee the consistency of molten brown glass and a 'Margherita' pizza, presumably named after the small Italian dog which had given birth to it in the kitchen. I closed my eyes and ate: it wasn't bad. It almost tasted of something. It filled me up. There now, that didn't hurt, did it? By now time was pressing. Desperate remedies were in order. I got up, paid the bill ('Have a pleasant evening') and went back to the table where the two girls were still gossiping, each holding a Lambert & Butler King Size at precisely the same acute angle near their left ears.

'Excuse me, could you give me some advice. If you had time to kill, what would you do in Edinburgh?'

The girls glanced at each other, nonplussed.

'I mean,' I continued, 'I have a few hours to kill before my train leaves and I was wondering what I should do. Are there any good plays or films or clubs on?'

'I dunno,' said one of the girls, 'I never go out.'

'You want to go dancing?' asked the other.

'Perhaps – anything not too expensive – theatre or cabaret or classical music – I don't mind. Jazz. Rock 'n' roll.'

'Well, mostly it's out by the University. The clubs and that.'

'How far is that?'

'No' far – you can get a bus.'

'Okay. Do you know the number of the bus?'

'D'ya ken the number, Kirstie?'

'No.'

'No. You could ask.'

I smiled resignedly and thanked them.

'So, anyway,' Kirstie went on, 'she told me he was interested, an' I said gettaway, he's all mooth 'n' troosers, besides he's too tall an' he's a nose like Cyrano de Bergerac's brother wi' the big hooter, an' she says, "Aye, ye ken what they say aboot men wi' big noses" . . .'

'Cheeky coo.'

'Aye! Anyway . . .'

I lingered in the warmth of the restaurant. Near the door were an American woman and her son. I unhurriedly put on my coat and fiddled with my camera bag so that I could eavesdrop. Mom had evidently just arrived in Scotland; Junior had been in Britain for a few weeks and was showing her his snaps.

'This is near Loch Ness in, er, Stirlingshire. It's some kind of castle built, I dunno, 16-something, maybe one of those med-eevil kings . . .'

I sneaked a look. It was the Wallace Memorial. 'Gee,' said Mom. 'Willya look at that afforestation!'

Out on the long bus track of Princes Street once more, the Italian family were posing for a photograph in front of the statue of Allan Ramsay. The thin, dapper father backed further and further into the doorway across the road, while *mamma* and *bambini* shuffled sideways precariously on the opposite kerb, teetering out over the bus lane. Finally he snapped, capturing the family, the back of a taxi, part of the statue, the front of a bus close to take-off speed, and a small wizened man in a hat constructed from semi-digested noodles by Jackson Pollock.

I wandered disconsolately along to Waverley Bridge, paused momentarily to glance up at the magnificent purple and gold sunset above the mighty citadel, and went back to the car. Blodwen looked ludicrously out of place in the carpark, stuffed as she was with cooking equipment, sleeping bags and laundry, and sticking up like a bandaged thumb amongst the svelte BMWs and Audis. I paid the extortionate parking fee, left Edinburgh and hit the motorway. I hated the inside of the van already, and I had three full weeks to go. I had lost my momentum by spending two days at home, and after my visit to Scotland's capital, I felt completely unrefreshed. Common sense dictated that the next letter should not be too distant; so why did I feel so guilty arriving in Falkirk, a mere 25 miles to the west?

FALKIRK

Familiarity, family fun, and farming fraught with freakishness

I didn't pay much attention at first to the shallow hole in the greensward next to my parking space in Falkirk. It looked as if someone had skidded to a halt in a JCB, creating two parallel ruts which had filled up with litter and broken branches. I was sitting behind the wheel feeling miserable and trying to summon up the energy to walk around Falkirk Town Centre. Not for the first or the last time I had a strong urge to drive straight on to my next destination and justify myself retrospectively by claiming that to anyone with one functional eye, Falkirk could be summarised accurately in a minute's cursory inspection: dead boring. Dead, boring.

I think only my extreme fatigue dissuaded me from this precipitate action, which is just as well, since I had the opportunity to discover at my leisure just how completely dead boring Falkirk is, and thus feel thoroughly holy about probing this dullness to the full. That, and a small metal plaque on the wall which bordered the carpark. I got out to read it, thinking that it must refer to the historical origin of the wall to which it was affixed, which did look quite old. It told me instead that the shallow scrapes filled with empty Coke cans and crisp-bags in the middle of the grass marked the foundation of the Antonine Wall. This temporarily deluded me into thinking that Falkirk might actually be more interesting than I had suspected, and persuaded me to stay.

The Antonine Wall, unlike Hadrian's, was a gimcrack affair of (mostly) earth and timber, and was the Roman equivalent of the M25; everyone could tell it was completely useless as soon as it was finished. It was built in the 140s AD but quickly proved its obsolescence as an anti-Pict device and the frontier was subtly replaced a hundred miles to the south. In fact, although Hadrian's wall was much more substantial than that of Antonius Pius, its success was largely the result not of its superb fortification and subtle placement but of a series of treaties made with the tribes immediately to the north, who were Britons, not Picts. Britons probably helped to garrison the wall too, whereas Antonius's effort was manned by Roman legions alone. So the poor old Britons were persuaded to act as a buffer-zone between the might of the Roman Army and the hairy loons to the north. I don't suppose they had much choice, but Hadrian got the credit, whilst Antonius's little scrape quickly filled up with empty mead cans and disposable tubes of woad. *Sic transit gloria*, I thought; what was once the end of the world is now a carpark in Falkirk. I glanced around at the neat tower blocks and a long, low slab of concrete which looked like a public urinal but was in fact a nightclub. Banal, yes, but hardly apocalyptic. For a couple of hours I wandered around the deserted town centre. It was so unremarkable as to be remarkable, without any distinguishing features what-soever, either tawdry or pretty. Admittedly there was a Chinese takeaway called 'The Family Way' which struck me as puzzling until I realised it was owned by the Wei family. And the tourist office is housed in a curious building with a spire, known imaginatively as 'The Spire'. But the shops were the same shops as anywhere, housed in ordinary Victorian buildings, with the predictable precinct and the new one-way system. As in many Scottish towns there were as many empty shops as new building sites. I had marked Falkirk down mentally as rather grim and industrial; far from it, the town is surprisingly green and clean, the tower blocks look well-built, even desirable. There is a huge park, and despite a great deal of litter, no vandalism beyond the ordinary. My impression was of a very comfortable bourgeois shopping and commuting town.

I drove around the outskirts, more in hope than expectation of anything to see. The modern estates were very large, very uniform, very grey, but well-kept and tidy. Only the view from some of them was unusual: the vast expanse of the petrochemical complex on the Forth at Grangemouth lit up like a Steven Spielberg spacecraft and belching smoke and steam.

By now feeling that I had at least scratched the surface of the town I resolved not to stay there but to drive the 40 or so miles home and return in the morning to try to discover Falkirk's hidden secrets, if any. By the carpark was a noticeboard headed 'Choose Falkirk for Leisure'. Falkirk's dazzling nightlife had this to offer:

Ballroom Dancing
Youth Music Festival
Falkirk Youth Theatre presents *Oliver!*
Vienna Festival Ballet in *Swan Lake*
South Pacific

. . . well, I thought, so much for the over–55s. I wonder what everyone else does. I was soon to find out. Every newsagent's shop in the town centre carried the same range of postcards. Of 20 or 30 pictures available, only one was actually of Falkirk itself. It showed the Boating Lake. With leisure like that, who would ever need to leave town?

At 11 o'clock the next morning I entered the offices of the *Falkirk Herald*, and talked to Raymond Harvey, a reporter on that worthy journal. Like all good reporters the first thing he did after writing down my name was to ask how old I was. I couldn't remember. Neither he nor I could spell 'dyslexia', either. He pretended to take offence at my suggestion that Falkirk was extremely ordinary, but when I challenged him to produce evidence to the contrary he could think of absolutely nothing interesting that had happened there since James Watt was working at the Carron Iron Works in the early days of the Industrial Revolution. That factory is now closed, as is all of Falkirk's heavy industry; most of the town commutes to Grangemouth, and Falkirk is exactly what it appears to be, a Victorian town (little remains of the medieval market town) which has been cleaned up and is now almost entirely devoted to retailing and services.

The 1980s were Falkirk's boom years; it was a model of Thatcherite post-industrial development, at least on the surface. Falkirk attracted big shiny new retail developments and prospered, but all that had really changed was that the population became commuters. There were not really any more jobs; they were simply not in Falkirk anymore. Conversely, Grangemouth lost any claim to be a dormitory or shopping town. In the new recession of the early '90s Falkirk is faltering a little. The biggest new shopping development has gone bust, and stands half-completed at one end of the main street; small retailers are closing again, and new businesses are being squeezed, some terminally. Unemployment, low by Scottish standards for the last ten years, is rising. It might be said that towns like Falkirk are more vulnerable to economic downturn than previously. Although it may not be wise to put all your eggs in one basket, even an iron one, it cannot be comfortable to depend almost entirely on decisions made in Edinburgh or London or New York, and to make your money from things which people desire rather than need.

Still, on this weekday morning the town seemed bustling, the citizens well-fed and clothed. Their conversation was not about the recession but the Poll Tax, the Orkney 'Satanic abuse' allegations, and Falkirk FC's chances of promotion to the Premier Division for the first time. I had the impression that by rights Falkirk ought to be a struggling dowdy little place, a Burnley or Whitehaven, instead of this cheerful if uninspiring Pooterville. Before leaving the newspaper office I asked Raymond what was the most extraordinary story he had covered. He looked blank. 'Quads?', I prompted, 'A cow with two heads?' Immediately his eyes lit up. Apparently there is a very long-running dispute between a local farmer and a chemicals company which had had a factory adjoining his fields. A succession of malformed calves had blighted the man's business. Didn't this worry local people? Not a great deal, it seemed. As at Dounreay, you cannot afford to bite the hand that feeds you.

So I went to look at Falkirk's saviour, Grangemouth. The couple of miles of land between the towns are a flat, dusty waste full of dumped household crap and wrecked cars, with tattered plastic bags hung like bunting on every barbed-wire fence and the outlandish refineries and chemical works ahead growing more gargantuan by the minute. Here and there curious terraces of industrial cottages spring up amongst the fields, seemingly transported from some town centre or other by supernatural means; a single street or one at right angles to another, without any attendant factories or shops.

The outskirts of Grangemouth, as Raymond the Reporter had warned me, were grim; Falkirk has managed to give Grangemouth all its worst housing in exchange for Grangemouth's shops. Ugly and decrepit '30s to '60s mid-rise tenements line the main road, meaner and more demeaning than anything I'd yet seen. But the town centre was a surprise. Grangemouth is a place struggling to be a town rather than a collection of factories, and the result is peculiar, with streets of well-tended semi-detached houses, each with a privet-hedged garden laid out with roses and dahlias such as you might see in Chelmsford or Slough or Kidderminster, but right up against the huge snaking tubes and fairy-lit gantries of the refinery. It was as if someone had moved the Pompidou Centre to Bournville and set it on fire.

On the way out I pulled off the road by an abandoned row of shops and houses, the only remnant of what must have been a substantial Victorian town now replaced by new industrial sheds and vacant lots. Behind the old shops was something that may have been a small workshop or factory, and the corner of the row had a rather elegant little clock-tower. Elder bushes sprouted from the crumbling black brick, and buddleia from the gutters. There was still an enamelled street sign, 'Grange Place', and a plaque on one of the walls dating it to 1900. It had been abandoned for at least a decade. I picked my way around the back through the thorns and dumped mattresses and broken glass, trying to find some clue as to what had been made there, but apart from a tramp's camp-fire and scuttling rats, there was nothing to see. Even the wiring had been stripped out. Seventy years didn't seem a very long life for a building which had evidently once been a focal point of the local streets. The little ornate clock-tower insisted that it was ten past one, but it was two-thirty and time to move on.

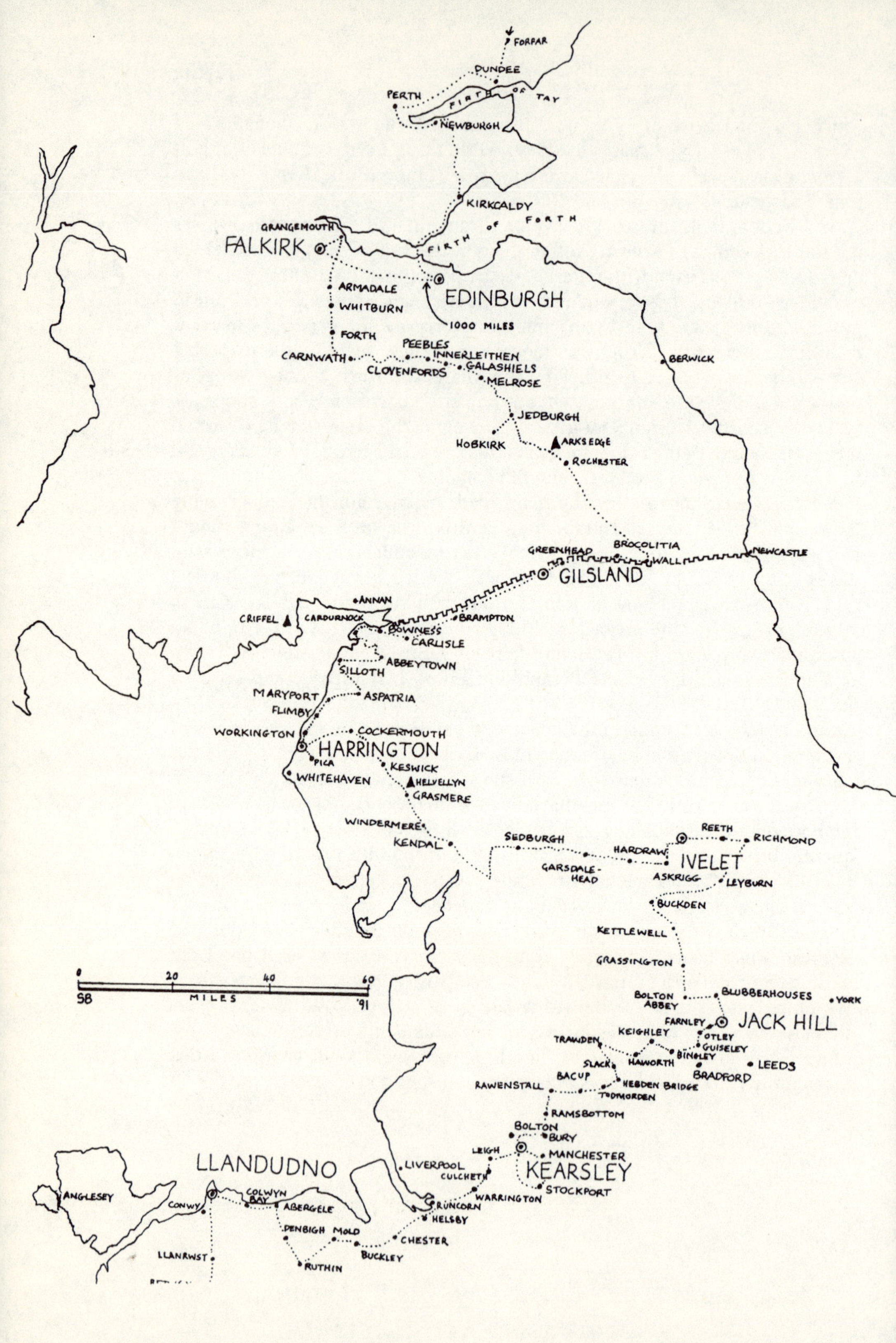

FORFAR
DUNDEE
PERTH
FIRTH OF TAY
NEWBURGH
KIRKCALDY
FIRTH OF FORTH
GRANGEMOUTH
FALKIRK
ARMADALE
WHITBURN
EDINBURGH
1000 MILES
FORTH
PEEBLES
CARNWATH
INNERLEITHEN
CLOVENFORDS
GALASHIELS
MELROSE
BERWICK
JEDBURGH
HOBKIRK
ARKS EDGE
ROCHESTER
GREENHEAD
BROCOLITIA
WALL
NEWCASTLE
GILSLAND
ANNAN
CRIFFEL
CARDURNOCK
BOWNESS
BRAMPTON
CARLISLE
ABBEYTOWN
SILLOTH
MARYPORT
ASPATRIA
FLIMBY
WORKINGTON
COCKERMOUTH
HARRINGTON
PICA
KESWICK
WHITEHAVEN
HELVELLYN
GRASMERE
WINDERMERE
KENDAL
SEDBURGH
REETH
RICHMOND
HARDRAW
IVELET
GARSDALE-
HEAD
ASKRIGG
LEYBURN
BUCKDEN
KETTLEWELL
GRASSINGTON
BOLTON
ABBEY
BLUBBERHOUSES
YORK
FARNLEY
JACK HILL
KEIGHLEY
OTLEY
TRAWDEN
GUISELEY
BINGLEY
LEEDS
SLACK
HAWORTH
BACUP
BRADFORD
RAWENSTALL
HEBDEN BRIDGE
TODMORDEN
RAMSBOTTOM
BOLTON
BURY
LEIGH
MANCHESTER
LIVERPOOL
KEARSLEY
CULCHETH
STOCKPORT
WARRINGTON
LLANDUDNO
ANGLESEY
COLWYN
BAY
CONWY
ABERGELE
RUNCORN
HELSBY
DENBIGH
MOLD
LLANRWST
CHESTER
BUCKLEY
RUTHIN
0
20
40
60
SB
MILES
'91

GILSLAND

Ghosts, guesthouses and gales

I took a wrong turning into somewhere called Westfield, an unentertaining diversion except that there was an LP lying on the white line in the middle of the village street; evidently they go for middle-of-the-road music there. As it turned out this was the most exciting thing on the way south from Falkirk towards Lanark, climbing the Pentland Hills. The bright spells and swift April showers of the morning gave way to a howling gale and lashing rain; this stretch of countryside (and I use the term only after consideration) is perpetually windy. It is also unrivalled as the most dispiriting in Scotland. The road itself is poor – narrow, deeply rutted by heavy trucks and frequently broken up into potholes five inches deep and three feet across, a road such as you might imagine running between Timbuktu and Ouagadougou, except that that is probably a superhighway by now. The B8084 rises and falls like a rollercoaster every 20 yards or so, making overtaking impossible and limiting travel to about 35 mph, and passes through three of the most ugly and depressing little towns on Earth: Armadale (no relation), Whitburn and Forth. These ex-mining, ex-industrial, execrable towns are all hilly places through which battered artics and dump-trucks crawl like slugs. They are surrounded by vast brown unlandscaped slag-heaps and their buildings are singularly unprepossessing; grey pebble-dash and chipped concrete ruin many Scottish towns but there can't be many which consist solely of these materials.

Abandoned by the whims of Thatcherism to the mercy of a market force which simply doesn't exist, these Lanarkshire towns reminded me of the kind of shock one gets when one sees a black and white film of Britain in the early 1960s. How dowdy everything looks! Did it really rain all the time? Were all the streets cul-de-sacs blocked and blackened by factories, full of smoke and women scrubbing the doorsteps with Woodbines dangling from the corners of their mouths? One of Britain's saving graces is that the worst excesses of its industrial past are usually adjacent to pleasant country-side; although the North-west and Cornwall have some exceptions, the grim sprawls of Leeds, Sheffield, Derby, Birmingham, Leicester and Newcastle are all within striking distance of, and in some cases actually surrounded by, lovely scenery. Alas, these Scottish coal towns lie in an upland waste of purgatorial grottiness. A blasted expanse of bog, tussocky fields and moor, scattered with leprous twisted trees so stunted that it was a long time before I realised that they were for the most part beech and birch. They are the colour of, and look as hard as, cast iron, as if they have been spellbound by some particularly vile demon with a predilection for art-nouveau metal-work. Here and there the land had been ploughed up for, or planted with, small conifers. It was actually an improvement. I congratulated myself on choosing Falkirk rather than Forth for my sixth destination; Forth made Falkirk look like Monte Carlo.

Only as the road descends towards Carnwath do things gradually improve; the beeches become tall green things which botanists might recognise in a moment, particularly if like me they were almost forced to drive up one by a combination of a sharp corner, hurricane-force winds and a lorry-driver with the instinct of a rottweiler. I stopped to get my nerve back in Carnwath, a farming village which is almost pretty, noted (I presume) for its unrivalled production of manure, an alp of which steamed by the lay-by. The car smelt of it for days; more unfortunately the coffee I was drinking tasted remarkably rich in phosphates also. As I drank this nutritious, health-giving beverage, I watched hundreds upon hundreds of geese struggling northwards in the teeth of the gale. Flying in Vs of 20 or 30, honking like veteran cars, they laboured into the wind, making little or no progress, apparently driven beyond reason by the call of the tundra. A few gave up, and honking a joyous farewell shot away south-westwards, presumably to rest on the Solway until the storm abated. But most carried on, some actually moving backwards during the most ferocious gusts.

At Newbigging I passed the first Tourist Route sign for many miles and knew that I was entering the Border Country. The road was as terrible as ever but I suppose the local authorities hope that their natural good-fortune will distract the motorist sufficiently. Big rounded hills, wide, shallow valleys full of stoneless red earth and scattered with drumlins too steep to plough and crested by pines; simultaneously the small houses become picturesque and the larger ones grand. All the most charming little tracts of riverbank or hillside seemed to be occupied by elegant Queen Anne or Georgian homes, and the vernacular farms began to lose their bulky small-windowed Scottishness and acquire an airiness which looked flimsy and, judging by

84

the climate, foolish. The road down to Peebles is like a drive through a Noddy book; everything seems too pretty and childishly simple to be true.

By now I had given up hope of reaching my next destination that day. I wanted 'G' to be in England, but the first examples were still a long way south. Peebles is a tourist centre and little else, its long, once-elegant main street now a riot of signs for hotels, crafts, cream teas and knitwear. I didn't stop, not being in the mood for a lesson in bowdlerised 'romantic' Border history, although Neidpath Castle, just before the town, looked terrific. I think I was put off mostly by the sign on the outskirts yelling 'PEEBLES FOR PLEASURE'.

Innerleithen, the next village, is neither as attractive nor as pretentious as Peebles; I shall remember it, unfairly, for being trapped behind a tractor towing a trailer which I thought at first was completely covered in rust, but which proved over the next ten minutes and from a distance of two feet to be liquid cowshit which was slowly forming glutinous stalactites and slopping off on to the road. Dear reader, the subtle but extraordinary complexity of colour and texture would have amazed you, and I sincerely hope that one day you too will have the opportunity to examine this bovine by-product. By the time I got past I could have chosen 'Diarrhoea in Cattle' as my specialised subject on *Mastermind*.

Into the bigger, barer scenery of Ettrick and Lauderdale and at Clovenfords – what a wonderful name – we passed the thousandth mile of our journey. The dark day was getting rapidly darker, and I decided to stop for the night at or near Jedburgh; after a few soft nights I felt I ought to rough it once again, and I wanted to have plenty of time to seek out a suitable hidey-hole before nightfall. Galashiels was next, still more concerned with textiles than tourism, with a rash of new housing placed unforgivably along the steep wooded hillside above, a prime example of someone selling a view for a quick buck at the expense of everyone else's pleasure. The road twists around the base of the weird Eildon Hills, two steep, spooky-looking peaks, and dips down towards St Boswells with the uninviting line of the Cheviots masking the southern horizon. Here the distinction between England and Scotland is becoming blurred; St Boswells is a low-lying village with a vast green and a cricket-pitch; Jedburgh, ten miles further south, is a very Scottish hilly border town with a rugby ground. The rain petered out leaving a fine evening sky. Jedburgh is a wonderful place for an evening stroll, its beautifully-preserved medieval streets climbing steeply from the pretty little abbey up to the ridiculous toy-town fort, which looks as though it ought to be garrisoned by wooden soldiers. For some reason Jedburgh also has the prettiest girls in Scotland; maybe it's all the red meat they eat, for the town has more butchers' shops than would seem strictly necessary. There were very few people about, which made the number of tall willowy flaxen-haired girls more remarkable. Perhaps they were all related. I ate a wonderful meal of sausage, egg and chips in a café and went in search of a home for the night.

It took me hours. First I selected a likely area on the map, a village not far to the south under Wauchope Forest called Hobkirk. When I got there – it was further than I had supposed and down a fairly awful road – I couldn't find anywhere that was sheltered enough. All the field entrances were swamps of tractor-churned mud after the day's downpour, and there were no quiet dells which weren't already occupied by houses – not surprisingly, since the country round about was exceedingly bleak and windswept. The villages were unassuming, pretty prosperous little places huddled around steep stream valleys, and Hobkirk was well-named, with a squat, strange, little brick church with a stumpy tower. I was glad to have seen it, but by now the dusk was gathering and I had not found anywhere remotely like a campsite or a parking-place. I headed back towards Jedburgh, thinking that I would have to pay for accommodation after all, but then noticed a track leading into a conifer plantation which I had missed on the way down. It was too late for second thoughts; I reversed down the narrow gully between the spindly black trees until the road was out of sight and turned off the engine. The sound of the wind moving the crowns of the trees was like the ocean; apart from the creaking of their branches nothing else was to be heard. I walked a little way into the forest, which was called Swinnie, and by the time I got back to the car, my head full of the pungent smell of pines and stinkhorn fungus, it was dark. I brushed my teeth and clambered on to the back seat. Once I had found a reasonably comfortable position I found the strongest FM signal on my Walkman and settled down. The song playing was *They Don't Make Cars Like They Used To*. How true, I thought; nor, if they have any sense, do they live in them. For a while I lay awake looking up at the bright stars through the soughing pines. Then I slept solidly for more than nine hours, waking only once to remove the iron bands from my knees.

I walked around Jedburgh again first thing in the morning, determined after a day in the saddle to get some proper exercise. The Rhinemaidens had vanished but it was a calm sunny morning and the town looked lovely. Neither a tourist centre nor a shopping town, or rather a little of both but mostly just a country town which makes a good living from the land, you have to look closely to see which are the new buildings and which are old, at least in the centre. It is a wonderful example of what development can mean if you have something worth preserving to build on.

Here is as good a place as any to say that I resent having to pay to get into historic buildings, ruins, museums or galleries, and I hope some enlightened government will one day ensure that entrance to such places is always free. I say this in the knowledge that such places are expensive, but they are not luxuries, as the system of entrance fees implies. At Jedburgh I was in two minds whether to pay to see the interior of the abbey; because

I was in a hurry I decided that the fee wasn't worth it, yet if there had been no admission charge but instead a collection box inside I would certainly have contributed. People who are not really interested in historic buildings may not pay to get in, but they will go in for free, and may become interested in historic buildings as a result. You could argue that it is fairer if those who actually 'use' the place pay the most, but this is a nonsense. The buildings do not exist because they ought to be used, but because they are worth preserving. They have been saved, as we are always told, 'for the nation', not for the tourist.

All along the road south of Jedburgh are signs saying 'LAST CAMPING IN SCOTLAND', 'LAST SHOP IN SCOTLAND', 'LAST PETROL IN SCOTLAND' . . . only the most fanatical patriot would be swayed by the latter, surely. English petrol! Ugh! I climbed the big series of hairpins up to Ark's Edge, the brow of the Cheviots from which you can look back over a huge expanse of the Border uplands. Shortly afterwards the Border is marked with due ceremony on the English side by a hot-dog stand. The hills here have for the most part English names; Oh Me Edge is the best of them. The Cheviots do not give the impression, after the initial scarp, of being hills at all, but rather a single undulating upland plain. As the road descends gradually into Redesdale, the true moorland is quickly left behind, and most of what you see is rough upland pasture, the colour of pale cream sherry and almost without features. A lot of it is taken over by the Ministry of Defence, and red flags flutter here and there, although neither sight nor sound of troops could be detected. It is a sinister place, as if the crimson flags warn against some invisible malevolent presence, a baleful spirit of these dreary uplands.

I stopped high up the valley and wrote notes (I had not had time before dark the night before) and postcards for a couple of hours in a lay-by. The wind whistled around and through the car; by the time I had finished my feet and hands were numb. Then I got out the road atlas, for shortly afterwards I knew that I would be faced with a major choice. The road forks and I would be committed either to the North-east or the North-west of England; my schedule would not permit me to cover both. In the end I chose Greenhead, which lies on Hadrian's Wall, almost equidistant from Solway and Tynemouth; this more or less inevitably meant that I would not see the North-east. I love Newcastle and its satellites, and like Geordies, and there were some tempting Gs, notably Guide Post, a town near Morpeth. Gateshead, too, with its odd combination of old industry and ultra-modern development, would have been fascinating. But I remembered a promise I had made to myself once on a plane over Solway, and besides, if Greenhead proved dull there were several other Gs not too distant.

I have made several flights over Britain in recent years, usually from Edinburgh to London and back. I flatter myself that my knowledge of British geography is pretty good, but no matter how fine the weather and how clearly the flight engineer enunciates the route, I can rarely relate what

I see below to anything I can remember from a map, unless a city or a stretch of coast is in sight. Otherwise, one corner of green and pleasant land or one set of brown wrinkled hills looks much like others. Flying to London, for example, I am lost soon after take-off as the plane heads south-west along the border hills. Soon though, I pick up the Solway Firth and the Cumbrian coast (Sellafield is unmistakeable), and shortly afterwards the long, straight line of the Manchester Ship Canal. But from then on I'm lost until the wheels are scraping the rooftops of the semis in Hatton Cross. A few weeks before my journey with Blodwen was due to begin, I had to fly to London on business. My thoughts were full of the trip and, as I gazed down upon the Solway Firth, entranced by the fractal geometry of the tidal mud and sand, I decided that if I could I would drive along it on my journey. I had no idea what it was like; from the air it looked weirdly complex and fascinating. If when I got there it was dull, I could at least look up and say, 'I was there'. It was like sticking a pin in a map. It seemed to fit in with the premise of the trip. A little further on I picked out the Ship Canal and the huge plain I knew to be Chat Moss, west of Manchester. I suppose I ought to go there too, I thought. I had made an uncomfortable promise to myself that I would try to balance the rural with the urban, the beautiful with the banal. And, having once seen Wigan and Warrington, the environs of Chat Moss, from a train, I knew that they had a kind of grotesque attraction. It's not often a place lives down to its reputation so completely.

At the top of the A68 one is greeted by a series of signs bearing huge exclamation marks warning you to take extra care on its series of blind summits, steep dips and sharp bends. '93 ACCIDENTS IN PAST 3 YEARS', one of them says encouragingly. Amazingly, most drivers obeyed these admonitions even when sorely provoked by a prolonged view of Blodwen's back end as we crawled up the hills. One immediately obvious difference from similar stretches of upland in Scotland is that here the beech trees stand up tall, 60 or 70 feet in height, despite the constant wind. Only the oaks still look a little fragile and gnarled and overcome by grey lichen. At Ridsdale, a village which looks like a Hollywood set for *Jane Eyre*, I got out to stretch my legs. It was bone-splinteringly cold. The dark-brown terraced cottages ranged across the top of the hill trailed smoke sideways over the fields, and as I tried to take some photographs bits of my camera bag blew away into a cow-field whilst the wide-angle lens fell down a crack in a dry-stone wall, necessitating ten minutes demolition work to retrieve it and ten minutes rebuilding under the blank but to me suspicious eyes of the houses. I wasted a few frames and gave up; it was impossible to avoid camera-shake. The wind had a way of punching you in the face and then whipping around you like Mohammad Ali and tapping you on the shoulder and then when you turned around laying you out with a right hook. I don't know what people do in Ridsdale; not a lot, if the number of For Sale signs on the houses was anything to go by – seven or eight of the village's 40-odd houses had one, and so did many others throughout Redesdale, whereas Jedburgh had had none. It must be a pretty terrible place to do nothing in.

The road continues to give the impression of going up as much as down, but the vegetation gradually begins to become lusher and greener and then you notice that you are among hedges rather than walls, and that there are copses and green rather than brown fields. I turned west and down to the North Tyne valley, meeting the Wall at Low Brunton near the big fort of Chesters/Cilurnum. Shortly afterwards I passed a reasonably substantial hamlet called Wallwick which was entirely absent from my map, although it didn't look as if it ought to have offended the Ordnance Survey in any way. Indeed it had a remarkable four-storey Georgian building, with a dozen or more windows in each floor, which might have been an inn or just as easily a warehouse, but which definitely existed. Perhaps it is the headquarters of something we 'need not know about', such as CRETIN, the Committee to Re-Elect Thatcher In the Nineties.

Hadrian's Wall may be a masterpiece of military engineering, but the land across which it runs is hardly gripping, and it beats me why anyone should want to walk along the thing from end to end. Because it is there, I suppose, but then so is the M1, which would probably be a good deal safer to hike than the narrow, dead straight B-road which follows the wall. Nevertheless, people do, including one poor soul I passed near Wallwick, a young man whose legs were literally giving way under the combined strain of the wind and a rucksack which looked as if it contained lead ingots.

I stopped at Brocolitia (some signs say Procolitia but this sounds less like a Roman vegetable farm), a small fort where a Mithraic temple has been unearthed. The carpark, which was by far the most substantial building to be seen, provided a terrific 180° panorama southwards, over row after row of long flat-topped hills. As the site of the fort was immediately next to this carpark it struck me as curious that the Romans had chosen to build it where nothing could be seen to the north, but perhaps they were struck by the potential for a picture window. Their modern descendants, however, showed no such sentimentality, and sat in their cars resolutely facing the Pictish Peril and studying the expanse of tarmac.

The temple lies a little to the south of the earthen bank which is all that remains of the main complex, and now consists solely of a paved floor and three small concrete pillars marking the altar, the originals of which are safely indoors in a museum at Newcastle. Despite its minute size (which brings home just how much Homo sapiens has grown in the past 2,000 years) it is an affecting place. Mithraism originated in the Eastern Roman Empire, in what is now Iran. It found great popularity among the legions, and it was one of the direct antecedents of Christianity, to which it was very similar in many ways: drinking the god's blood in the form of wine was one, a belief in the resurrection of the god another. This goes a long way to explaining the relative ease with which the Roman state embraced Christianity under Constantine; no great leap of faith was involved, contrary to the impression given by both historians and the Church ever since. We are supposed to believe that Christianity arose suddenly and swept away paganism; far from it, it developed slowly, and with many false starts, weird variations and heretical sects. In the catacombs of Rome is a wall-painting which represents Helios, the Sun God, and Jesus Christ as one and the same. Christianity is an amalgam of ancient Jewish and later Roman cults which in many cases have simply had their heroes deleted and replaced by a new set of names. This doesn't deny the validity of Christianity or the existence of Christ, though it does highlight the ludicrous ignorance of fundamentalists of any persuasion. Religions evolve, like species, like cultures.

No mention of all this is given on the 'explanatory' plaques provided by English (sic) Heritage at the site. The visitor who wonders what an ancient Persian sect was doing on the top of a hill in Northumbria is informed, by the implication of a load of sentimental claptrap, about how cold the Romans must have felt, that the wall was garrisoned by soldiers from the Mediterranean who brought the cult with them. But this is a half-truth. Some followers of Mithras at Brocolitia may have been 'Romans', or indeed Persians at one time, but they certainly included Germans, Britons and Gauls. So the true meaning of the temple, that it represents not the homesick expression of a lot of miserable Latins, but a common faith among the mass of Europeans, is censored in the interest of conveniently packaged and uncontroversial 'history'.

Still, I did find myself muttering, 'Oh, for a beaker full of the warm South,' as I fled back to the van. Once there I sat drinking coffee, facing the wrong way so as not to draw attention to myself, and watched the arrivals and departures. I think you can learn more sociology than history at Brocolitia; I find it bizarre that the British insist on dragging themselves and their children around 'Sites of Historic Interest' in the rain. I admit I do it myself and I resent being prevented from doing it by entrance fees or ridiculously paranoid self-styled 'guardians', as at Stonehenge. But surely any normal child forced to examine a mud bank in freezing April rain on a windswept hilltop is going to be put off history for life? I watched family after family arrive, spend three minutes wandering around the site, then either play football in the carpark or drive away. What is this weird compulsion we have to examine our so-called 'heritage' in the field rather than in warm, informative libraries or in front of the fire watching television? We are conned into believing that such visits are the 'real' way to learn, that they are 'educative' (although often little or no information is provided) and therefore good for us. But when we get there there is little to see and nothing to do. A good many such sites, of course, are very substantial, or very attractive, and we enjoy them for aesthetic reasons; we picnic in the ruins. Thus 'heritage' has come to indicate leisure rather than education; it is a less frightening word than 'history'. Nevertheless, the British are completely indiscriminate when it comes to visiting the sites where their ancestors lived their miserable lives; the smallest fragment of tumbledown wall, the dimmest depression in the mud will require a carpark, fencing, a ticket-hut and a plaque to tell you some 'facts'.

Why aren't we one of those cultures which spends its time sitting in nice warm cafés, arguing about politics and football, clicking beads or picking teeth and moaning about the cost of keeping a mistress? I have the feeling that we've always been like this; it would explain a lot.

The big Roman settlement at Housesteads was crawling with anoraked schoolchildren; I drove on. Greenhead, on a cursory inspection, seemed dull, but Gilsland, a few miles further, looked promising. At first it was difficult to put my finger on what was so unusual about it. It lies in a shallow bowl between rolling green hills; the floor of the bowl is full of steep humps which punctuate the houses. The village is further divided into bits by these mounds, the main Newcastle to Carlisle railway line, Hadrian's Wall, the Poltross Burn and the old Northumberland/Cumberland border. As if these interruptions weren't enough, it consists very largely of enormous detached Victorian houses, set far apart, big, square and of red or yellow brick, so that the general effect is of a number of big brightly-painted cubes sprinkled at random across the valley. On the hillside above are two substantial Victorian buildings which look like hospitals or country houses, long and low. It was this scattered, oddly decentralised layout which I found appealing; it was quite unlike anywhere else I had seen except perhaps those Swiss alpine villages where big wooden chalets are arranged loosely across a valley. I parked in what might have been the middle, next to the stream which marked the old county boundary, and wandered along the road. Turning off to see if anything remained of the railway station (nothing did), I found a path signposted to Milecastle 48, a fortlet in rather a good state of preservation on a steep slope above a series of waterfalls. From the path one can see the Wall, here only three or four feet high, snaking away over the tumps and incongruously through the gardens of houses and bungalows.

Back on the main street I found a wonderful shop, part antiques and bric-a-brac, part restaurant and part guesthouse; unfortunately they were booked up. The old Station Hotel pub was now a rather smart country hotel, and I enquired at four or five other places before I found a room, but it was in a lovely big Victorian house and had an enormous bed with a walnut headboard which almost filled the room. The owners, Mr and Mrs Newrick, gave me lots of helpful information about the area; I also found a small guidebook, *Gilsland, Past and Present*, by Marc Alexander, which I acknowledge and commend, not least because it is full of wonderful phrases: '[Gilsland lies] in the bloodied hunting ground of Scottish reiver and harsh

Border Lord', for example. Gilsland had done its best to be an ordinary Saxon settlement while all this reiving was going on, and managed to see off a series of rather nasty Norman landowners, only to become a health spa in the 1740s and a popular Victorian weekend resort for the workers of Newcastle and Carlisle thanks to the waters and the railway.

Shaw's Hotel, now Gilsland Spa, one of the big buildings on the hilltop, was the first major commercial venture, though the naturally sulphuretted springs had long been celebrated. Walter Scott stayed frequently at Wardrew House, in the woods behind the spa, and Robert Burns visited too, though we only know this from a cursory note in his diary; presumably the waters didn't agree with him. I'm not surprised; turning on a tap produces a pronounced whiff of bad eggs. Large guesthouses sprang up to cater for the increasing number of invalids and trippers in the 1800s, giving the village its peculiar aspect today. By the Edwardian era, the spa was in terminal decline, along with the fashion for regularity and inner cleanliness. Eventually the railway station closed, leaving Gilsland a stranded collection of enormous houses in the middle of nowhere. Gradually, thanks to the Wall and the motor-car the village is once again becoming a centre for tourists, but it is largely unknown and the visitors tend to be more interested in the Roman rather than the Victorian remains, which is a pity.

I spent a blissful night in the King of Beds, and went down to breakfast to find a charming group of Irish archaeology students and their lecturer/chaperone. Prompted by Mrs Newrick I explained my trip, which led into a long story about the teacher's own Morris Minor, Puggsy, a learned debate about a number of small pots which Mrs Newrick had been told were dug up in the garden by the former owner but which proved to be modern tourist trinkets, and the pleasures of the Glasgow to Dublin shuttle, known universally as 'The Vomit Comet'. Margaret Newrick mentioned another local attraction, the Popping Stone. This is a large boulder by the River Irthing upon which Walter Scott, on a visit to Wardrew, popped the question to a Mlle Charpentier, and was accepted. Apparently it was later much reduced in size by Victorian maidens who fancied that fragments might magically encourage their own beaux to do the same. Vandalism, it seems, is not new. The Irish girls – I suppose they were from a private school, since they were not old enough to be at university and would hardly be studying Roman archaeology otherwise – found this story charming. They asked what I hoped to find beginning with G, and I told them what I had read in the guide. Once upon a time there lived at Triermain Castle, just outside Gilsland, a Norman baron whose brother had left his only son in his care upon his deathbed. The Baron had no offspring of his own, and the boy was the heir of Triermain and would become its Lord on his majority. The Baron found that he liked the privileges of the lordship too much, and one day abandoned the small boy on the moors during a hunting trip. For days the boy wandered through the rocks and bogs crying piteously until, worn out and starving, he crept behind a boulder and died, his small frozen corpse being discovered by the villagers and brought back to the Castle. The Baron pretended grief at this 'misfortune', but the villagers kept hearing the child's ghostly cries through the mists and fumes of the moor, and suspicion grew. The Baron's guilt began to prey on his mind; his health failed and he took to his deathbed. As he lay dying, surrounded by his servants and retainers, he complained of an icy cold in his bones, though the room was warm enough. At that moment a small, pallid figure clad in dripping rags appeared at his bedside, and cried:

> Cauld, cauld, aye, cauld!
> An ye'll be cauld for evermair!

The nasty little brat did this to all the Baron's descendants, too (apparently he had managed to have some in the end). Another version has the boy's Wicked Stepmother lock him in the cellar. At any rate (cue high-pitched spooky music) even today walkers and shepherds out on the moors sometimes feel a sudden chill come over them, and a small, icy hand slips into theirs.

The Gilsland Boy became a popular northern nursery tale, and presumably helped bring more visitors to look at the Castle, long since ruined. Scott also wrote about Triermain, in an excruciatingly bad poem called *The Bride of Triermain* which reads like a folk-story but which he probably invented:

> Where is the maid of mortal strain
> That may match the Baron of Triermain?

Strain is right. I'll spare you the rest. His novel, *Guy Mannering*, is also partly set in the Irthing valley.

The sentimental creepiness seemed to strike a chord with the Irish girls – they all but wiped their eyes – so I cheered them up with another little gem which had been told to me by the landlady of the pub the night before; she knew someone who had felt the hand of the Gilsland Boy, but she easily topped that story. A friend had bought one of the big Victorian houses not so long ago, and liked it, but a guest had found it inexplicably creepy. Still, there didn't seem to be any local ghost stories attached to the house and although the feeling persisted, the guest decided not to worry her host with it. Until, that is, she woke up that night to see a man hanging by the neck from the rafters above her bed.

It was a good breakfast.

The rain had cleared away but despite the blue skies, the wind was more ferocious than ever; it was bringing down branches. I drove up to Gilsland

Spa on the hill, now a private nursing home, and found a path which led into the woods beyond. It dropped steeply into a deep gorge through which the Irthing ran between cliffs of sandstone. From the village there is no indication that this chasm exists. Once down at the bottom, although the river roared over the stones and the treetops high above echoed it as the wind lashed them, all was peaceful and warm in the sheltered early spring sunshine. I found the drinking fountain with its supposedly diuretic properties; it stank, but I risked a gulp or two. Strangely it tasted all right. Nearby was the empty bathing pool where the residents of Shaw's Hotel had splashed their way to health, or an early grave. Trees grew from its tiled floor. For 20 minutes or so I wandered along the riverbank, meeting nobody and enjoying the dappled light and the rushing water, and I found the Popping Stone, still a fat boulder even if it was eroded by desperate Victorian spinsters. Certainly it is a charming place; I should imagine it would be pretty difficult to resist a proposal there, and possibly a quick consummation as well, provided one doesn't mind the occasional waft of sulphur to remind you of the torments awaiting those guilty of fornication.

As I meandered back, pausing on the little wooden footbridges to watch the tiny trout flicker in and out of the shadows, I was startled by a loud screeching sound. Simultaneously something fell vertically into the water at the river's edge. I clambered over the rocks to see what it was, and found a sparrowhawk, its wings spread, flapping around in a shallow pool and eyeing me malevolently. It made no attempt to fly away, and at first I thought that it had been shot and injured – the gale might have prevented my hearing the gun. After a moment, another movement caught my eye and I saw the reason why it didn't escape; a jackdaw had got the hawk's leg firmly clasped in its beak. It was difficult to say whether the sparrowhawk was holding the jackdaw down with its foot or the jackdaw was pulling on the hawk's leg; at any rate the jackdaw was coming off worst, being almost completely submerged. Finally the sparrowhawk broke free and flapped heavily away into the trees across the river. The jackdaw, so waterlogged as to be almost immobilised, crawled under the lip of a boulder out of sight. I went and peered under the rock; the bird, sitting on a ledge with its tail in the water, watched me morosely with a pale blue eye and shivered uncontrollably. I couldn't have removed it to see if it was injured without getting severely pecked; whether it was shivering mostly from cold or from shock, I couldn't tell; both, I should think. So I left it in peace. I couldn't imagine what had caused this palaver. Perhaps the jackdaw, doing aerobatics in the gale above along with several chums, had accidentally barged into the hawk. Or maybe the hawk had mistakenly attacked the jackdaw because it hadn't had a square meal in weeks and the sparrows were on strike. The birds are about equal in size, though the jackdaw is a good deal heavier. Normally they would avoid each other like the plague, though jackdaws, like all crows, will mob and tease hawks on occasion. The most likely explanation is that the jackdaw was chasing the hawk out of spite and got more than he bargained for, a bit like the school wimp felling the captain of the rugby team with a swift upper cut. A few hundred years ago, I reflected, this would have been a Sign or Portent of something. As usual when something freakish happens in nature, it left me uneasy.

Wardrew House, above the Irthing gorge is easily the saddest house in the area, for its downfall came not from the passing of time but through greed and carelessness. In the early 1970s the house was empty but intact, a substantial Italianate mansion in a beautiful and spectacular landscape with important historical connections, as the estate agents would say. It was bought by a company who applied for permission to turn it into a sports complex and health farm, with squash courts and so on, although it was fairly inaccessible and had an interior which was a valuable example of its type. To the amazement of local people planning permission was granted (I hope the persons responsible blush if they read this) and the new owners set about completely destroying the interior, ripping out all the floors and ceilings and taking off the roof. At this point they ran out of money, and abandoned it. Since then it has been sold again and a new house constructed in the shell, though it is only two stories high and the end walls protrude several feet above the new roof.

Back in the village I went into Dacre House, the antiques/café/bed-and-breakfast place, and spent a happy hour browsing through an extraordinary selection of books, bugles, baubles, bangles, beads, and brass bricollage and chatting to the proprietor over coffee and cake. Restored I ventured once again into the wind to try to photograph the village and the spa beyond. I perched on a low section of Hadrian's Wall and waited for the zephyr to momentarily abate; it pushed me off into the mud and I gave up. Instead I went to photograph Triermain Castle, holding the camera firmly to the top of a stone wall. Only one tall column of rubblestone remains, but surely that small bluish shape drifting across the field wasn't there just now . . .

HARRINGTON

Historical heart-failure

From Gilsland, on a Sunday morning, I drove down to Carlisle, which was closed. The 'Great Border City', as it advertises itself, is in reality a rather poky market town which gives the impression that it has become a kind of nature reserve for that unendangered species, the consumer. A great swathe of the city centre has recently been pedestrianised, leaving a sahara-like expanse of coloured brick where the market-place used to be, and several medieval streets have been glassed in to form an 'upmarket' atrium called 'The Lanes'. The local Sunday Trading laws must be incredibly strict, because the only place open was McDonald's. My footsteps echoed along the marble and chrome shopfronts of The Lanes and from time to time I heard other steps coming nearer and then fading away, without ever catching a glimpse of anyone apart from a few distant figures wandering across the horizon of clean, bare brick pavement. I drove out westwards thinking, can a place so wholly dedicated to shopping really be described as a city at all? Here we have an ancient place which has become a series of compartments for living, shopping, working; when one sector is alive the others are dead. Is this what people want? It seems to me to be an almost literal interpretation of Thatcher's 'non-society'. The logical conclusion of a policy of social control based on money rather than social intercourse, where shopping is a form of 'leisure', spending money is entertainment, and forms of leisure which have in the past not been paid for must now be purchased by 'the consumer'. As a result, if there is no money to be spent (because you are poor or because of religious prejudice against Sunday Trading) there is nothing to do. To participate in this version of 'society' at all, you must pay. All right, so that is a fairly over-the-top, over-simplified, over-critical assessment; but you go to Carlisle on a Sunday and see if you disagree.

I drove on into Cumbria cogitating on the 'Carlisle factor'. One of the great ironies of post-industrial consumer society has been the way in which capitalism has led to exactly the 'nightmare scenario' which capitalists have been warning everyone was the inevitable result of communist totalitarianism. Orwell's *1984*, for instance, has been held up over the years as a warning that we face a future in which everyone dresses alike, partakes of the same sanitised books and television, is forced to carry identity papers (the loss of which means expulsion from society), and so on and so forth. The communist régimes of China, Romania, pre-Gorbachev Russia have been pointed to as evidence that Orwell (a democratic socialist) was right. Consumerism and capitalism have been championed as the natural consequence of democracy and the only safeguard against the Orwellian nightmare. Yet we now live in a society where our civil rights and liberties have been eroded to a point where they have become an international embarrassment, where without the 'identification' of a credit card or cheque card or cashpoint card we are increasingly helpless, where the police have become a political weapon, and where everybody watches the same television programmes, reads the same newspapers, and wears the same clothes. We are told consumerism = choice. The reality is that we live in a society where 'choice' has come to mean the right to choose from a limited (and declining) number of options. The *right to choose* is not in doubt, but what may be chosen has become the first business of the State. 'Choice' in education means the ability to choose from a curriculum designed by the Department of Education. 'Choice' in the Health Service means the ability to pay for attention ahead of those who need it more. 'Choice' in shopping means that wherever you go you will find the same 20 chainstores owned by the same half-dozen multinationals. 'Choice' means your 'right' to buy a house or buy shares in a utility which is being sold to you, who own it already, by people who do not and have never owned it, so that a small number of already very wealthy people can cream off the profits henceforth. It is as if you were to buy a pound of cheese, give it back to the shopkeeper and then pay for it again. Your 'right to choose' not to pay your union dues means your 'right' to ignore the democratic decision of the majority, and denies them their right to protection from unfair exploitation, but mysteriously you do not have the 'right' to ignore the democratic decision of the majority (actually a minority under our electoral system) to pay taxes towards the cost of arms, nuclear power, or the salaries of incompetent ministers. To choose, you must be able to pay; without money, you not only have no choice, you increasingly have no rights. I consume, therefore I am.

One thing above all dismayed me while I was making this journey. This was the realisation that wherever I went I saw towns and cities which had become more or less identical: regional diversity, both cultural and economic, is largely a thing of the past. I do not mean that all regions are economically equal; far from it. It seemed to me, however, that the replacement of traditional local economies and industries with a blanket of consumer and service industries has tended to wipe out diversity even though these new industries perform far more efficiently in some regions than others. To find a place which did not conform to one's expectations to a very great extent was usually to find a place which was so poor that it had fallen out of the economy almost completely.

To some extent this is because people are increasingly mobile, though they usually are people who get in the Sierra rather than on their bike. Places which retain a strong regional identity – Glasgow, Liverpool, Tyneside – have done so in no small part because they have been denied economic opportunity. Dundee is a prime example. 'Successful' towns such as Southampton, Reading, Banbury and Colchester have become anodyne, cloned expressions not of a local identity but of a polycorporate strategy. What remains of their traditional identities is expressed in the language of 'Heritage', packaged remnants of the past now outside the day-to-day experience of their inhabitants, 'attractions' and 'leisure opportunities' pinned to the town like costume jewellery.

Carlisle haunted me all afternoon, a nightmare vision of a future Britain. I drove, as I had promised myself on the aeroplane I would, along the southern shore of the Solway Firth, still following Hadrian's Wall. It is a strange region of dazzling light, of dunes, marshes and wind-flattened bushes, of mirages and mud. From Burgh-by-Sands to Bowess-on-Solway the road is a thin lifeline across the tidal sand and silt, with frequent signs warning that it is covered at high tide by up to four feet of water. The villages are low-slung white places built on almost imperceptible headlands; they seem to be trying to keep their skirts out of the water and duck the wind at the same time. Between them, every farm seems to have a huge stone barn, many evidently very old, which struck me as odd in a region where no natural building materials were to be had. Even stranger, none of them had been converted into bijou residences, though doubtless their time will come. I crawled across the dunes and marshes toward Drumburgh; even Hadrian's Wall is here a mere bank and ditch of mud like a disused railway line. The light was so fierce, the air washed clean and the dust blown away, that everything seemed to have been flattened by the weight of the sunshine. Rather than clarifying objects, the brightness distorted them. Across the Firth the industrial town of Annan with its four huge cooling towers spewing acid steam sideways jerked and buckled in the heat-haze, although it was far from warm.

The wall ends at Bowness; beyond it the road continues in an enormous semicircle to a hamlet called Cardurnock, where there is a collection of spindly radar towers in a field grazed by sheep happily oblivious of the signs reading 'DANGER – HIGH VOLTAGE'. I found myself heading inland again, watching the peak of Skiddaw on the horizon grow larger. The mountains of the Lake District, from this low coast, seem to begin abruptly, with no foothills, like traffic cones, and to form an immense barrier cutting off this curious region from the rest of the world. It had lived up to my airborne expectations, a secret country of subtle shifting elements and colours, somehow too insubstantial for anything as massive as the Wall to begin or end in, a vague half-finished watercolour seen in tricksy light. This odd disorientation continued as I crossed the marsh country called Wedholme Flow and came to Abbeytown, where a strange barn-like church in dark red sandstone crouches amongst a few old white wooden cottages and new bungalows. I spent some time photographing the church, unable to decide how old it was. There was not a soul on the streets.

Only when I reached Silloth, a small semi-industrial resort, did I feel I had stepped back into reality. Silloth is a rather sad place, with a couple of good fancy Victorian terraces on a cobbled main street and a seafront dominated by a huge mill. It looks as if it grew up as a place where injured or wheezing miners from the Cumbrian coalfield could convalesce; it was never grand, or even brassy and blowsy in the way that British resorts used to be. It was a little dour and poker-faced, but it was certainly bracing. I sat on the esplanade and watched a line of squalls blow in from the Irish Sea, tracking up the Solway Firth or over the distant hump of Criffel, a lonely hill on the Dumfriesshire coast. One of these mean, black little storms swung south as if spotting the strolling T-shirted Sillothians taking the air, and within a minute preternatural darkness had descended and the people were scurrying for cover as the sea apparently lifted itself into the air and dumped itself on to the prom. A small ice-cream stall with 'Mr Longcakes' painted on its side had been doing steady business in the sunshine; now the owner hitched it to the back of his car and drove away although by the time he turned the ignition key the sun was shining again and he was soaking wet.

They seem to go for unusual place-names in Cumbria; apart from Silloth I passed a sign to a place called Jericho on the way to Aspatria. The road, like all English roads which traverse completely flat terrain, indulged in a series of 90° bends just to keep me on my toes. Aspatria proved to be a village of Victorian red brick interspersed with a few medieval buildings (the Sun Inn looked particularly ancient), but with only three interesting points apart from its name. Firstly the church, a mid-Victorian horror of such ugliness that it ought to be condemned on aesthetic grounds alone. Secondly, a memorial to a local public benefactor, Sir Wilfred Lawson, in the form of a superb statue of St George and the Dragon, with a plaque of Wilfred himself on the base looking like Leonardo da Vinci. Lastly, the Job Centre, which was for sale, surely a bad sign. I remarked as much to two men who had stopped to admire the van. 'Aye,' said one, and they both nodded glumly. I explained what I was doing in response to their enquiries about my transport and received in return much helpful information about a man named Bert who worked in the same garage as one of them. Bert is dyslexic. He knows letters, but cannot read words, and when he tries to write he puts the letters one on top of the other instead of in a line. The older man demonstrated this foible at length, drawing letters with his fingertips on the dust of Blodwen's rear door. I remarked that dyslexics are often good at maths even though unable to cope with writing. 'Oh, no,' said the man. 'He's fookin' hopeless. Hopeless.'

And the younger one nodded and chipped in, 'Aye. Hopeless.' The older one demonstrated how poor Bert puts numbers on top of each other as well as letters, and as final proof volunteered that Bert had once tried to sell a spark plug for £450 instead of £4.50. It struck me that Bert ought to have realised that sparkplugs are not made of platinum and might well be incredibly stupid rather than, or as well as, dyslexic, but before I could pursue this point the older man launched into a history of every car he had owned since 1948 describing in detail their cubic capacity, brake horse power, top speed over level ground, usefulness in attracting young ladies and level of comfort for two people placed horizontally on the back seat for the purpose of sexual gratification. He had, naturally enough, once owned a Morris Minor van; it came off rather badly on all counts, but was 'as reliable as a dog'.

After this, conversation flagged, until the younger man nodded towards the Wilfred Lawson memorial and said I ought to take a picture of it. I already had, I said; I thought it was great. 'Aye,' he nodded, 'that's History, that is.'

On to Prospect, which may once have had some. Prospect is the first industrial village of this famously industrial Cumbrian coast and, until a few years back, marked the boundary of one of the biggest and worst slums in the world, stretching more or less uninterrupted from Maryport to Whitehaven, some 25 miles of black, stinking misery. Crosby Villa consists of a single terrace of workers' cottages along one side of the main road for half a mile; Crosby is the same except that both sides are occupied. Here and there in the land between a little brook runs through a fragment of pretty land, and often a substantial Georgian or early Victorian house occupies the bank, but for the most part the land looks as if it has been chewed up and spat out. What is not waste is covered by allotments or forms grazing land for small, hairy ponies, munching around the wheels of wrecked cars. Maryport seems to be trying to pull out of what looks to have been a catastrophic depression, but although the old harbour has been cleaned up and converted into pleasant little flats, with a 'marina' (mostly empty) and a bistro, the backstreets are cluttered with more-or-less derelict houses, and many of those with half a roof and missing windows appear to be occupied. There is a new industrial estate, but it is largely for sale.

100

Between Maryport and Workington, enormous coalyards line the shore, some in use, most apparently not. What few new factories there are stand like plastic toys in a landscape which looks poisoned and dead. More allotments everywhere, bordered by flimsy fences of scrap sheet metal and old doors held together with plastic twine, the soil black with coal dust, the decrepit tool sheds and pigeon lofts padlocked but falling down. Workington appears on the horizon like a broken black tooth. Flimby, another long collection of identical terraces, bowed and cracked by subsidence, with four out of every ten houses displaying a dusty 'For Sale' sign like a flag of surrender. Seaton has a vast refinery on the landward side and a field of sheep on the seaward, more allotments, more terraces, more waste ground covered in shreds of plastic and metal.

'WELCOME TO WORKINGTON, TWICE WINNER OF CUMBRIA IN BLOOM' is the message that greets the visitor, but it's not easy to see how. Immense, tumbledown, satanic, encrusted with soot, Workington gives the impression that the Industrial Revolution stopped only a few minutes before you arrived, and nobody's quite sure what to do now. Compared to other great Victorian cities, such as Leeds, Sheffield, Birmingham, now modernised and clean, this is the Stone Age; there seems to be nothing new here, nothing that isn't falling down or cracking up. From the higher ground one can see endless rows of back-to-backs, like a sea of fossilised ribs. Harrington is joined to Workington by a couple of miles of unvaried council estates. The houses, built in the '20s and '30s in pebble-dash, looked in a bad state, with repairs of repairs and patches of bare dust instead of gardens. Harrington itself occupies a steep little valley running down to a small bay; climbing up the other side one comes to High Harrington, an earlier development than the late Victorian houses at the bottom. I drove up and down a couple of times, then turned towards the shore, passed under a long, low railway viaduct, and emerged in an immense area of nothing. It was obvious that between the railway and the sea about a square mile of the town had been completely demolished, but there was no sign of anything being put in its place apart from grass-seed. The street continued past two remaining buildings, a pub and a public urinal, which stood 400 yards apart. At the end of the road a concrete sea-wall adjoined a tumbledown harbour-bar and a beach which consisted of large stones, bricks, chunks of concrete and rusted pieces of iron. Across the harbour, low cliffs of crumbling whitish soil were crowned by a landscaped tip on which new houses had been built, and on the hillside behind the railway a row of pretty, late eighteenth-century cottages, brightly painted, stood out against the darker terracing and a grim church with a tower. I turned off the engine. I had come 118 miles from Gilsland and 1,383 miles in all.

There didn't seem to be anything to see on the front, but close inspection revealed that the harbour was built of titanic blocks of stone and must once have been of great importance. There was a new building at the back, under the railway viaduct, and four or five pleasure boats hauled up on to the quay, but no clue as to what had surrounded the harbour before. I wandered along bent almost double against the wind, enjoying the sensation of cold spray on my face after a tiring drive, and discovered that the council had begun to lay out part of the field with paths and flowerbeds and benches, but these had been left unplanted and isolated by the immense swathe of grass. A few people had driven out to the shore and were sitting in their cars eating fish and chips or listening to music; on the greensward tiny figures hurled invisible sticks for dogs. When I got back into Blodwen my face felt as if I was wearing a mask of salt.

My first priorities, as usual, were to eat and to find somewhere to sleep. I had little hope of finding accommodation in Harrington; it isn't the sort of place where there is any demand. But up the hill in High Harrington I noticed the Riverside Hotel, a name which puzzled me until I realised that a stream ran in a dark brick conduit below one side of it. A little old man opened the door. 'Sorry, she's not in, and she doesn't take anybody on Sunday nights anyway.'

Harrington didn't look like the kind of place where one could fall asleep in the car and wake up with your wheels still intact, so I found a Chinese fish and chip shop on the Workington road and sat in the van eating a most delicious meal before setting off into the boondocks to find a quiet spot. As I ate, I watched the world go by; the world drives an incredible assortment of ancient cars – I saw nothing later than a B-registration – and the world's offspring have stick-like legs, ragged hand-me-down dresses, bruises and sores. Entertainment for the Harrington young seemed to consist of getting as many hulking crop-headed young men as possible into an old Fiesta and burning rubber up and down the street again and again and again. A very fat woman in a soiled nylon overall laboured up the hill towards the chippy; when she arrived I saw that she was wearing pink bedroom slippers with pom-poms. She bought a giant bottle of cola and toiled away again. She must have been about 20, though she looked closer to 40. She had a black eye.

It was now nearly six o'clock. I headed out of town towards Distington, hoping to find somewhere to park for the night in the stretch of land between the coastal towns and the Loweswater Fells, the beginning of the Cumbrian Mountains. It was the longest evening of my life; I drove about 40 miles until, exhausted, I settled for a bleak hilltop lane having investigated West Cumbria in microscopic detail. Road after road, in miserable ex-pit villages on the plain and among the burglar-alarmed cottages of the fells, proved unsatisfactory. My final choice had at least the benefit of a wonderful view; I hunkered down with the earphones on. Once again, the first tune made me smile: Warren Zevon's *Splendid Isolation*.

From my eyrie on a windy hilltop above the River Keekle (yes, Keekle) I had a spectacular view of the fells turning flame orange as the sun went down, but when I awoke nine hours later the mountains, though only four miles away, were invisible in mist and drizzle. I spent three hours breakfasting and writing my notes before cold and damp forced me to move on. I drove down to the village of Pica (pronounced Pyker) where a magpie (Latin name *Pica pica*) was sitting on a fencepost. One for sorrow: Pica is a dump. In fact the whole of the coastal strip inland as far as the river is a dump, since almost all of it has been dug up, dug into or dumped on at one time or another; there were both opencast and underground mines here. I parked at the railway station in Harrington and walked up the street to the Post Office. I stopped to read the advertisements on cards in the window, as good an indication as any of the state of the place, I supposed. There were the usual MOT failures, offers of Plumbers' and Builders' services at 'very cheap rates', and this, which I thought balanced its sales pitch with friendly reasonableness:

> 'STONE CLADING' (sic)
> 'DECORATIVE'
> Only Ten Pound The Lot.
> Come + have a look + see What you think.

Inside the shop I asked the woman at the counter if she could tell me a bit about Harrington, but she was from Workington. She turned to a man stacking shelves and explained what I wanted.

'So what goes on here?' I asked.

'In Harrington? Nothing. Dead boring really.'

Startled by this flood of information I pressed on regardless. Was he from Harrington? No, he'd only lived here 15 years – but it felt longer.

'Look,' he said, 'You want to talk to our local historian over the road.'

He pointed out the house. A woman in curlers answered the door. Her husband was at work but if I came back at one I could have a word. I thanked her and headed down to the harbour.

The front was completely deserted, except for three men sheltering from the bitter wind and drizzle in the lee of the public lavatories. I went over and talked to them. They were all Harrington-born and bred. As we talked they gradually became enthusiastic in their explanations; up there on the hill the magnesium works had stood, during the war. Before that the iron works was up there. All round where we were standing had been streets, a 'separate little town' around the harbour. At the side of the harbour had been the slipway for the shipbuilders yard, and at the back the railhead for the coal and coke wagons. There had been a big steelworks, too, across the harbour, over the tip where the new houses had gone up; one of the biggest steel towns in the world, Workington was then. Now they bring the steel in from Middlesbrough and just shape it into rails. Used to be three, four thousand men in that steelworks; barely four hundred today. Their reminiscence flagged, as if in their enthusiasm they had prematurely run dry. 'Aye,' one said. 'There used to be seven or eight pubs down here. A separate little town of its own, like, it was, this side of the railway. For the shipworkers. Always a lot of pubs round a shipyard.'

'So what happened to the houses?' I asked. 'Were they condemned?'

'After the War, aye. But they were good houses, mind. Bloody good houses. It were never a slum down here. Real artisans' houses, they were.'

'So what happened? Subsidence?'

'No, no. It were the war. During the war they built the magnesium works, see, and they pumped sea water from the harbour to help the process. It produced this white powder which got everywhere. They didn't care about pollution in them days . . .'

'Well, there was a war on,' chipped in one of the others.

'Aye. This powder, it ate into the stone. Metal, stone, anything, it just rotted it away. After the war the whole lot came down.' He gestured away beyond the viaduct. 'That were never Harrington in them days. It were here. The real town was here.' And his friends nodded and smiled.

'And they never built anything to replace it. Are there any plans to?'

'Aye, well . . . they talk about building flats down here, but there's no money, you see. There's no money in this town now.'

'Still, at least they kept a couple of useful buildings,' I said, nodding towards the pub and the urinal. 'So there's not many jobs round here anymore?' They shook their heads, still smiling except with their eyes. 'What do people do nowadays, then?'

'They come down here and stand behind the toilets,' said one, and the others laughed.

After that I walked around the dock and tried to pick out signs of the past, but they were few. Where the marina now stood had been the Salvation Army hostel and the Coastguard HQ; where there was now a piled shingle beach the rails had run out over the sea on a wooden jetty and the trucks had dumped slag into the water. Old railway lines, now green scars, crisscrossed the town; ships and trains had unloaded steel and coke and ash, iron ore, limestone, magnesium . . . now a two-car diesel crept along the shore beneath the crumbling cliff and pulled up at the station. No one got in or out. I could hear the guard's buzzer telling the driver to move on from 40 yards away. The three old men hadn't seemed unhappy. They surveyed the wasteland with rheumy eyes and wry smiles, as if they had always expected it would come to this. There was no anger in them, yet their voices and expressions had become animated as they had recalled the vanished streets and factories and yards, and there had been a note of pride, almost of wonder at the place, its power and dirt and money. They surveyed the gutless corpse of their town, now, as if sharing a secret, ironic joke.

It began to rain. I drove up the street to the house opposite the shop, and the door was answered by Geoff Johnstone. In the hall hung a watercolour showing Harrington with all its industries in situ; not as it had been, he said, at any one time, but a sort of amalgam of local history showing where everything had been. Some of it was unclear; the shape and even the sites of some of the important buildings were now uncertain. He had put together as much as he could and directed the artist, using old photographs. We sat in his sitting room for an hour and he patiently explained the history of Harrington and Whitehaven, Maryport and Workington. Mrs Johnstone offered me tea and biscuits. The memories of the three wise men down on the front were obviously fading; Mr Johnstone put me right as to the position of the magnesium works, the slipway, and the number of pubs around the docks (17). But they had been right about the toxic white powder, and about the quality of the houses; they weren't late Victorian terraces but late Georgian to early Victorian villas. The powder combined with rain to form a powerful alkali or acid which 'ate everything it touched', just as the others had said. God knows what it did to people, I thought.

He talked about the various railways, both heavy and light gauge, and the early history of the port; serious shipbuilding was begun in the 1760s by a man called Thomas Ellwood. He and his successors seem to have been benevolent employers, to judge from the remaining pre-Victorian houses and the description of the old town. The shipyard had closed in 1879. Coal, which had been mined on a small scale in the area since the 1600s or earlier, had become the great local business, underpinning the iron and steel works and being shipped out from the docks. The rich seam which provided it is called the Lowca Seam. The last pit, Harrington Number Ten, closed in 1968. There is now talk of starting a new open-cast mine above the town, but the remaining coal may be too low-grade and sulphurous by modern standards.

Geoff Johnstone has worked in the local shipping industry all his life and has been a councillor for many years. He had written a brief history of the town for use in the local schools, a copy of which he gave me. Again, I caught no trace of bitterness or disillusionment in his voice, even when we were discussing the Salterbeck Estate, the vast, dingy and bedraggled housing scheme which lies at the back of the town and towards Workington proper. It was into Salterbeck that the population of Low Harrington was moved when it was demolished. Unemployment among those gimcrack, slipshod boxes is currently over 20 per cent. I found myself half-wishing that the new open-cast project would come off; although it would be an environmental nightmare it would at least give people some work. Geoff Johnstone seemed to have his doubts.

I thanked them both and got up to leave. They wished me luck with my journey and said they would look out for the book. As I stepped out into the little front garden Mr Johnstone pointed to something in a corner of the flowerbed: 'Take a look at that.' It was a small sundial which he had rescued from the demolition. It had belonged to Thomas Ellwood, the shipbuilder, and it was inscribed in beautiful crisp letters:

T. ELLWOOD 1770
WELCOME FRIENDS

Geoff Johnstone had tested it against a modern satellite navigation system; it is accurate to the minute.

I went back down to the harbour and traced the positions of the railhead and the shipyard and the poisonous factory. One of the old men was walking back across the grass. He waved and called, 'Good luck, lad.' I drove up to the Salterbeck Estate, and learned only that it was as bad as I had at first suspected. When I parked, men walking along the street – and there were a lot of men on the streets, walking dogs or just walking – gave me frowning, suspicious looks. I wasn't welcome in my poofy car. I drove away again, parked down at the railway station and bought some food and drink; on my way back to the car I noticed a poster on the fence by the platform:

> Looking at the pleasant modern landscape of Harrington, who would dream that this was once one of the most heavily industrialised areas of Workington. But the steelworks to the north still supplies rails for the world's railways! The delightful sand and shingle beaches and sun-trap breakwaters to the south of the harbour opened in 1760 are ideal places to relax, while on a clear day a pleasantly invigorating headland walk further south offers views across the Solway Firth to the Galloway Hills and even to the Isle of Man. Many ships were built here for the Irish coaling trade and, in the 1860s, tall sailing ships for trade all over the world.

I looked out at the sea across the 'pleasant modern landscape', the flat empty space where Low Harrington used to be. Available now, I thought, with vacant possession. Sun-trap coastal site with bags of scope and character. Lovely views. No environmental or planning problems, skilled local workforce.

Come + have a look + see What you think.

IVELET

In arcadia ego

It was already after 2.30 p.m. by the time I found myself on the road to Cockermouth and the Lakes, and I didn't stop until Keswick, where I fought my way through its pretty but crowded streets in search of camping gas (easy) and bottled water (strangely difficult). I ended up in a queue in a healthfood shop behind a woman who was buying two of every organic vegetable in the world, presumably to start some kind of vegetable introduction agency. In all she spent £15, which will buy you a lorryload of potatoes in Tesco's. Meanwhile her daughter Tamsin set about trashing the joint ('Darling, PLEASE! Mummy's trying to think . . . two starfruit please . . .') whilst outside on the pavement husband Dirk ('Dirk gave up a promising future in futures to run the Coriander Wholefood Non-Smoking Hotel with ex-publisher wife Sara near Keswick') wrestled with three-year-old Tarquin, who should have been in a straitjacket. A few E-numbers would probably have quietened him down. The whole family was clad in what can only be described as organic sweaters, possibly a wool/seaweed mix. I felt a quiet glow of satisfaction when, as Sara tried to extract money from a drawstring purse handcrafted by Peruvian lepers, Tamsin broke open a pack of Kelp-O-Krunch snack-effect ozone-rich biscuit-style food, and ate one. Serves her right.

Keswick's shops were mostly given over to horrendously expensive 'County' goods – floral porcelain, saddlery, waxed jackets – and horrendously expensive souvenirs – Wordsworth tea-towels, Edwardian Lady pot-pourri in containers labelled 'From The Lakes', Windermere Honey Gift Sets – with the residue taken up by camping shops. I ate a belated and hurried lunch in the carpark, including some kind of wholesome wholegrain whole earth chewy bar which I think must have been a pet food product in a different wrapper, and hurried on. I had planned to go to a place called Ings, but changed my mind for two reasons. Firstly, I passed straight through it at 65 mph on a dual carriageway and was ten miles beyond it before I realised my mistake, and secondly, I had a growing urge to get as far away from the Lake District as possible as fast as possible. Not to put too fine a point on it, I hate the place. Always have. Not without good reason, however; I was once forced, while on a Geography field trip, to climb Helvellyn in March during a blizzard. Apart from this, what I saw now convinced me that the Lake District is not real countryside at all. It is a theme park. Wordsworthland. The Daffodil Experience.

Between Keswick and Kendal, Ullswater and Ennerdale, there is not one unkempt acre, not one mountainside, lake shore, tree or rock which does not look as if it has been hoovered. Every turn of the road opens up a delightful new vista of tumbling rock and water, baize-smooth meadows, charming islets and soaring fells, and not one feature is out of place. Nothing jars; even where the dry-stone walls have fallen down it looks as though the farmer has called in a landscape architect to push them over just . . . so. This powerful impression of watching a hologram is amplified by the fact that it is all traversed by a large modern road, carefully hidden behind rocks and trees, so that the people picnicking on the tailgate of the Saab across the lake aren't put off their foie gras by all those ghastly trippers. What wouldn't the residents of Caithness or Wester Ross or mid-Wales give for roads like these: fast, smooth and efficient and tucked out of sight like plastic surgery scars. I'm not blaming anybody for this, except perhaps that old coot Wordsworth ('You would have to go and open your big mouth, William . . . look at them all!'). But nobody could describe it as 'rural'. Even in April the roads are crammed and the villages bursting: the area has to cope with a population equivalent to a major city, and needs the infrastructure to keep them moving. The effect on the environment is massive. It's no use encouraging golden eagles to nest on the fells if four miles away it looks like Blackpool's Golden Mile crossed with the M25. It's probably too late for anything but damage limitation, but the problem arose because it was people who were given all the attention, rather than the environment which people wanted to see. 'Lakeland' – the brochures make no bones about the theme-park – has the shops, the hotels, the advertisements, the cafés, the pubs, the pollution, and the *convenience* of a conurbation, and like any city it has much that is fine and much that is not. It is a microcosm of the British countryside: the city of woods and fields, full of people enjoying an artificially sustained, unnatural and in the end, self-defeating 'leisure experience'.

Windermere and Grasmere were choked with people in immaculate outdoor gear and gleaming, mud-free boots. These poseurs were interspersed with 'serious' walkers, who can be divided into two types. Type A are the 'Climb Every Mountain' brigade, whose spiritual leader is Chris Bonington rather than Julie Andrews; their idea of fun is to die in a rockfall suspended 500 feet from an overhanging ledge by a rope clenched in their teeth. Type B are older, wiry middle-aged couples who carry small knapsacks and wander around the lower slopes frowning at maps and trying to find the Public Footpath whilst thousands of people in blue nylon windcheaters stampede past them like wildebeest, heading up the mountain in a frenzy of trespass. Finally, of course, the multitude of Good Old British Tourists, who very sensibly wouldn't climb anything higher than the steps into the Red Lion, and whose idea of relaxation is to sit in the Cavalier eating Hula-Hoops and listening to the football on Radio Two; the important thing is that they want to do this in Keswick and not Kensal Green. And so they should.

Despite my mindless, ill-informed, ideologically-unsound, shallow, dismissive prejudices, I did find myself admiring the odd vista as I tore through, but only in the sense that one admires a pretty postcard. I didn't want to get involved, let alone climb anything. I have a great admiration for the work of A. Wainwright, a fine prose writer as well as a great draughtsman and designer of guidebooks, and like him I don't really like people *en masse* – yet many were here on his account.

I was just congratulating myself at having escaped the Attack of the Daffodil People when I hit Kendal and its murderous traffic system, which is exacerbated by signs which direct you only to Penrith, Northallerton or Skipton. I, in common with 99.99 per cent of sane people, have no desire to visit any of these, and inevitably found myself on the wrong road. Any readers still awake at this point will spot that this implies that I knew where I was going by now. I was a long way south by the time I had an opportunity to turn off, and I backtracked up the motorway in a foul temper. But this abated when I turned east toward Sedbergh and found myself in a lovely valley, that of the Lune, with the Howgill Fells ahead and not another vehicle in sight. The whole of the rest of the afternoon's drive over the Pennines took place on roads almost completely deserted (except by battered Landrovers and wayward sheep), yet the countryside was easily as impressive as anything Lakeland has to offer. The Pennine dales were a revelation to me; television vitnery doesn't do them justice. I found myself grinning with delight after the sad waste of Harrington and the grotesque abuse of the Lakes. I pray that the day doesn't come when there is a banner across the road welcoming you to 'James Herriot Country'.

As the road climbs from the well-wooded valley the dry-stone walls begin to break up the land like filigree between cut emeralds, until in the high dales they form astonishingly dense patterns of tiny fields, each with a neat stone barn looking as clean-cut as the day it was built. There are no loose stones in the fields, so the walls appear to have come from somewhere else, as if someone had made a sand painting on a snooker table. At the top of the valley a long viaduct brings the Settle to Carlisle line in across the moors, and beneath it stands a tiny chapel with a little allotment garden instead of a yard, with chickens and, over the road, a pigsty. No house was apparent.

Having crossed the watershed one enters Wensleydale, and the road descends gently to Hawes. In the 20-odd miles since Sedburgh I hadn't seen a single house which looked out of place; no mock-Georgian villas, no bungalows in yellow brick, no Alpine-style chalets. What is going on here, I wondered. Surely not Responsible Management of the Countryside? Where are the Strictly Limited Developments? The Tasteful Conversions? The Well-Camouflaged Caravan Parks and Exclusive Security-Patrolled Timeshare Villages? Could it be that as I drove in rapture down that last slope we attained a speed which took us *back in time?* Had I entered a mysterious dimension where stone cladding had been outlawed by The Wise Ones?

I turned off to the hamlet of Hardraw, a place as lovely as its name is ugly, and continued to Askrigg, looking for a road marked on my map that would take me over into Swaledale. No signposts were in sight; I took a chance and headed up the hillside on a narrow track of bumpy grey macadam. Thus began the sternest test that Blodwen had to face on the entire trip, and probably the hardest she has ever taken. Nothing on the roads of northern or western Scotland, the Grampians or the Lakes had been remotely as tough as that little road over Askrigg Common. My road atlas has the serious fault that steep inclines are not indicated in minor roads – a major oversight, since this was a very dangerous road indeed. I was not in the least prepared, and as soon as I was on it I realised that it would be impossible to go back; the track was barely wider than the van, with a wall on one side and rocky ground on the other. I watched the speedometer fall from 35 to 25; third gear; 20; second gear; 15 . . . 10 . . . 8 . . . 5 . . .

Now Blodwen is an old car. She does not have exotic luxuries such as synchromesh in her gearbox, and when she is hot and tired she has been known to refuse to go into first gear, as on the evening in Baddidarach under the disapproving gaze of the wealthy. All you can do is to let in the clutch and try again, or stick it in second and accelerate hard. She was almost at rest; if I had had to do either of these I would have been travelling backwards at high speed before I could say 'Oh, bother'. I actually closed my eyes, rammed the gear lever forward as hard as possible and hit the gas. After a noise like someone attacking a bus with a chainsaw we proceeded up the hill at a steady 4 mph. It seemed to me to be a 1 in 2 slope, 45°. There were no bends at all. But I was moving up it, and that was enough. I warn you now: don't do it. Especially in a Morris. It's like trying to climb Everest in a diving suit. At the top I got out and sat on the grass and smoked a cigarette.

On the Swaledale side civilisation has advanced to the stage where they have realised that if you put in some hefty bends the downward motion of the vehicle is usefully reduced. You still travel at something approaching mach 3, but you are so grateful to be alive that this is exhilarating rather than an occasion for underwear concern. Occasionally your tyres even touch the ground.

Ivelet is a mile east of the place where I landed. It is not signposted, and lies across the River Swale, and I had gone a mile or two beyond the turn before I realised my mistake. As it happened, this was fortunate because in coming round via the next village and doubling back I avoided a bridge which is so steep that one has to get out to check that there is nothing coming on the other side, run back to the car in case something does, and then more or less take off as you come over the hump. Ivelet is so small that I wasn't sure I had arrived. I got out and hailed a young man standing by the telephone box, which is one of the more major structures. It was eight o'clock.

'Is this Ivelet?' I asked.

'Yes.'

'Thank God for that.'

We talked for a few minutes. I said I hadn't expected to find a telephone box, and he told me I was in luck because there was a guesthouse along the road too. I began to like the place. I knocked at the farmhouse door; it was plastered with 'Highly Commended' signs. A woman opened it, accompanied by a delicious foody smell.

'Now, then,' she said.

'Good evening. Would you happen to have a single room for one night, please?'

''Appen.'

I paid too much for a tiny room with a bigger en-suite shower, but slept like a dog. I was too late to get an evening meal so it was supper in the van again, but the next morning I got a splendidly cholesterol-rich breakfast with more meat in it than I normally consume in a month.

Swaledale was enchanting with patches of bright sunshine zooming across the slopes. I walked down to the Swale, following a beck which is spanned by a modern road bridge and just below it an ancient one in danger of collapse, where there was a sign saying 'NO TIPPING', but of course people had tipped. Most of the rubbish seemed to be farmers' – plastic bags and chemical tins. The heap of rubbish was next to a waterfall, which I photographed, trying to decide whether to turn the camera so as to censor the tip or whether to leave it in. In the end I did both. At the bottom where the beck meets the river is the alarming bridge I mentioned earlier, and 200 yards up the opposite slope is Ivelet; 50 yards more and you are through the village. The half-dozen cottages were silent; I sat down in a flagstone at the foot of a dry-stone wall and waited in the pleasant sunshine for something to happen, not really caring if nothing did.

Pheasant call. Kestrel hovering. Chaffinch and blackbird song, curlew's call, crows' and jackdaws' chatter. The walls of the fields are the walls of the houses. Dog's howl. Sheep making a variety of entertaining noises, cockerel's crow. Water bubbles and drips. Stones clink and scratch. The sound of the Swale is the sound of the wind in the trees, is the sound of the cloud-shadows racing across the hillside. A polythene bag stuffed into the dry-stone wall. Deer crossing a distant field. A red bus bounding up the dale. A woman, old and bent, comes out of her house, lifts a heavy stone from the dustbin lid, pops something in and goes back indoors. The closing door starts the dog off again.

I stand for a long time waiting for the light to be right for a photograph, watching a patch of sunlight coming down the dale. It seems to be moving fast but takes an eternity to arrive: I don't mind. I enjoy every minute of it. Time moves with the speed of lichen. You might walk around a field and find you have returned a hundred years hence. Nothing will have changed, I hope.

I drove down Swaledale to Richmond. The road seems to follow every twist, and feels as bumpy as the bed of the Swale. Through pretty villages, like Gunnerside, Low Row and Healaugh, completely at ease with their surroundings. A sign to a village called Crackpot. If these villages were in the Cotswolds, they would be overrun by coaches and cars. Healaugh in particular is a stunner. I had shot a whole roll of film in Ivelet, despite my determination to resist the merely picturesque. It was my last roll, which was no bad thing or I would never have got out of the dale. As the valley descends, the villages get bigger but no less attractive; Reeth and Grinton are like little market towns. I half-expected to see John Bull coming out of the pub. The Swale slows and meanders through rich meadows; then, as the valley opens out it becomes rocky again, and the road climbs high on the southern slope and runs through beechwoods, across little cliffs and scars and wooded bluffs. Below, a caravan park, 'Swaleview', ends the idyll.

Richmond is often cited as an example of the best kind of English market town, particularly by the *England Uber Alles* type of historian. This is because its architecture is mostly Georgian or older, and has been well-preserved. It is certainly fine, and not over-run by visitors; it gets on with its own business. But here, as in Keswick, there is a noticeable tension between the traditional business of the countryside and the new country money. There are lots of shops selling up-market furniture and crockery and fashions, and a large number of well-groomed young men driving big German cars whilst talking on the phone. I decided these must be estate agents; the property crash in the South doesn't seem to have reached here, judging from the shop windows. A rather hideous modern four-bedroomed bungalow on the outskirts cost £300,000. Coincidentally, the cottage I had been sitting next to in Ivelet was on the market; three bedrooms, double glazed, centrally heated, 1760s, it seemed a snip at £165,000. Broad Yorkshire voices clashed with the piercing tones of the chattering classes; the butchers sold plovers' eggs as well as black pudding and tripe, shit-splattered Land Rovers dripped on to Golf Convertibles. Around every corner were the same urbane Georgian features slightly differently arranged; I fancied I could hear Alec Clifton-Taylor's well-oiled vowels and unruly false teeth with every step. The castle, a simple square red box, flew the flag of English Heritage as if it were the headquarters of some nasty little Fascist group determined to preserve one last bastion of roastbeefery. At least, I thought, I don't have to worry about leaving my car here; if they wanted to steal my hubcups they'd probably have to call out that nice little man from the garage.

JACK HILL
J. M. W. T.

Before I began this journey I tested a few possible routes on the map, and on most of them the letter J was supplied by Jack Hill. This was because I wanted to travel both to Wales and East Anglia before swinging back westward across southern England, and in order to fit all this in I had to get far enough south by the letter J to leave enough of the alphabet to divide up the rest of the country into manageable bits. Although there are plenty of Js further north – Jedburgh, Jarrow, Jesmond, Johnstonebridge, there is only one which falls at the right latitude for my purposes. Admittedly there is a temptingly-named place, Jump, 30 miles further on, but this was too far to be comfortably reached from Ivelet. I only mention all this to illustrate the way in which the trip was constructed; most people I explained it to were amazed that all but one of the letters could be found, let alone visited in the correct sequence; in fact, although there were a couple of rare letters which I had to plan ahead to reach, most of the time I was able to keep to my original rule of deciding on my destination one day at a time. A couple of people rather cruelly suggested that since the journey was for dyslexia I should have done them in the wrong order, which simply proves that the Sick Joke is alive and well.

Jack Hill caused me some concern because I wanted to visit a variety of types of place, and, like Ivelet, it was a mere dot on the map of Yorkshire (it's a little to the north of Otley). I needn't have worried. South of Richmond the land became greener but increasingly less attractive, and largely taken over by the MOD. Near Downholme, an army housing estate with a splendid view across the sewage works, I passed a shepherd and his dog standing in a field devoid of sheep. Everywhere there were large signs warning of Ministry of Defence firing ranges, usually with sheep grazing insouciantly around them; and there were several disconcerting bangs; although I didn't actually see any sheep get wasted maybe that was the explanation for the shepherd's puzzled expression. At Bellerby a sign said GO SLOW with an arrow pointing to a picture of a duck. 'I know they do' seemed the only appropriate response.

The countryside got prettier again as we left the environs of Catterick, and there was as usual a noticeable increase in the number of large Georgian houses in all the best spots. I found myself wondering whether the houses had been built in the best spots or whether they were the best spots because of the houses. Leyburn, by contrast, had the first terrace of red brick cottages I had seen since leaving Harrington, and they were the particularly livid red which you get from industrial Yorkshire south to about Leicester; so red that they create weird optical effects when seen against green fields. The farms all had new buildings, long shiny plastic barns, and shiny metal sheds; there had been none of these up in Swaledale. Perhaps they are forbidden under the terms of the National Park. I bet the Swaledale farmers would give their eye-teeth for a nice new prefabricated milking shed instead of those draughty stone byres.

Across the Ure and into Wensleydale, which is on a much grander scale than Swaledale, broader and greener below and with big rock sills along the tops. Big, prosperous farms predominate, some big enough to have stopped being farms and become country houses; I passed a number of fancy model dairy buildings and parks and follies, including a mysterious little Italianate rotunda in a copse, boarded up. The road was too steep and narrow to stop and investigate further. Then, as the road climbs up next to Bishopsdale Beck to Langstrothdale Chase, the farms decline again with the impoverishment of the land, until there is a farmyard full of rusted cars and tractors. Again, I wanted to stop, but could not do so until I reached a lay-by; in trying to turn round I nearly fell backwards into a ravine, and I gave up.

On the high ground between the dales it is once again the walls which draw the eye. They differ from dale to dale in colour, texture, and mossiness, in the size of their individual stones, and in the shadows stone casts upon stone as the light varies up hill and down dale. Frequently in the smaller valleys one wall stretches from the riverbank at the bottom straight as a ruler up the valleyside to the scree at the top – more than a mile in some cases. In all there must be tens of thousands of miles of these walls in the Pennines; only in the lower parts of the dales have they been replaced in some cases by wire; I hope the walls survive. It is impossible to visualise the Dales without them, and letting them go would be like painting out the trees in a Constable landscape. Or, come to that, a Turner.

It is a long fall into Wharfedale, the rockiest and grimmest of the dales

I saw, and by a long measure the busiest. There were walkers and caravans and coaches everywhere, for Wharfedale opens out just north of the Leeds/Bradford conurbation, and is a favourite escape from urban Yorkshire. All the villages have substantial carparks, conveniences, cafés and souvenir shops; caravan snackbars sit in the lay-bys. Huge limestone sills run along the valley sides, often forming the entire slope, and people dangled on ropes, crawled like spiders or abseiled down like multicoloured hopping fleas. I stopped high up at Kettlewell, where there is a youth hostel, tearooms and a snackbar, a busy pub and plenty of accommodation. I walked up the lane, nearly getting mown down by the traffic more than once. It was a powerful, still wintry landscape, with an almost prehistoric look. I felt as if everything here must be of stone, the tables and chairs and beds, like a Yorkshire Bedrock. But Yorkshiremen don't say 'Yabbadabbadoo' (thank God) when they meet you in the road. They say 'Ey-up', 'Grand day' (it was drizzling), or simply nod and grunt.

Kettlewell also contained a number of fabulously ancient buses. It looks as if they have simply been left there when, after years of carrying trippers up from the cities, they have finally wheezed their last, and now sprout nettles. Lower down, many of the farmhouses have become hotels, and a rash of signs tempt the jaded businesspeople of the West Riding with saunas, jacuzzis, squash courts and salad bars. Here something happened for the second or third time that day which made me laugh; a car in front, out for a spin with gran and the kids, pulled over to let me pass. Seeing a battered Morris in the rear-view mirror I suppose the driver presumed I was some kind of wacky rural type, on my way to fetch emergency supplies of clogs and tripe. Since Blodwen has a slow and steady approach to hills, this usually meant that they were stuck behind me for rather a long time.

At Burnsall the river is broad, with sand and shingle beaches on the bends, and there were picnickers all along it despite the dreary weather. Suddenly the road shoots up and teeters along the top of the valleyside, just as in Swaledale, through woods of beech and oak, with glimpses of the river far below. Then it descends gradually to Bolton Abbey. A fast dual carriageway took me across the moors to Blubberhouses – much prettier than it sounds – past a collection of giant golf-ball buildings which must be some kind of radar establishment; they look like spacecraft from a late-1950s horror movie: *Quatermass and t'Pit*.

I was almost there; the Swinsty Reservoir glimmered ahead, and I began to watch for a sign to Jack Hill. I climbed a long hill up to a conifer plantation in the centre of which was a huge radio tower, parked to look at the map, decided I had miscalculated, drove on down a very steep hill and across a dam, found myself in Farnley, too far south; turned and drove back; still found no turning; parked again and turned the map upside down and squinted at it; drove off to look for a turning near the reservoir; missed it; had to go on to Farnley again before I could stop; turned; swore a lot;

116

drove three miles back to the aerial; stopped; looked at the map; started off the wrong way; turned down a tiny track which seemed to be almost vertical in places, followed this for three miles before realising that it was the correct road, and emerged at the other end, having seen no sign of a village, to find a sign pointing back the way I had come reading 'DOB PARK'. I was at the top of the dam again. I turned left up the steep hill and eventually off again down the same tiny track, this time going as slowly as the forces of gravity would allow and keeping my eyes peeled for anything that might be a village disguised as a cow or a telegraph pole. At the very bottom of the valley I found another track leading off to the right; 'A-ha!' I said, and turned into it, only to find an 'UNSUITABLE FOR MOTOR VEHICLES' sign. So I reversed and continued along the valley, emerging by the Dob Park sign again none the wiser, whimpering 'I want to stop, I want to stop,' over and over. Not only had I not found Jack Hill, I hadn't even found this alleged Dob Park, which wasn't even on the map, whereas Jack Hill was marked as a substantial village; not just one dot, but a little group of dots, implying *lots of houses*, yes? SO WHERE THE HELL ARE THEY? Are you seriously telling me that I have driven 95 miles, gibbering into a tape recorder all the way about the subtle gradations of dry-stone walls, in pursuit of a *misprint*? Is Jack Hill in fact not in Yorkshire but in Dorset, or Burma?

I rang home. Kate asked how I was getting on. 'I think it'll have to be "Jiggered in Jack Hill",' I replied. 'It doesn't seem to exist. How about you?'

'WILL YOU SHUT UP. I'M TRYING TO TALK TO DADDY! Oh, all right. In fact, apart from warming my feet up at night I'm not really missing you at all.'

Round in a circle I went again, back to the hilltop under the aerial. Nearby was a farmhouse with a Bed & Breakfast sign; I needed no further encouragement. Jack Hill could wait. In fact, if it existed at all, it could go stuff itself. A teenage boy opened the door, yelled 'MUM!' and vanished; when Mum appeared she did not have a room free. But she did tell me where Jack Hill was, and I learned that I had been pronouncing it wrongly. It isn't Jack *Hill*, like a bloke, it's *Jack* Hill, like an invisible village.

I spent the night parked at the back of a picnic area above the reservoir under a stand of pines adjoining a denser wood on the steeper valley slope. Because the picnic spot wasn't signposted on the road I guessed that I would be relatively undisturbed, and so it proved, except for a middle-aged man who parked his car for an hour and read a paperback, and later that night after I had turned in three young men whose idea of a good time seemed to be to sit in the car and listen to Dire Straits whilst drinking Pepsi – clean-living lads they have in Yorkshire these days. I had been asleep when they arrived, and they swung the car around under the trees a couple of times so as to examine Blodwen carefully in their headlights but then left me in peace.

The morning was hazy and humid. After breakfast I set off down through the woods in search of the teeming metropolis of Jack Hill. The edge of the picnic area was covered with litter, and all down the footpath the young pines had been snapped off or uprooted by vandals. Beneath the trees, covered in a thick cover of pine needles, the tumbledown remains of old field walls could be seen. It was curious to be able to discern the pattern of the open countryside in this dank, close and very dark place.

The woman at the farmhouse had told me that there had once been a thriving community at Jack Hill, employed mostly in tannery. The ruins could still be made out, though she was a little vague ('under the trees') as to their whereabouts. When the valley had been selected for water storage it had been compulsorarily purchased, she thought, and the villagers moved out.

I emerged on to the lane near the sign saying 'Dob Park', and turned right towards the bottom of the valley, keeping my eyes peeled for anything that might be a village. A mile or so later I reached the junction marked 'Unsuitable for Motor Vehicles' and, reasoning that tanning would require water, turned down it towards the brook which flows between the reservoirs. The lane became a rutted track, extremely steep, and then a loose amalgam of sand and boulders with a small stream flowing down the centre. At the bottom was a paved ford, its flags now smoothed and buckled by the passage of water and time, and a delicate stone footbridge which might well have been medieval. There were trees all along the waterside, but no ruins; still I stayed there for an hour or so, on the excuse of waiting for the light to improve so that I could photograph it. It was very quiet. I thought how unusual it was to find an ancient bridge which had not been widened and strengthened for motor traffic; nothing could get down here except perhaps a tractor. The farmer had of course dumped empty weedkiller tins on the bank; that is what farmers do best. Up the valley the weird white golfball buildings near Blubberhouses began to appear through the lifting haze.

The light remained sullen; I grew cold and walked back up the streambed and up the lane in the opposite direction to that which I had driven the previous day. I peered over hedges and behind byres, climbed on to walls and ferreted around under trees, to no avail. The lane began to swing up the slope towards the aerial on the hilltop; I decided that either I had missed the ruins or that they must lie off the lane altogether. But what puzzled me was that my road atlas marked a considerable number of buildings on the lane, and I had passed only three or four isolated houses. They were ex-farms, now gentrified, with two-car garages, pernickety gardens and carriage lamps beside the door. I came at length to another, where there was a man in the garden. I hailed him and feeling as self-conscious as always in these situations explained what I was doing. To my relief, when I asked him where Jack Hill was, he replied, 'You're in it.'

The ruins, it seemed, were only a couple of hundred yards further up the lane. They were under some tall trees, and on the opposite bank of the road the village stocks were still standing. I asked if he knew anything about its history, but he didn't think he could help much. I told him what Mrs Beaumont at the farmhouse had said about the village falling into disuse when the valley was flooded, but he thought that it had been in terminal decline long before, and few if any occupants would have had to be removed. There had, however, been a pub which had remained in business almost to within living memory. Now Jack Hill was more of an address than a place; his house and the farm just above the ruins were still in Jack Hill. I said that the 'Dob Park' sign had confused me; it confuses everyone, he agreed, because the area along the lane is called Norbert's Bottom. I didn't hold out much hope of finding anything in Jack Hill beginning with a J, so I didn't mention this aspect of the journey. I thanked him and remarked that it was a lovely valley. 'Yes, isn't it?' he replied. 'Turner used to come and paint it; he stayed at Farnley Hall quite often.' So J for Joseph Mallord William Turner made my day.

The 'couple of hundred yards' turned out to be a good half-mile of one-in-four, but I found the place easily, under a group of tall beeches. The trees were immense, and were growing out of the ruins, which put the abandonment of the village at least a hundred years ago. Beyond their protection, nothing remained to be seen; the stones had presumably been stolen for field walls. On top of the bank, just as he had said, stood two stone posts, each grooved on the inside to hold the wooden trap of the stocks. I picked my way around, boots crunching over a thick carpet of beechnut husks, trying to decipher the ruins, but to little avail. A couple of walls had windows in; something now mostly below ground level might have been a fireplace; an empty door with a cracked lintel stone led into an old chicken run. One of the buildings stood, but only just, its roof sagging and sprouting ferns and willow-herb. I tripped over something half-buried, and picked it up; a half-bottle of Moët champagne, unfortunately empty. I balanced it on a wall and wondered how long it would be before the roots of the beeches tipped it off again.

The remains were too small to be particularly interesting. There were no signs of a church or chapel if there had ever been one, and none of the walls looked as if they had belonged to anything bigger than a small cottage. It was too far gone to be melancholy or atmospheric; coming along the lane, unless you knew what you were looking for, you would ignore it as simply the remains of a couple of old sheds. I tried to imagine the people born and bred here, who worked quietly in their valley and thanked God that they didn't live in the blackened monstrosities half a day's walk south. The smoke of Bradford, Leeds, Keighley and Shipley would have darkened their sky. They have no memorial except confused memories and a misleading map. Joseph Mallord William Turner, if he came back today, would doubtless miss the pub, but he might appreciate the ghostly giant puff-balls of the radar station, the iron aerial spearing from the trees, and the glimmer of water along the valley floor.

It was a long walk back to the car. The sun broke through, pearly then hot. Beneath the conifers the air was thick and the ground slippery; I was sweating freely by the time I reached the picnic area. Five miles to the south lay Otley, and Otley is joined on to Burley, which is joined on to Menston, to Guiseley to Yeadon to Rawdon, Pudsey, Farsley, Calverley, Shipley, Bingley, Bradford. Between Merseyside and Leeds there is hardly a ten-mile stretch of open road in 80 miles, and what open ground there is is largely Pennine moor. It was time to look at another side of Britain, and I pointed Blodwen's nose at this vast conurbation and prayed I would emerge intact on the other side.

Shack with whale jaw, Armadale

Abandoned croft in Sutherland

Welcome to Camusterrach!

The terraced houses of Grange Place, Grangemouth, built in 1900

Milecastle 48 on Hadrian's Wall, near Gilsland

Ivelet, Swalesdale

All that's left of Jack Hill

Llandudno from Great Orne Head

The Shropshire Bedlams in full swing, Montgomery

The graveyard at Nantyglo

Oxford, city of secrets

Shops at Perry Barr

Chalk and bales, Brancaster

On the quayside, Wells

After the hurricane, ancient oak forest, Suffolk

KEARSLEY

Kaput

I hate large cities. Whenever I am in one, I can't help thinking about all those miles of stone and concrete spreading in every direction. If I live in a place that takes me more than an hour to walk across I feel claustrophobic. So my mood was not ecstatic as I drove into Otley and saw the first of those dark satanic mills which lurk in the valleys of West Yorkshire and East Lancashire, and whose stacks have stained the houses and rocks black so thoroughly that when a Victorian building is cleaned it looks as raw and out-of-place as Canary Wharf does in London's Docks. I drove all day through interconnected small towns, frequently getting lost, cursing road surfaces which had been pummelled into ruts and craters and shoddily repaired if at all, and worrying that Blodwen, who is at her most peevish and unco-operative in stop-start traffic, would do something rash. The worst thing about these towns is that none of them dominates; unless you go down to central Bradford or Leeds, you never seem to arrive anywhere. You pass housing of varying attractiveness, industrial quarries both derelict and new, shopping malls and retail warehouses and garages, the odd town hall or civic amenity, but nothing ever grabs you and says, 'Stop! Look, you're *here*.' It's like driving all day up the Old Kent Road and never reaching the Thames.

At first I tried to make the effort to distinguish the subtleties of place, the marks which set, say, Bingley apart from Shipley. But as the day wore on, and the punishing roads and traffic refused to loosen their grip, the terraces and factories and demolition sites and interchanges began to blur. When I tried to force myself to concentrate, to describe what I was seeing with the same thoroughness that I had been describing the countryside, I found that I simply lacked the vocabulary to do so. Or rather, I found that almost everything I said was negative and disparaging and I lacked the ability to counter that negativity even though I wanted to. It came as a shock; I thought I had outgrown the prejudices of a middle-class southern suburban upbringing. I dislike cities in general, not northern or industrial cities in particular. Indeed, although I hate the experience of urban life, I like the *idea* of cities even though so few live up to my ideals. But I found myself trying to distinguish between two areas of redbrick terraced houses by saying that one had been 'rather grim' and the other 'a little more upmarket', based on the facile observation that some had bay windows and stood in tree-lined streets whereas others were flat-fronted and stood in greenless cobbles. By what standards was I judging what I saw? Because to describe at all seemed to be to judge; I was so used to describing what I saw in aesthetic terms that not only did I lack all but derogatory words, but also my mind was simply not receptive to what I saw; after a few minutes it just switched off, to awaken whenever I passed something 'interesting', like a church or a river.

So it was ugly, yes, and unvarying and sometimes mean and squalid, and dispiriting and banal. Or it was, if you like, not half so bad as the sum of those words would suggest; it was intermittently green, modern, clean, convenient, friendly, surprising, impressive. I could imagine loving it. I could imagine feeling at home, feeling safe. As a Southerner I was surprised both that it resembled so closely the mythical North of southern prejudice, and at how much it did not. The difference between the myth and the reality was largely a measure of redevelopment; it was a long time since I had last been in the industrial North and much had changed; for a start, most of it didn't seem very industrial any more. There is renewal and regeneration everywhere, but it is piecemeal and has had a negative effect in some cases. Big, fast new roads occasionally spring from nowhere and cut through the old heart, only to leave you somewhere which looks exactly like the place at the other end. New shopping centres and parks have appeared, but to reach them you have to struggle through streets which would be crowded with half the traffic, and the old houses seem to push in around them and stifle them. Past experiments are half-abandoned; tower blocks and newish factories stand apologetically in seas of waste which never turned to streets of gold.

For all that I tried to see the positive aspects of this gargantuan spoor of a long-dead industrial beast, for all that I could see that little by little it was being transformed, I couldn't escape the feeling that the chief problem is its sheer size. Urban renewal and administration has been left to individual councils and micro-urban projects, with the result that everyone has been beavering away on their own little patches but no one had liaised with anyone else. One council's development duplicates that of next-door's; one new by-pass fails to connect with the next. This is understandable because it has never been a real city, only a loose confederation of towns, many of which have a history far older than the megalopolis. Or worse, new facilities are provided only after they become necessary; regeneration is locked into a cycle of crisis and response, dictated not directly by the needs of people but by the demand of the market to create those needs.

The modern concept of a city is a series of interdependent but self-contained 'villages' (the idea behind Milton Keynes); this is provided with a focus, even if it is as artificial as that of the 'centre' of Milton Keynes. But here in the West Riding the supercity has not yet been given a centre. The old centres have been rubbed out as the constituent towns merged, but no central focus has arisen to replace them. In the meantime it is a mess. Sometimes appealing, often appalling, it seems unable to shake off the weight of its own history, its haphazard origin, even though the days of unfettered development are gone. This didn't seem to me to be purely because of a lack of funds. There was plenty of money around in bits of it. In the more successful areas it is quite easy to forget the rest. But a city should equal more than the sum of its constituent parts, should generate its own logic. Logic is in shorter supply than cash here.

There was a good example of this in Keighley. I stopped to look at the terminus of the Worth Valley Steam Preservation line; Keighley station is shared between BR in the guise of the South Yorks Metro and the enthusiasts. The side devoted to keeping the past at full steam is, as you would expect, spic and span; the BR side isn't bad. But attached to this major tourist attraction is a row of 14 lean-to shops, ten of which are derelict. No other western country, surely, would be so careless of what it is pleased to call its glorious past. But even in Keighley, which was having a noticeably tougher time of it than its neighbours, there were new factories and houses and clean air amongst the sooty remains of the railway age. At the end of one half-boarded-up terrace was a house with a satellite dish; it seemed a neat if glib summary of what I had seen so far.

Also of note in Keighley was the most obscene poster I have ever seen in a public place, flyposted on to a derelict shop window by a local band called Pregnant something, featuring a woman's face clenched in a hairy male hand and being forced to give fellatio to an oversized and lovingly-detailed phallus. Subtlety, I reflected, reverting to prejudice, is not generally reckoned a Yorkshire trait. Lest we dwell too long, however, on the morality of the present generation, a stone's throw up the hill was a piece of Victorian cynicism on a grand scale: row upon row of tiny terraced houses, unrelieved by shops or trees or variation, with each street named after a different tree – Myrtle Grove, Elm Grove, Sycamore Grove . . .

Next stop was Haworth. Now I am ashamed to admit that I have read very little by the Brontë sisters and that I disliked what I have read. I had therefore no vested interest in finding Haworth romantic, moving or pregnant with cultural resonance, and I didn't. It is a beastly little town, which seems unable to manage the easy task of fleecing a lot of unsuspecting Americans properly. It is full of junkshops which do not even pretend to be antique shops, and makes a few rather unsubtle gestures towards its literary heritage; the Branwell Gallery, The Brontë Barn (a woollens shop) . . . I expect that there is a Heathcliff Hotel somewhere. One gets the impression that the residents are heartily sick of the Three Weird Sisters and their rather pathetic brother and wish that the whole lot had lived in Ilkley instead. Derelict mills, factories and chapels clutter up half of what never was a pretty view up to the Parsonage, and inappropriate modern buildings and an army of coaches do the rest. No wonder they were such a miserable family.

In revenge against my philistinism, the shades of Charlotte, Emily, and Anne (not to mention Sharon, who never wrote anything) removed all the signposts so that I was drawn against my will on to a tiny and precipitous road across the moors, or perhaps I should say The Moors. They are indeed the be-all and end-all of moors; when the moguls of Hollywood decided to wreak their particular brand of carnage on the Brontës' novels they at least had the good taste to put a few blasted rocks and tortured trees on Wuthering Heights. Nature, like the good folk of Haworth, can't be bothered to do the thing properly, and the result is desperately unromantic, a sea of lead-coloured grass. Trawden, the first Lancashire town on the other side of the hill, was out of my way so I backtracked along another fun-packed superhighway marked 'UNSUITABLE FOR COACHES', in fact unsuitable for anything except suicides. I came to a long procession of keen types with back-packs crossing the road, following the Pennine Way. They all looked utterly miserable which at least showed they were still sane, I suppose.

All day I had been fighting a mood of depression. The weather was a suffocatingly close confection of pallid sunlight and steam bordering on drizzle. The miles were beginning to tell; I was tired and aching and increasingly uncertain of my motives. Something told me that a day which had mostly been tedious was about to turn nasty; it was my symbiotic relationship with the Austin-Morris A-series four-valve engine again. Pain stored up progressively in the back of the neck paralleled, I suspected, a similar concentration of trouble under Blodwen's bonnet. As I came down off the moors into the village of Slack (even the place-names were repulsive), I saw ahead of me the figure of a man. Just as with the daredevil lady motorist near Culloden, I knew instantly what this man looked like even though I could see only his back and he was still 200 yards away. I suppose the nearest popular comparison is the character of Foggy in *Last of the Summer Wine*. Tall, gangling, po-faced, bespectacled, with a repressed moustache, the man ahead of me topped off this generic persona with three masterstrokes: a long grey gaberdine coat belted too tightly, a tweed hat which was too large and pressed down the top of his ears, and an oversized pair of PVC gloves. As I came abreast of him he turned and regarded me lugubriously. He looked exactly as I had imagined he would; his entire visage, outfit and demeanour had been accurately deduced from his loping stride and the back of his coat. I howled with laughter and immediately the car broke down.

I pulled the bonnet release, got out and peered at the engine, hoping that I would see something obviously wrong, since its subtleties are beyond me. All appeared well, however, which usually means something awful has happened. There had been no histrionic bang, whimper or gush of steam, merely a sudden and total loss of power. I checked all the bits I knew about, which took me about three seconds and, since it had started to rain, got back into the driving seat to make a roll-up and ponder my predicament. I glanced back along the road, thinking to ask the strange man how far it was to the next garage or telephone box. Although there were no houses in sight, and no cover, he had vanished. He had been, it seemed, either the peeved and unflattered personification of the region I had been bad-mouthing all morning, or the Morris Minor's Angel of Death. As it turned out, he must have been the former; having uttered the same scatalogical four-letter word 20 times and finished my cigarette, I turned the ignition key, the engine came to life and I drove away, suitably chastened.

We plunged (that's the word) down the hill to Hebden Bridge, where I left Blodwen to recover herself while I went in search of provisions. The town surprised me; I had always presumed it represented the grittiest of gritty milltowns, but it has become positively bijou. One clue as to the reason for this is the extraordinary number of Volkswagen Beetles to be seen there. In the early 1970s, when Hebden Bridge was still a ghastly, godforsaken little eyesore, it had been invaded by hippies and other alternative people attracted by the cheap property. They had set up little businesses, wholesaling healthfoods, running bookshops and making furniture and pottery, and gradually, as they aged and the old industries closed, they came to dominate the town. Hebden Bridge became trendy, ceased to be cheap, and thus became desirable. Now it has shops selling hide sofas costing £3000, and designer muesli, but it is still full of wiry men with long hair, grey now, pottering around in purple Volkswagens. It has also become a place to retire to, since it is now clean and gentrified and gradely.

I said somewhere earlier that wherever I went people insisted on living up to their stereotypes; there were two Yorkshire stereotypes in Hebden Bridge. Both were in the supermarket. The first was a girl talking to a friend face to face as if she were a hundred yards away, with the Yorkshire way of projecting the voice from the very front of the mouth, the words forced out as if through a sausage machine, and the hard flat vowels compressed into a cutting edge. Legend has it that this mannerism developed in order to make speech audible over the racket of the looms.

In Lancashire they wisely learned to lip-read and gave up vocalisation altogether.

The second stereotype was a conversation between two ladies waiting in the queue for the checkout. They both looked as if they had been created by Alan Bennett, like most of the population. But I had no idea that Mr Bennett's dialogue reproduced the daily conversations of his subjects so closely: 'Well, of course,' said one powdered lady to the other. 'They asked Malcolm if *he* would do it. But he had to decline on account of his bunions.' Hebden Bridge deserves its success; it is a pleasant place, full of little Victorian architectural gems now cleaned and spruced after years under soot. Blodwen seemed to have regained her composure there; we continued down the narrow, increasingly black valley to Todmorden, which has not kept pace with its upwardly mobile neighbour but is a pleasant enough straggle of chimneys and terraces. What saves these towns is their extremely steep location; I don't suppose their buildings are in essence different to any other little mill town's but the way they are piled and staggered up the valley side gives them a romantic air.

Odds and sods of terracing, strange deserted little factories and tumble-down battery sheds loosely connect Todmorden to the Lancashire town of Bacup, which like Otley felt like a country market town which had become attached to the industrial development by accident. Otley is the outlier of the Leeds/Bradford chain, Bacup of the Lancashire/Cheshire equivalent which includes Bury, Bolton, Stockport and Manchester. Beyond Bacup were dozens of shoe factories along the road towards Bolton, interspersed for added interest with shoe wholesalers. I had been under the impression that the British shoe industry was a thing of the past, but here suburb after suburb seemed to depend on it; the factories looked prosperous enough, too. Maybe they were all owned by Spaniards or Cantonese. Rawtenstall is simply in-fill along the main road up to the Pennines, unplanned, unwarranted and unlovely, but not as unlovely as Ramsbottom, where the serious urban pressure begins, a chaotic mixture of old, crumbling factories, half-built or already abandoned developments, and vast tracts of rubble-strewn waste. In downtown Ramsbottom, a dingy street of small dowdy shops, I stopped to phone a friend and beg a bath and a bed. Then I took a look around, hoping as at Falkirk that I would find something to disprove my cynicism. There is another steam railway, but that was all. Neither wholly industrial nor wholly a suburb, formless and shoddy, it is worse than any innocent southerner has a right to expect. But such places, and there are still many in Britain, make up for what they lack in civic amenities by their warm-heartedness, character and deep-rooted sense of community. Or so they tell us.

My friend didn't get off work until nine that night, so although technically today was one of the one-in-four 'rest' days I allowed myself – days when I could afford not to reach my destination without upsetting my schedule

– I decided to kill time by going for a quick look around Kearsley. This was a mistake. It was getting on for five o'clock, and the traffic was building up rapidly. I got lost any number of times in the maze of suburbs around Bury and Bolton and spent more time stuck behind buses, sitting at roadworks, or parked at the kerbside studying the road atlas than actually on the move. It was after six when I got there, and it was a raw, dull evening. Although I was expecting Kearsley to be – well, not exactly Cannes – I had rather hoped that it would have some noticeable features, either good or bad. Sadly, Kearsley has no character at all. It is simply the name of a stretch of the main Bolton to Manchester road along which, in the last decade of the last century, a developer constructed a few lines of terraced housing, leaving sufficient space for the local council, 30 years later, to fill in the gaps with semis. To make matters worse Blodwen had been coughing and spluttering intemperately as we negotiated the charmless maze, and I had grown increasingly paranoid about becoming marooned in some famously unsafe area after dark. Having made Kearsley it seemed foolish to press on straight away, so once more I left Blodwen to recuperate and I set out with my head throbbing and my brain in neutral.

After a few minutes walking the deserted streets I had more or less decided to go on tomorrow to Knutsford or Kidsgrove or Kirkby, since there seemed to be even less to the place than met the eye. But I had made a vow never to renegue on a random choice of destination except *in extremis*, and there was certainly nothing extreme about Kearsley, so I took a deep breath and tried to convince myself that this had to be the place.

Some places are boring enough to be interesting: Falkirk, for example. Some are grotty enough to be photogenic or romantic; some sordid enough to be heroic. Kearsley is boring in an almost indescribable way. If I could put my finger on the essence of its banality I could describe it to you and then it would not be quite so boring, but there is nothing on to which the scaffolding of words could be attached. In fact, to bother to describe Kearsley would be to infer an interest which has no justification. The most interesting thing about it is that it is pronounced 'Kersley' rather than 'Keersley'.

Very well, I exaggerate; nevertheless that was the impression I got that first evening, and it took a lot of footslogging and an almost superhuman devotion to duty to bring Kearsley, as it were, out of the darkness of deserved obscurity and into the glaring light of the dissecting theatre which is the prose you see before you. But that was the next day. I stumbled back to the car, Blodwen swung out into the dense stream of traffic, drove a hundred yards up the road to where a major series of roadworks had necessitated a single lane controlled by temporary lights, chose the only position where traffic could be completely brought to a standstill, and went dead.

I would like to take this opportunity to thank the citizens of

Greater Manchester for they way in which, in their thousands, they responded as I attempted to push a ton of useless metal out of their way. Their offers of assistance, colourfully phrased in quaint northern dialect, were music to my ears, and I found, I must admit, that I could barely hold back a little tear of gratitude and humility that I, a helpless stranger in their midst, should be the subject of such warmth and generosity. Having managed to push the recalcitrant medieval relic out of their way at the cost of several pints of sweat and a few hundred kilocalories, I felt I ought to offer some token of my esteem to the assembled queue of selfless philanthropists, and I spent a happy moment or two telling them clearly and precisely the exact nature of the relationship their ancestors had had with a variety of diseased dumb beasts. Luckily they were all too intent on getting home to their suppers of microwaved Dralon steakettes to be bothered to get out and belt me one.

Blodwen was only trying to help; seeing the waste of space that is latter-day Kearsley she spotted the potential of 'kerbside' and 'konked out' at once. Once again, a much-needed cigarette later, I found that she started up with her usual alacrity, and off we went down the dual carriageway into Manchester, only occasionally doing the odd kangaroo hop. Nevertheless it was clear that something was badly wrong, and I devised a cunning plan to keep us moving on schedule through the wonders of the alphabet. The next time it happened I would play my ace; I'd call out the AA.

My friend was required at Waterstone's Manchester emporium that evening until nine in order to hand around bowls of peanuts and glasses of plonk to a throng of literati assembled to discuss the various ways humans do each other in; Crime Fiction is as big in Manchester as the real thing. I sat in the staff room while the ghouls debated the merits of the cheesewire noose, catching up on my protein and alcohol. We then repaired to a pizzeria, where the waitress caught sight of my jumbo box of kitchen matches, the camper's friend. 'Ooh, you're like me,' she gushed flirtatiously, 'a REALLY SERIOUS smoker!' When the pizza arrived I checked it for dog ends.

The finest bath and bed Stockport had to offer were mine as promised. Before either I did more talking than I had done for weeks; it was so long since I had had a sustained conversation that I gibbered like a drug-crazed Brazilian sports commentator. Luckily my audience, a dog called Foxy, didn't seem to mind; my friend had gone to bed.

Next morning, having returned to Kearsley in an apparently happier vehicle and a fresh pair of underpants, I set about the kind of detailed warts-and-all investigative journalism which has made the *Wisbech Bugle* what it is today. Kearsley may once have been a village but the only building which predates the terraces of red-brick houses along the Bolton road is the pub. The terraces themselves are of a very fine-grained hard brick which has barely weathered; the buildings are relatively free of encrustation so it would appear that the houses were built very late in the industrial period. It was never an industrial centre itself; the houses are not the smallest or most basic of their kind and it would appear that Kearsley was developed as an area for skilled artisans, clerks or white-collar workers whose wages enabled them to move out of the most oppressive areas of Salford or Bolton into what must at that time have been a semi-rural area, commuting to work by train (a disused line borders the suburb on the northern side) tram or bus. It was never intended to be anything but a dormitory area; no formal centre or focus was given to the ribbon development, and only basic corner shops opened, one of which survives along with a small garage and a hairdresser's. In the inter-war period the area to the west of the road was developed as an overspill estate, and the greatly increased population resulted in the incorporation of an Urban District Council with a small Town Hall. Schools and a recreation ground were also built. The ground to the east of the road falls away down to the floodplain of a small river, and was thus unsuitable for development until in-fill in the 1970s enabled a small industrial estate to be laid out near the surviving railway line. A larger factory located at the Salford end of the road provides some additional employment, but Kearsley today is still mostly occupied by commuters, and as always represents a relatively quiet, secure, predominantly white, white-collar and skilled working-class constituency. Latterly, due to public concern as to the lack of entertainment for the young and the rise in street crime, burglaries and car thefts (though these are still at a relatively minor level compared to neighbouring areas such as Farnworth and Salford), a Civic hall has been provided in the form of a temporary building bordering the recreation ground, where karate lessons were to be had until they were discontinued. The Civic Hall houses the day nursery. Kearsley is also the site of the council's Department of Works depot. A small new council estate, of noticeably poorer quality than its predecessor, was inserted into the last available space during the 1960s.

Well, I did warn you. On the recreation ground I met three boys playing truant from secondary school. They reckoned it was dead boring too. The only thing to do of an evening was go to the sports hall at the school or, if solvent, nightclubbing in Bolton. Otherwise it had nowt going for it. Since these were the only living persons in sight I set off around the estates and along the abandoned railway line in search of clues to Kearsley's hidden secrets. The council estate was well-built and very clean and tidy; neat, well-kept gardens were separated by immaculate fortifications of privet. There was no litter. Most of the garages and driveways were empty; employment was high. Although solid, the estate appeared at first completely unvaried architecturally or socially. However, more than half the houses bore testimony to their occupants' approval of Mrs Thatcher's 'Right to Buy'; the proud tenants-turned-owners had signified their entry into the property-owning democracy by installing double-glazing, mock-Georgian front doors, bottle-glass and front porches. Variations on these four basic improvements formed the only distinction from one house to another.

The reason for the estate's suspiciously spotless demeanour became obvious as I walked along the railway cutting behind Pilkington Road. Like most such places it had been used as a dumping-ground, not merely by those mysterious people who take infinite trouble to transport mattresses and lorry engines over considerable distances so as to foul up any green space as completely as possible, but also by the residents of prim Pilkington Road itself; a huge scree of household and garden waste descended from the back fence of each house. I poked desultorily at various of these glaciers of pollution, hoping to turn up something noteworthy such as a soggy cache of porn or a late fourteenth-century Flemish burgomaster's beechwood ossuary inlaid with plaques representing the Stations of the Cross carved in walrus ivory, but found only bits of polystyrene, the remains of Chinese takeaways, and indecipherable electronic components.

So I went to the shop to buy a Snickers bar and quiz Pat, the proprietoress, on the seething mass of repressed desire which I felt must lie barely contained behind the ruched blinds of Pilkington Road. Pat gave me to believe that the place was changed beyond recognition in the five years since she had moved there; it had been 'like a village' then. Now car-thefts were getting ridiculous, it were the kids, there was nowt for them to do of an evening. So those boys had been telling the truth, I realised; I had the case figured all wrong. Pat vouchsafed that Kearsley gravitated towards Bolton rather than Manchester; Farnworth, the next bit of Bolton up the road, was where you went for a good pub crawl. But the pubs in Farnworth were getting dead rough. It were dead quiet, Kearsley.

'Like a village' – she meant in terms of community, not design. The bland and straitlaced order of the estate evidently masked a changing population, increasingly transient. You felt you no longer knew your neighbours. There were worrying signs that something interesting might be going to happen one day soon. Kearsley is a Frankenstein's monster of a place, cobbled-together bits which do not add up to an organism. But these are freakish days, charged with the social electricity of sex, drugs and rock 'n' roll, immigration, religious bigotry, political radicalism . . . one day someone will pull the switch, and Kearsley will rise from the dead.

OK, perhaps not.

LLANDUDNO

Leisure and Liverpudlians

Kearsley was not easy to escape. I missed a motorway junction and plodded around for hours in the suburbs; then Blodwen threw a tantrum again. I thought it best after that to keep off the motorway, and more or less deliberately found myself traversing Chat Moss on the dual carriageway towards Warrington. After a while I took a small country road, bored of the noise and tension of the main road – nearly all the traffic had been lorries. Open countryside, although flat and dull, and the first of the black and white half-timbered houses which typify Cheshire farmland cheered me slightly; I felt as if I had emerged from the morass of Manchester reasonably unscathed and was entering new territory. On the little road I was driving behind a bus which stopped every 200 yards or so. Blodwen grew hot and at the entrance of an industrial estate in the middle of a flat sea of beet fields she broke down once again. I walked into the estate and knocked on the door of the first unit; a kind employee of Heroncraft Ltd allowed me to use his phone to call the AA.

It is often said that the most stressful thing that can happen to you is the death of a loved one, and that this pressure-raising disaster is closely followed by being divorced, burgled, married or a fan of Crewe Alexandra. Moving house is another oft-cited heartstopper; this is called 'flitting' in Scotland, although the sight of four burly men wrestling with a piano seems at odds with this delicate word. To this invidious list I would add two others: buying a car and breaking down (the car, that is, though spending three weeks in a National Health mental institution is probably about as debilitating).

I decided that the time had come to buy a car when I learned that I would be moving to Scotland. For some reason I had never felt that I needed one while living in Norfolk, despite that county's rarefied public transport system. But there was no way I was going to miss out on the banks and braes, so I scrounged £500 from my long-suffering father ('Just remember this when *your* kids come whining to *you*') and began to scour the second-hand car lots of Norwich to little avail. There seemed to be depressingly few Bentleys on the market for my kind of money, but a colleague told me of a couple of brothers who restored Morris Minors for a living; since he was the proud owner of a faithful Traveller and a Scot to boot I sensed a bargain. I found the brothers Smith in a wilderness of sheds somewhere off the Drayton Road. They were pleasant, but apologetic . . . the only thing available was that thing there. I looked. A multicoloured assemblage of pirated body-parts, four flat tyres and a profile like a pregnant wombat. I thanked them but thought, on the whole, not. Later that day I investigated a Renault Five. It looked, and drove, all right . . . but under the wheel-arches I found enormous scabs of rust which could be twanged like Jew's harps. I walked home. Time was short; we were moving in two days and I wanted if possible to get the whole thing done with before I had the additional worries of a new home and a new job. I went back to see the Smith brothers, and gradually saw the machine in a different light. Solidly built; restored by enthusiasts. Street-credible. Breaks the ice at parties. Faster than a Reliant Robin . . . almost as fast as a Churchill tank, and about as heavy. Could I test-drive it? Sure, they said, come back in the morning.

So I test-drove and fell in love. One of the Smiths came along to make sure I remembered to turn off the indicators. As I pottered around the ring-road I remembered that the only time I had ever been car-sick was in a Morris Minor. Still, everyone said they went forever. Rugged, practical, cheap . . . how cheap? Five hundred and no haggling. I heard myself say 'yes' as we swung back into the yard. The steering was superb, like a very, very slow Lotus Elan. Any particular colour?, they asked. How about white? They had lots of white paint.

The next day was hot and sunny. As I entered the yard something flashed in the distance. As I got nearer it began to hurt my eyes as if I were approaching a supernova without the benefit of Ray-Bans. I realised that it was my car-to-be, resplendent in bridal white. The Smiths emerged from their shed.

'For Christ's sake,' said one of them, 'get some dirt on it quick.' I got in and pulled the door closed; the handle came off in my hand.

'Minor problem,' they quipped. The interior smelled like Sullom Voe oil terminal. My eyes watering, I wrote out a cheque.

I parked outside our flat and ran inside. 'Look out of the window, then,' I said to Kate, '. . . but put the baby down first.'

She went over to the window. There was a long silence before she very quietly said 'Oh my God.' Gaining control she added, 'It's very nice, darling.'

Thus Blodwen (which means 'white flower', although at the time I was under the impression that it meant 'white pig') came into our lives. And I can honestly say, my hand firmly on my heart and the other just as firmly touching the wooden top of this desk, that she had never let us down. Except at the top of the Schiehallion road about 2,000 feet up, and then on the M90 on a couple of occasions. And in Kearsley, and in Cheshire. Well, what do you expect? She's older than most of you. Have some respect.

The AA man identified the trouble immediately: it was the fuel pump. He showed me how to dismantle it and clean the electrical contacts, and advised me if all else failed to hit it with a spanner. While Blodwen's engine was idling sweetly we sat in his van discussing the merits of Morris Minor vans, which were once standard AA issue. His considered opinion was that their greatest drawback was that the heater 'fried yer plums' – he indicated a podgy groin encased in brown terylene. I personally only wish Blodwen's heater would get hot enough to slightly defrost mine. He then tried in vain, via his radio, to get my details from the computer; I had lost my membership card although my subscription is paid by standing order. I gave my address, the address before that, and so on, back until my original joining date in 1975 but according to the operator I had never been enrolled. Now one of the famous side-effects of AA membership is the incredible volume of junk mail you receive. One of the things which annoyed me most about this was that the letters I received in envelopes which screamed 'OPEN NOW! YOU MAY HAVE ALREADY WON A VALUABLE MYSTERY PRIZE!!!' were 'signed' by a computer called Stephen Butler. I suspect that they had taken the name of one of their members whose address they had lost (me) and put it to good use. So when, in darkest Cheshire, I required for the first time in five years their excellent rescue service, I was miffed to say the least to find that I had vanished off the face of the earth. However, if there is one organisation more administratively mysterious than the AA it is my bank, so I couldn't be sure who was to blame. I had no choice but to rejoin on the spot, and sign umpteen forms directed at my bank, their bank, a person such as a JP or Doctor who had known me for at least 20 years, and so on.

I bade farewell to the man with the sweltering testicles and continued as far as Warrington. To my surprise what little I saw of the town was gleamingly modern and consisted almost entirely of spanking-new factories and roundabouts, of which there were so many that by the time I got out I felt as if I had been spin-dried. It was a warm day and Blodwen soon began to splutter again, although Mr Friedplums had assured me that heat was nothing to do with it. With my new-found technical mastery I pulled over and whacked the fuel-pump with a socket wrench. This had no discernible effect, so I decided to go hell-for-leather down the motorway to Chester, where I intended to take the rest-day I had denied myself in Kearsley.

I remember the first time I saw the stretch of land along the south end of the Mersey estuary. I was a callow youth starving to death in a rock 'n' roll band, driving a van loaded with dodgy amplifiers to a gig in North Wales. I had never seen anything like it: a desolate, hellish waste dotted with gargantuan, weirdly-shaped structures belching orange flame and black smoke. The intervening 14 years haven't changed it much, but whereas then I had difficulty believing that any part of Britain could have been allowed to degenerate into such a state, now I found myself actually admiring the sheer majestic brutality of the place. With dark, beetling cliffs on the left hand side topped with snaggled trees and crumbling ruins, flinching little villages beneath, and a vast flat plain to the right looking like a scene from Jonathan Porritt's worst nightmare, I felt a strong desire to be hurtling down the motorway in something like a Mack truck, the exhaust farting plenty of lead, with the *Ride of the Valkyrie* playing at full volume; fear and loathing in Runcorn, crushing a Maestro here and a Lada there, carrying bulk nitro-glycerine and swigging Jack Daniels . . . Driving a Morris does give you a thirst for revenge.

By Chester I had calmed down enough to notice that far from looking like a venerable Roman city, it is very largely modern, looking more like Slough than anywhere historic has a right to. But I was too far gone to care much. I spent a day talking nineteen-to-the-dozen with my godmother, a woman of wisdom and perspicacity who loves to talk as much as I do, and who had thought through most of the ideas that the trip had set buzzing around my head far more deeply than I over a much longer period and in considerably more trying circumstances. There is nothing like intelligent conversation to gee you up, especially if you have been trapped in a mobile biscuit-tin for two weeks. I set off into Clwyd feeling a good deal more optimistic about the validity of the exercise. As I wound down the window I noticed a curious smell. For a moment I couldn't place it, and then I realised that it was the smell of warm earth, growing grass and spring flowers. I was in the South.

The most curious thing about going into Wales is the very sudden transition from English to Welsh place-names; it implies a cultural separateness which has surely not been so severe for hundreds of years. The English-Scottish border is not nearly so linguistically distinct, and Scotland has many more English place-names than Wales. Most odd of all, I suppose, is the scarcity of pre-Anglo-Saxon placenames in England in anything like their Celtic form. Wendover (Gwyndowr), Helvellyn, and Pen-y-Ghent notwithstanding, even where it is evident that British and Anglo-Saxon tribes lived side-by-side it seems to be the 'invader's' place-name for the British village which has survived: Walton, for instance, the 'town of the *Weala*' (Welsh). I suppose the Welsh thought that if these German yobs were going to remove all traces of their language from the map they would bloody well make sure that Wales got Welsh names. They always have had a bigger chip on their shoulder than the Scots, and with some reason.

The Clwydian Range, a line of steep little hills cutting off North Wales from Cheshire, is a delightful area, but something about it bugged me as I laboured up it. It was noticeable that as the border is crossed the ornate, opulent-looking Cheshire farmhouses patterned with timber and fancy brickwork gave way immediately to the rather drab vernacular stone cottages which one sees throughout Wales, but that wasn't entirely it. It took me a good many miles of pleasant rolling countryside to put my finger on it . . . *there's nothing there.*

Driving through Scotland and England there is always, over and above the countryside itself, something to see: a big house, a ruin, a medieval barn, a church, a standing stone. Wales must have these things, but where are they? Why are they so much fewer and further between? The countryside of Clwyd on that sunny afternoon was undeniably pleasant, but it was a kind of basic, no-frills countryside, the visual equivalent of muzak. Still, I did find something which made me turn back for a closer look – a small factory in the middle of open farmland outside which was a line of rusting anti-aircraft cannon. I can't imagine what they do with them – maybe give them a lick of paint and flog them to the Papua New Guinea Army. While I was taking a photograph of them I was stung by a nettle, so Spring was definitely here. Indeed in the green, still valleys I was too hot for the first time in the entire journey.

The towns were mostly dull. Buckley, Mynydd Isa, Ruthin, Mold and Denbigh were all very full of both people and traffic. Whenever I got out and strolled around I was struck by two things; firstly the ordinariness of the architecture (it isn't ugly, just mediocre) and secondly by the almost complete absence of Welsh voices. Only in Denbigh did I hear both Welsh accents and the Welsh language being spoken. Everyone else seemed to be from Liverpool. Also in Denbigh a farmer wearing patched green corduroy trousers held up with string, a cowboy shirt straining under the weight of his enormous beer-belly which flopped over said trousers, a waistcoat smeared with greenish stuff of uncertain origin, and a shapeless tweed hat squashed down over a face like the setting sun with muttonchop whiskers. The stereotype strikes again; the only improvement might have been to replace the cigarette dangling from his mouth with a stem of grass. Maybe he was a stockbroker.

I suppose as an Englishman it's none of my business, but why is it that the Welsh insist on having all their public signs in two languages even where the Welsh word is the same as the English? (Or vice versa, if you see what I mean. The English words are almost always put first.) TOILETS/ TOILEDAU seems a bit unnecessary. A very helpful sign at Llanferres tells you that the *toiledau* are seven miles away, surely news to weaken the strongest resolve.

I pottered along at 40 mph through the undulating, sleepy countryside until I emerged on the North Welsh Coast at Abergele. I must admit to some trepidation about this part of the trip. I expected the resorts of North Wales – Rhyl, Colwyn Bay, Abergele, Llandudno – to be rather too similar to the town where I grew up, Clacton, for me to be very dispassionate about them. I have a sort of love-hate relationship with British seaside towns. On the one hand I find their cheerful egalitarianism encouraging; it seems that the British, after all, can let their hair down when they want, and don't particularly mind who's looking. I suppose that the Seaside Holiday has taken the place in British culture which Carnival has elsewhere; it has the same tinselly, slightly fake jollity, the same rather forced atmosphere of over-excitement. On the other hand, I dislike the very striking similarity of most British resorts, although they can be loosely divided into two sorts: those which are 'posh', which means that they are full of geriatrics and there is nothing to do except Old-Tyme Dancing – Frinton is almost in a class of its own in this camp – and those which are not, which means that they ape Blackpool, but have never spent the kind of money which Blackpool has lavished on its attractions. Only places which originally had another function, usually as a fishing port, tend to add any variety to these tendencies; purpose-built resorts are nearly always one or the other.

The British Resort is not what it was; it has had, and is having again, some lean years. The scare-stories of the Costa del Crime were not enough to revive it; the Conservatives' taxes have dealt its hoteliers a near-mortal blow. I can remember as a ten-year-old standing on the esplanade next to Clacton Pier and being unable to see any beach under a sea of white, pink and tan flesh. On Bank Holidays the entire population of the East End seemed to converge on a couple of miles of litter-strewn, wasp-plagued, dog-turded sand in their hundreds of thousands. It was as if a Cup Final crowd had mysteriously disrobed. Nowadays what gives our resorts their charm is their faded, slightly desperate gaiety, like old music-hall comedians playing to three pensioners on the end of the pier because they don't know what else to do. They have a dingy, peeling tawdriness which is almost poetic; they have become more and more desultory in the provision of entertainment; they are places to use for a weekend of slot-machines, take-aways and sex if you are young; for the old they provide a slow euthanasia of bingo and whist.

They will never recover. Some have managed a second career built around huge conference centres and new luxury hotels, but not many. Most couldn't afford or attract the investment. They do what they have always done, providing cheap, uncomplicated fun and accommodation, unreliable weather, cold, dirty water for bathing and greasy, sticky food for people who cannot afford but would doubtless like something better and are determined to have a good time if it kills them.

Colwyn Bay is a classic good-time resort. It makes no bones about its purpose, which is to give as many people as much of a good time as possible, and it has done it with enough success to be able to spend money on fairly grand bits and pieces of Public Works. The esplanade is as pink as the Mall but three times as wide and forty times as long; behind it the town seems a bit lost, like a very small man with a vast handlebar moustache. I parked by the beach. There were quite a few people around, but the scale of the seafront made them seem insignificant. I watched two nuns struggling arm in arm towards me out of the far distance, against the wind. Their feet moved in perfect unison and seemed to slightly cross over each other, as if they were practising a silly walk for the convent's annual talent competition. They passed, silent, watching their feet, and slowly, slowly made their way to the horizon, as though they were doing some kind of penitential pilgrimage through the latter-day Sodom and Gomorrah that is Colwyn Bay in April.

I went to find some cigarettes, and discovered that Sodom and Gomorrah is about right. I had to go into five or six shops to find the brand I smoke, and I have never seen so much pornography as was on the magazine racks of that chilly, antitumescent resort. Most British newsagents have, I suppose, ten or a dozen different 'girlie mags' – how should I know? – but the first shop I entered had twenty feet of shelving groaning under a library of bulges, wobbly bits, leather thingies, pink crevices and pouts. Since they didn't have Marlboro Lights, I had the opportunity to investigate whether this was the one-off lifetime's research of a connoisseur or a hitherto unsuspected side to the famously puritan Welsh. It turned out to be the rule, rather than the exception, but I don't think the Welsh have anything to do with it. All the shopkeepers were either Lancastrians or Liverpudlians of Asian or Anglo-Saxon descent. This implies that visitors to the resort, mostly working-class Northerners I suppose, demand prurient reading material in vast quantities, although back in Lancashire and Yorkshire I had noticed no such fascination with the hurly-burly of the chaise-longue. The one shop run by a Welsh couple had no porn at all.

The wind dropped and the dead calm of the evening added to the air of anticipation in Colwyn Bay; it was spruced up and ready for the season. I drove along the gigantic dual carriageway to Llandudno to find that here business had already started. The strange thing was that the gaggles of people on the seafront were all young men and women in smart business clothes. They roamed the amusement arcades and burger joints, pubs and hotel bars like Hell's Stockbrokers. For a time I thought I had stumbled upon a hitherto unrecorded youth subculture; none of them appeared any older than 20. But closer inspection of the plastic lapel badges they all wore proved that they were in town for the annual conference of the Association of British Travel Agents. This surprised me; if ABTA can't get a good deal on a group-booking in Antigua, rather than North Wales, who can?

Enquiries at three or four guesthouses led to a single room at the back of a creaking terrace for £8.50 – the cheapest of the whole trip. Mind you the hall smelt strongly of urine, but I was too tired to care. The bedroom was clean, if shoddy; there was satellite TV for those armed with 50 pence pieces for the slot. But freedom from the clutches of the Box was one of the great delights of the journey. I went out instead in search of the Real Llandudno and food.

Seen from a distance Llandudno is pretty; from within it is grand. Not posh but solid and attractive. The gigantic hotels, spread in a long white crescent along the eastern esplanade, reminded me of Brighton without the tat; Llandudno is easily the most attractive large seaside resort I've seen, a feast of late Victorian and Edwardian opulence which manages to be impressive without being exclusive. The setting on the perfect crescent of Llandudno Bay helps, and the rocky limestone headlands which frame it. The town occupies the neck of a promontory which runs northwards into the sea, so that it has a second, less grand but very pleasant western promenade 'at the back'. This traditional prosperity seems to be continuing; the town has plenty of new developments, including the ubiquitous super-stores. But the accent is on providing the Traditional Family Holiday, squeaky-clean and fun for all ages. I suppose the conference trade has helped a great deal; indeed Llandudno seems the ideal Labour Party Conference town, a grand expression of the spending-power of the workers. It easily outclasses the tawdry sprawl of Brighton, the geriatric monotony of Bournemouth and the unabashed vulgarity of Blackpool.

I spent an unpleasant night, kept awake by howls of laughter emanating from the lounge downstairs until three in the morning. All the other rooms in the place were taken, and in the best British tradition their various occupants were having a good old get-together. There is nothing more miserable than trying to get to sleep in a hotel while listening to people having a good time. Unless, of course, you are listening to people fighting in the next room, or the rhythmic creaking of bedsprings and the sound of a Dralon-padded headboard pounding the wall, both of which followed the merriment. Breakfast next morning, at 'eight sharp', was a quiet affair although the room was full. Most of the guests were middle-aged couples, though there were two couples in their 20s, and one family with two toddlers. Nobody looked as though they'd had a decent night's sleep, and the grease-soaked 'traditional breakfast' was eaten with some care. A half-hearted conversation was going on about the town's various enticements: the Miniature Golf Course, the Dry Ski Slope, the 'Happy Valley' gardens; it was as if they had never met before, let alone spent several hours telling filthy jokes. Most were on first-name terms with the landlady; they had been coming here for years. I couldn't face the inquisition which would be the unavoidable preliminary to my asking questions; I was in a zombie-like state due to sleep deprivation and a cholesterol overdose. I ate up and got out.

138

The presence of the spotty overgroomed travel agents almost persuaded me that my 'something beginning with L' should be 'Lost Luggage', but in order to avoid legal proceedings for libel I abandoned this. I spent three hours wandering from one end of the town to the other and back again in the chilly sunshine without finding anything very noteworthy beginning with L. The preponderance of Scouse was the best I could do. So I repaired to the Tourist Information Centre; Llandudno was built for Leisure and as we are entering a new Age of Leisure (or so they keep telling us) it seemed a fair subject to tackle, especially since my brain resolutely refused to come out of neutral. The Centre provided me with vast quantities of Leaflets. It was staffed by Lovely Ladies who Live to Lighten your Life with Lots of Literature to Lead you to Local Landmarks and Lists of Low-Cost Laughs. Whaddaya want, poetry? It was tough out there.

MONTGOMERY

Murder, morris dancers and a meritorious mobile motor mechanic

I chugged sleepily up the valley of the Conwy into thick and chilly mist, too tired to notice anything but the thankfully sparse traffic. Oddly, of the dozen or so vehicles I passed in the first half-hour, four were Rolls-Royces and four were police cars. The Rollers were at home here, amongst the big luxury bungalows and manicured gardens of the Conwy estuary, where everyone seems to have a three-car garage and a boat. The boys in blue tore around apparently without purpose, squealing their tyres. Gwynnedd looked an unlikely place for a major drug-bust or a nest of forgers. Perhaps they were the Rolls Theft Squad.

The Conwy has the lush gigantism of the West of Scotland, nourished by the Atlantic rains but protected from the westerly gales. Holly grows to 50 to 60 feet; pines look like giant redwoods. It's all rather unreally perfect. As the road climbs over the rim of the Snowdon massif the vegetation thins out and the walls and cottages are built of frangible slaty rock. The Fairy Glen is a twisted gorge choked with vegetation, very unelfin these days due to the big crash-barriered road which scythes through it; beyond is a broad upland valley where the rock has degenerated to the extent that the field walls look like they are constructed from millions of tiny biscuit-sized flakes. The villages have no pattern or building-line, and there are none of the roadside temptations which would be noticeable in Scotland or Yorkshire; I saw only one craft shop. Suddenly the slate gives way to huge boulders and chunky walls. The road still climbs but so gradually that the dwindling vegetation is the only clue. Again, there is a curious absence of visible history. The Welsh have as long and as bloody a story as the Scots; why

140

isn't it writ as large on the land? I've never seen countryside as empty as this.

By the time the long hump of Berwyn mountain loomed through the haze I was exhausted. I pulled into a lay-by and slept for a couple of hours, leaning on the steering wheel with my head on my arms. I dreamed that the van had broken down. When I woke, unrefreshed, the sun was shining feebly. Two buzzards were hunting over the field to my left. A raven flapped past and took a playful swipe at one of them, getting chased down the valley for its cheek by both.

Bala was a dingy collection of council houses and bungalows with a Victorian church which looked very aptly like a waterworks. The lake glimmered; sailboards appeared and vanished in the mist. I thought of the graffiti which made the place famous: 'Please Piss In This – The English Drink It'. The carpark was full of coaches; blue-rinsed matrons come here from all over the country. Why?

As the road wound up Berwyn I caught sight of a small metal plaque attached to a massive boulder some 50 yards from the road. At last, I thought, a Site of Historic Interest. I laboured over the slippery grass imagining a legendary battle between dark princes, a Druidic sacrifice; it turned out to be the site of the first recorded Sheepdog Trials, in 1873. There's interesting. On Berwyn the farms are ramshackle affairs, the local stone too poor for building. Barns are rusted corrugated iron wrecks, field walls mere heaps of stone across which sheep wander at will. Having criss-crossed the Gwynnedd/Clwyd border all afternoon, the Powys boundary ushered in the first really spectacular landscape, as if that county has a monopoly. A long and steep descent begins on the upper lip of a huge valley between great cliffs. A tall slender waterfall feeds the river far below; no barriers protect you from a drop of several hundred feet and the road is littered with fallen rocks and stones. Gradually moorland gives way to fields. The daffodils were out but it still looked and felt more like November than April.

At the bottom of the valley, completely surrounded by steep hills as if in a bowl, the village of Llangynog was the first attractively arranged place I had seen all day, despite being host to a caravan park and a cluster of chalets and having a big quarry as a backdrop. The traditional stone or whitewashed cottages, their windowsills painted black, all looked for once as if some care had been taken in their construction and placement. By contrast, the metal barns and sheds were still common, weathered into more shades of rust-red than I would have believed possible. One of the cottages nearby was painted blue and cream, and I realised that this was another clue to the odd lack of focus I had found in Wales; in any English village there is always some wacko who has painted his house purple or green. The Welsh only seem to paint their houses by the seaside, and then go for tasteful pastels or white and cream.

At Penygarnedd many of the houses appeared to be caving in; the roofs bowed and sagged. A lot of the houses, including the farms, were for sale, and what new buildings there were had been made of alien brick. Most of the farms eked out their existence with a tent-pitch and a couple of caravans. The air of impoverishment accentuated the impression of having missed out on summer – the trees were still bare and thick with grey lichen and the mist gave everything a pallid, frosty look. But a mile or two further down the horse-chestnuts were in full leaf, and the next village, Llanfyllin, is a surprise, for here there are no Welsh cottages at all, but a street of three- and four-storey brick early Georgian terracing and a brick church. We had come to the Marches.

There were immediate signs of prosperity; a new Youth Centre, a butterfly farm. The air of quiet provincial civilisation, the soft red of the brick and the sudden switch from walls in the fields to neatly-clipped hedges made me feel as though I had suddenly entered an eighteenth-century landscape painting. I wouldn't have been surprised to have seen gentlemen in white knickerbockers and knee-boots carrying muskets or posing graciously by their prize steeplechasers. Wooden clapboard barns replaced the tin ones, and farmhouses had classical or Gothic features crudely carved from brown sugary sandstone. Then a wonderful ancient brick barn, immensely long and patterned with diamond-shaped groups of holes between the bricks under the eaves. A little further along the road was a modern barn built in exactly the same style; not simply trying to *look* like a traditional building, like a Tesco superstore with a Georgian façade and a silly little clock-tower; it *was* traditional.

In my entire journey this was the only new building in a traditional style that I saw. There were hundreds of new blocks of flats which aped the past, with local stylistic tics stuck onto an ersatz Georgian (why always Georgian?) shell. There were superstores aplenty, all in the same orange brick, with the same little clock and the same arched walkway to the carpark and the same trolley-park disguised as a Disneyland market cross. There were thousands upon thousands of mock-Georgian, and even a few mock-Jacobean houses complete with UPVC leaded-light double-glazing and bottle-glass and fanlights. These aren't objectionable in themselves; they are a great deal more pleasant than most mass housing, flats and shops erected in the first 60 years of this century. What irks me is that they are taken to be in a 'traditional' style, that they somehow show that we have become sensitive to our 'cultural heritage' (whose?), despite the fact that millions are built in areas where no buildings remotely similar ever existed. We are creating a blanket of sort-of-neo-Georgian because we are ignorant or uncaring of the past and terrified of the modern. Those new buildings which aren't neo-anything are either the casually unstylish boxes which small builders put up speculatively or attempts at 'post-modernism' which could consist of anything as long as an atrium is involved somewhere. It

142

seemed to me that as 'unspoiled' villages are prettified and over-restored and as new development is limited to a casual rehashing of incoherent bits of the past, we are heading for a situation where the distinction between old and new will blur in a welter of sham historicism. This would be a disaster, not aesthetically, but because we would be burying any chance of understanding the past. It is often said that the public have rejected modernism as impractical and ugly, but you can count on the fingers of both hands the number of truly modernist buildings constructed in Britain this century. The British have been subjected to a gigantic con, in which the ill-digested lessons of modernism were applied inappropriately and usually on the cheap to schemes which ignored the basic premise that buildings are to be lived in. This is why planning in this country has acquired such a bad name, because our architects are not trained to produce functional buildings and because our planners are not trained in aesthetics. As a result, when at last we have the chance to build a real modernist building such as Mies van der Rohe's glass tower, it is attacked as hideous and alien. We are making the same mistakes again with the new domestic 'style', ransacking details and ignoring function, placement and context. And in the commercial field we have the ghastly shitheap of the Docklands development, a lame-brained, asinine series of meaningless doodles about as useful and attractive as sandcastles on a beach. If modernist architecture was such a failure, you had better go and demolish New York.

I arrived in Montgomery in the early evening and fell in love. I had been all over Shropshire and Herefordshire and parts of the Welsh side of the Marches before, but had somehow missed it; it is my ideal town, set in my favourite countryside. Small, compact, on a steep hill with a ruined castle on a rocky summit above, built in the mellowest of mellow red bricks, architecturally stylish without the least bit of pretentiousness; not spoiled by inappropriate new buildings (though admittedly not graced by any appropriate new buildings); with a chip-shop and a number of delightful pubs; a fine early eighteenth-century Town Hall and a good big church with a tower, streets quiet as the grave, overshadowed by enormous old trees.

I went into the chip-shop and talked to the woman who ran it. She was from Yorkshire but never wanted to leave Montgomery. I explained my journey and she immediately gave me a pound from the till for the Dyslexia Association, the first person to make an unsolicited donation on my trip, and the last. I asked her what she would suggest for my M in Montgomery; any good murders, perhaps?

'Well, not quite, but they did hang a man here for robbery and he swore that he was innocent, and no grass ever grew on his grave. So that was sort of a murder, wasn't it?'

Indeed. Delighted to have found such a place and to have nailed the M-problem so quickly, I ate fish-and-chips in the van – they were superb – listening to the collared doves, the distant bleats of sheep and the rumble of conversation from the open door of the pub. Then, having phoned Kate with a much more enthusiastic report than of late, I set out to find my dormitory, which turned out to be a grassy verge beneath an oak, with the Long Mynd on the eastern horizon, a hill which belongs to the National Trust, largely because of the efforts of my grandfather to save it for posterity. There is a memorial to him there in the form of a stand of trees. The Marches have a quality which is best expressed by the French term '*domaine*', in the sense that that word is used by Alain-Fournier in *Le Grand Meaulnes*. It means a secret country, self-contained, mysterious, pregnant with meanings both evident and subliminal. In Shropshire, Powys and Herefordshire this takes the form of an exact balance between two fundamental but antipathetic tendencies in British culture: the Western, wild, romantic, Celtic, feminine, arcane tradition and the Eastern, ordered, civilised, urbane, Anglo-Saxon, masculine, logical one. In the Marches these poles are in balance, miraculously combining to produce a landscape on to which we can project very powerful cultural inheritances, and 'read them back' like a Tarot spread. Other places in Britain still have it, but the Marches is the most extensive of these domains, from Shrewsbury to the Severn estuary. Its landscape has been enhanced rather than desecrated by human activity, in the way that the Chinese traditionally ensured that what they did to a landscape amplified rather than interrupted its natural beauty.

There was a frost that night, and it was still bitter, though promisingly bright, when I awoke ten or eleven hours later. I changed my clothes in the lane; only one car had passed all night. Some sheep wandered over and jeered accusingly as I removed my underpants, 'Bare! Bare!'

I sat shivering in the front seat writing and munching semi-frozen muesli for as long as I could, then turned the key in the ignition. The engine turned over but wouldn't fire. I tried a few more times, then resignedly set to work dismantling the fuel pump. My fingers were already fairly numb; after five minutes they were about as useful as pieces of asparagus. The sheep watched me with smug expressions. 'Bare?' 'Yeah.' 'Where?' 'There.' 'Bare?'

'SHUT UP, MUTTON!'

After half an hour I had put it back together. This time she started immediately and we set off down the lane, managing 300 yards before conking out again. I pushed Blodwen 30 feet into the drive of an isolated cottage and knocked on the door. No reply. I peered in at the windows; there was another car in the drive. 'Hello? Anyone in?' Nothing. A few empty paintpots and a Black-and-Decker lay on the floor of the living-room: weekenders. But this was a weekend; where were they? I scribbled a note, 'Broken Down; Gone for Help', and stuck it under a wiper, then set off down a track towards another cottage half-a-mile away. A dog barked as I knocked, but nobody came. I knocked again. The dog barked again.

Then silence. Knock; bark. Knock; bark. Was it a recording triggered by sound? I never found out. Back up to the lane, and along past my overnight parking-place; there was a farmhouse a mile or so beyond.

'Bare!'

'Woof!' I responded.

'Moo!' Great. A smart-alec sheep.

The farmer let me use his phone; 40 minutes later the AA van came down the lane, by which time the occupants of both cottages had turned up. The AA man couldn't find anything wrong. Blodwen started first time when he tried the ignition. 'She always does that,' I protested.

'Try hitting it with a spanner,' he suggested.

'Yes, I know . . . trouble is, I've got about a thousand miles to go.'

'Ah, well, she may not give you any more trouble. Funny things, Morrises.'

'Hilarious. Oh, well. Here's hoping. Thanks.'

'Where are you headed just now?'

'Montgomery first, then down to the Valleys later today.'

'You'll maybe find a spare down that way. I'll follow you along the lane, make sure everything's okay.'

Everything seemed to be all right. At the turning for Montgomery he pulled alongside and said, 'Don't make the same mistake as one bloke; I told him to hit it with a spanner and a couple of hours later I got another call because it hadn't worked. Said he'd given it a fair old whack. I took a look, found he'd smashed the distributor to bits. Cheerio.'

It was by now 11.30 on a cloudless, hot Sunday. I left Blodwen in a carpark by the playing-fields where a scrummage of small boys meandered around – now and then a body or a soccer ball would fly out of the mêlée, to be almost instantly reabsorbed by the pipe-cleaner-like tentacles of the beast. I wandered up to the castle; from the narrow path above the roofs the insignificant sounds of people clinking coffee-cups and mowing lawns drifted up; otherwise only birdsong and the occasional church bell could be heard. The castle ruins are substantial enough to give you some impression of its famous impregnability; the massive walls are cleverly placed above a rock-cut trench, so that the keep, despite its narrow perch, had a deep, sheer moat on the only approachable side. But the most impressive thing is the view, which is breathtaking, across the wide plain of the Severn east and north to Stiperstones, the Long Mynd, Corndon Hill and Long Mountain. The blue, remembered hills.

I spent a long time taking in the view, the complex roofscape of the town with its fine big Georgian houses, a somewhat decrepit-looking neoclassical mansion hidden away off the main road, the outlying Victorian and '30s housing and the small factories and garages. Beyond was the road down which I had come the previous day. It speared straight as a ley-line across the floodplain and on the horizon the hills each seemed to have a significance, as if they might be read like a sonnet if only one knew how the cypher worked. I found to my annoyance that I only had two frames left in my camera and that I had left the spare films in the car. I tore myself away and descended to the market square, hearing as I came down the path a curious jingling sound from below. When I emerged by the Town Hall I found in the middle of the street a number of men in black stovepipe hats, coats made of pieces of multicoloured rag, carrying hefty rough-hewn sticks and with their faces blacked up. Oddly, below the waist they all wore Levi's, albeit with bells on, and white trainers. While they skipped and clunked their sticks together and whooped, a band of women in yellow and green stood on the pavement and played an assortment of instruments. At the end of the dance, the men suddenly all screamed at once and rushed out of sight around the corner down the street making a variety of animal-like cries, much to the consternation of a rather fragile looking woman who happened to be coming round the corner in a Daihatsu jeep.

A small crowd of townspeople and tourists had been watching, standing outside The Chequers pub with drinks in hand. The Morrismen came back, walking now, and took up the instruments while the women danced. A sign propped up in the road announced them as 'The Shropshire Bedlams and Martha Rhoden's Tuppenny Dish'. One of the men, very puffed, went round with a tambourine collecting money; I collared him and extracted a promise of an interview when he'd got his breath back. Then I ran down the hill to the carpark, anxious in case they would all have mysteriously vanished by the time I returned with my film.

I need not have worried; the two troupes continued for another hour, alternately playing and dancing; at the end of their dances the men sometimes sung an archaically obscene ditty before rushing out of sight like a pack of mad dogs, but Martha Rhoden's Tuppenny Dish were more decorous. I nipped into the pub to find a great many men gathered around a giant television screen watching the FA Cup semi-final. The beer was good, but whenever a black player got the ball he was the object of a torrent of abuse from the drinkers. I've often found that the most mindless racism is in towns without any blacks. Since neither of the teams happened to be West Ham United I went back outside with my pint, set it down on the pavement and clicked away happily with the camera between gulps. Most of the onlookers were women and children; the few men seemed to be all tourists, plus a mysterious Latin American in denims who looked as though he might be a professor of something at a Nicaraguan university, with a younger compañero in tow, both talking to a noticeably well-dressed Englishman in pinstripes. What goes on, I wondered, in this quiet little shire town on a Sunday? What brings them here? What do they make of these black-faced lunatics hitting each other and banging the road with bits of tree?

The Morrisman I had spoken to came back as he had promised (luckily, since I would never have recognised him again) and introduced himself as

146

Biggles. The Shropshire Bedlams perform Welsh Border Morris dances, an art which died out during the middle of this century but which has been revived from the careful notes taken by Cecil Sharpe, the great collector of folksongs and dances and lore. It had last been performed by miners in the Ironbridge area before the Bedlams were formed 15 years ago. The black-face is to hide the identity of the dancers – it's nothing to do with the casual racism of music-hall minstrels. The Bedlams perform some recorded dances and some of their own creations, but all carefully within the known parameters of the local tradition. Welsh Border dancing is entirely different from the forms found in Norfolk, Sussex and so on. It looks extremely demanding physically; none of the gentle hopping around with handkerchiefs one sees elsewhere. Bedlams is about right: 'Dervishes' would do. Martha Rhoden was a potter from Clun who wasn't very good. She used to sell off her failures, warped and wobbly pots, for tuppence each. The two groups don't always perform together, but do the rounds of villages and towns on Summer Sundays, usually two places in a day. Thanks to the efforts of these enthusiasts there are now several Welsh Border troupes, including one in the USA. And thank-you, Biggles.

I left them still screeching, jumping and clobbering and wandered around the town, finding on most of the central buildings small, discreet information plaques. These are the work of the Montgomery Civic Society, and received a Prince of Wales Award, whatever that is . . . probably an award given to towns with no hideous carbuncles. Actually, they are excellent, informative, concise and not patronising: 'From its founding in 1227 until 1885 the town was under the government of two Bailiffs, elected every year by the hereditary Burgesses, aided by a Town Clerk and two Serjeants-at-Mace. Thereafter Montgomery was established as a Borough until 1974, when it became a Community.' I don't suppose calling it a community actually made it one. Not in a place where the Town Hall clock is a memorial to a 15-times mayor called Alderman Nicholas Watson Fayldes-Humphries. I mean you could call Nicholas Ridley a Trotskyite, but that doesn't make him any less of a feudal anachronism.

And of course Montgomery *is* an anachronism, artificially preserved. The town's great good fortune is that it has not been on a main road since the advent of the motor-car, although it owes its existence to the command it provided over the strategically important ford across the Severn. Standing now in the castle ruins (it was deliberately torn down after the Revolution, in 1649) it is easy to imagine a column of marching ant-like figures coming down from the Shropshire hills and snaking across the floodplain towards you. These soldiers might be Iron Age tribesmen intent on nicking your sheep, or indeed returning having nicked someone else's, or a Roman legion, or a foraging Saxon war-band, or a troop of iron-banded Norman cavalry led by Roger, Seigneur de Montgomerie, or Henry II intent on knocking the stuffing out of the Welsh, or retreating Cavaliers, or

Cromwell's demolition experts. It is one of those places which seems to mean more than the sum of its parts, where the history of Britain – one might even say the Matter of Britain – seems to have built up the landscape in translucent sheets, so that one irrationally feels that what you are seeing *is* History, the 'real' Britain, the secret, mysterious, holy, bloodstained, marvellous, mystical Britain. Albion, a land with a destiny, now forgotten and polluted by rationalism and philistinism and leaded petrol. It's all bollocks, of course – I mean the feeling, not the history – but rarely is this feeling so seductive as at Montgomery Castle. It is a far more atmospheric place than Glastonbury, for instance, which has become the focus of much New-Age hoo-ha, both genuine and cynical, but where the nastiness of the town is difficult to ignore.

Children were flying kites from the top of the Castle Hill, an activity one seldom sees these days, which is a shame, for it teaches you how to master the elemental wind, and is much cheaper than sailing. (How to go sailing without owning a boat: stand fully-dressed in a cold shower and tear up ten pound notes.)

I realised as I came down the hill what it was I liked so much about it. I had been feeling – I suppose I have to admit it – rather guilty at having fallen so in love with it. I'm an inverted – well, confused at least – snob. Come on, I said to myself, act your age; what is this place if not a poky provincial little nest of monied True Blues pretending that the 20th century hasn't happened? They are all retired ball-bearing manufacturers from Smethwick, Thatcher's Chosen Few, the hang-'em-and-flog-'em brigade. It's not a *real* place at all, it's a film set for some Sunday-afternoon Classic Serial. Do people listen to Elvis Costello here? Do they read Hernandez Brothers comics? Do they have sex? Throw up at parties? Run out of loo paper? Of course they don't. They get confused between Arthur Scargill, the Bishop of Durham and Sinéad O'Connor. When they open their mouths, *Daily Express* editorials come out. Nevertheless, I loved it, I realised, because it was untypical. Its antiquated air was both unashamed and unadulterated – a rare combination. In the hot, bright light it didn't – this was it – seem *British*. In fact it feels very French, aptly enough, like one of those little towns where at midday nothing stirs between the faded, elegant, shuttered buildings, where life is a series of petty intrigues, feuds and jealousies, where mealy-mouthed respectability masks nasty, furtive, guilty passions. I suppose this could be the hidden Welsh element in what is to all intents and purposes a completely English town; it has a hint of Llareggubbian darkness behind its benign, periwigged exterior.

As I reached the level street at the bottom of the hill I stopped in the middle of the road (there was no traffic) to take a photograph of an old enamelled sign, still as bright as the day it was put up, advertising Jones's Sewing Machines. While I was wrestling with the focal length, or whatever it's called – one of those fiddly rings with numbers on – I heard a gentle toot, and along the street came the AA van. I waved, thinking that he was just passing through, but he stopped and got out.

'I've found you a fuel pump,' he said.

I was amazed. 'That's very kind . . . where on earth did you find it?' This was, after all, a Sunday in Wales.

'I went over to Welshpool, there's a scrapyard there. He was open, so I popped in and he had a Morris. I've tested it – it's okay. Cost me £8.50.'

'That's brilliant – thanks ever so much. How did you know I'd still be here? I was just about to go, in fact; you just caught me.'

'Oh, well,' he said bashfully. 'Just on the off-chance, really. Not a big place, Montgomery. Knew I'd probably see you if you were still around. I saw the van down the hill there. Hop in.'

So with further expressions of gratitude on my part we drove down to the carpark where in a trice he had the malfunctioning part out and the new/old one in. We talked for a while about Montgomery – he had been born there, I think, and was very fond of it. They call it 'Sleepy Hollow' locally. I remarked on the incredible prices I had seen in an estate-agent's window, and he said that he had had the chance to buy his house in 1964 for £400. These days it would fetch (it was a terraced cottage, I suppose) £60,000 or more; a farmhouse, £375,000, a big town-centre Georgian place upwards of half a million. The cheapest property I saw was a *derelict* one-bedroomed cottage: £40,000. It was, as I had supposed, Birmingham people who had started the property boom; the real 'locals' were now marginally sited, in the Victorian cottages and the little council estate and as ever in the tied cottages, though many of these had been sold off. (I mean, tenants' rights are such a *bore*, aren't they; I know they'd been there for years but the place cost a fortune to keep in repair – anyway we needed the money after all those death duties . . .)

And, of course, we talked about Morris Minors. I reimbursed him, thanked him again, said I'd put him in the book and asked his name. He grinned and said 'Trevor'. So thank you, Trevor, and may the sun always shine on your spanners.

I headed south towards Newtown, Llandrindod Wells, Brecon and the Valleys, into a golden afternoon, determined to get some dirt on the untarnished image of Wales I had so far seen. One thing was bugging me, though . . . what kind of a lunatic bastard *scraps* a Morris? Is nothing sacred?

Behind me the banshee screams of the Shropshire Bedlams echoed around the streets of Sleepy Hollow. The bloody British, I thought; you have to be in disguise to have a good time. And no one joins in; they stand around as if watching someone clean up a road accident. Strangely, on the day I was typing the Montgomery chapter I read this passage in a book by Duncan Fallowell called *To Noto, or London to Sicily in a Ford*. (His book is much better than mine, but then comparisons are odious):

The British are terrified of the Dionysiac, of anything getting out of control. The only Dionysiac event in the British calendar is the Notting Hill Carnival, which always puts the authorities into a panic (although New Year's Eve is increasingly wild). As a result of the general repression and attitude of denial fostered by the ruling class in Britain the Dionysiac emerges in a random way, making the country especially prone to outbursts of irrational or class violence and yobbery...

And Morris Dancing.

He's right, the British cannot Let Themselves Go; you could see it in the faintly embarrassed expressions of the onlookers, their polite, self-conscious applause at the bawled obscenities and maniac screams. The British have a dread of Joining In. They think they are being invited to make fools of themselves, like those hapless victims of Jeremy Beadle, *Candid Camera*, people invited onstage by comedians for humiliation. Who is the hero of Carnival? The Fool, he who is guided entirely by emotion. Dionysus. British representations of this figure, latterly, grotesquely display the stricture of the British's repression of this urge: Norman Wisdom, George Formby, Frank Spencer. Creators of Chaos, emasculated, gormless, pathetic. Later in his book I found this passage:

Here and there in Europe you may still find something cultivated but absolute in landscape, something which is perfectly beautiful because man is there and yet his parasitism and greed and ignorance are not. The borders of England and Wales between Hay-on-Wye and Montgomery... Everything balanced, connected, functioning, harmonious, belonging.

He's right about that, too.

KEARSLEY
LEIGH
CULCHETH
WARRINGTON
HELSBY
CHESTER
BUCKLEY
MOLD
DENBIGH
LLANDUDNO
COLWYN BAY
ABERGELE
RUTHIN
CONWY
LLANRWST
BETWS·Y·COED
SNOWDON
BALA
LLANGYNOG
PENYGARNEDD
BERWYN
LLANFYLLIN
MEIFOD
WELSHPOOL
CASTLE CAEREINION
THE LONG MYND
MONTGOMERY
NEWTOWN
LLANDRINDOD WELLS
BUILTH WELLS
2000 MILES
MAY HILL
LEA
BRECON
ROSS·ON·WYE
LIBANUS
MONMOUTH
BRECON BEACONS
RAGLAN
BRYN MAWR
ABERGAVENNY
MERTHYR TYDFIL
NANTYGLO
EBBW VALE
BLAINA
ABERTILLERY
BRISTOL
KEYNSHAM
GREEN ORE
WOOKEY HOLE
WELLS
GLASTONBURY
STREET
BRUTON

NANTYGLO

Non-conformism

Ten miles down the road from Montgomery, Newtown shows how lucky the little Norman domain has been, or perhaps unlucky. Newtown is mostly late Victorian to Edwardian, and has a wealth of new factories and businesses, including the St Giles Technology Park. It is a thoroughly ordinary, reasonably successful, absolutely bland little town. I suppose that Montgomery has been preserved at Newtown's expense. Or maybe Newtown has developed to Montgomery's cost; but it doesn't look that way. It looks as if certain groups of influential people have done a deal, unspoken perhaps, unrecognised even. A bit of mutual back-scratching. This is a big problem in a small country. People need to work, people need green fields, fresh air. People need houses. People need shops, schools, office-blocks. People need farms, parks, rivers. There isn't enough space for everyone to have everything they need. Sacrifices have to be made, both by the people and of the land. Compromises. Take the area on the edge of your town . . .

This land has been designated 'Green Belt'; it may not be built on. It forms a protective barrier between this town and that. This ensures that people have access to the countryside, that development is contained and guided. When that Green Belt was designated the area it encircled was 'zoned'. Such-and-such an area for factories; such-and-such for housing. But now all the land inside has been used up. Because there has been a moratorium on public housing, the zoned estates have mostly been privately-built, so that they were occupied not by people from the old houses in the crumbling town centre, but by incomers who could afford to buy nice semi-rural houses. So now there are more people, and more factories are needed.

Well, this bit of Green Belt here . . . it's owned by the mayor, by the Lord Lieutenant, by the local MP, by a business associate of the Chairman of the local party, who desperately wants to build a new town-centre pool/ school/precinct. Just there, where those old houses are . . . be an asset to the town, a service to the Community, would that . . . I think we can find an accommodation, don't you, Councillor? By the way, you live out at Thingummy, don't you? Well, you know that proposed battery chicken factory there's been all this fuss about? Well, I agree, it would be a shame, a great shame. Very desirable village, is Thingummy. Unspoilt, quite. Well, the bloke who wants to build it is a mate of mine, and I own a perfectly suitable bit of land over in Whatsitsname, you see, only of course technically it's Green Belt just the same. But, well, the damn thing's got to be built somewhere, and Whatsitsname, well, it's hardly what you'd call a conservation area is it?

That's how it works. Not all the time, but enough to make all the difference. It's not the compromise which is bad, but the way the compromise is achieved. We do need development. It might well be argued that some areas ought to be sacrificed in order to preserve others, if development is inevitable. But the areas which get off scot-free are the areas which have a vested interest in doing so; they are usually the areas of greatest historical or natural or aesthetic importance, but that is only because that is inevitably where the vested interests live. And when those interests find that it is to their advantage to compromise the purity of the area that they have 'fought' so hard to preserve, they will – they do. Bit by bit, acre by acre. It's *their* area. It was preserved 'for you', but they own it. And possession is nine-tenths of the law. The other tenth is graft.

It is a fact that over the past twenty years the population of this country has been falling. So has the population of London, of Birmingham, of all the old major conurbations. Pressure to develop the countryside and country towns comes from the mobility and the aspirations of people, not the number of them. Despite this obvious fact – the boom in the South and the wasting-away of the North – for the last ten years there has been no attempt to control this migration or mitigate its environmental side-effects. The market-force has been left unchecked, to build and destroy as it will. But the market-force has tunnel-vision; its eyes are on, and only on, the next profit. Even if the cost of that profit is the inevitable destruction of the market-force itself, economic collapse, over-heating, it will make that profit. As a result, the planning of new development has been forced out of the realm of social provision and into that of economic provision; it no longer gives people what they want, but what they now find they need. Planning has become a series of attempts to service the chain-reaction of market-led development. The market creates a factory here, a housing estate there, but it does not create the road that links them, the school that serves them, the doctor's surgery, the municipal pool. Areas in which the market-force has no interest, the inner cities for example, cannot develop. They have to scrimp and save, cut corners, cut jobs, cut services, because they have to make themselves attractive to the market-force. The councils forego their housing and build speculative office accommodation, increase local taxes to provide incentive 'grants' for businesses, and hope for the best. Then, if the best happens, the housing market booms, forcing local people out of the area, so that they have paid for other people's jobs. They are displaced, but the council has not been allowed to (and couldn't afford to) build new houses for them to go to. They end up in Bed & Breakfasts, hostels, prison, on the streets. If they have a little money, they head South. The inner city becomes a desert of offices, small factories, service industries. It has been developed to death.

I believe that people are motivated primarily by self-interest, that they are essentially anti-social. In this Margaret Thatcher and I agree, although we haven't actually discussed it over a Pina Colada at Groucho's. 'There is no such thing as Society', she is held to have once said; we differ there. Society is the result of a compromise between the self-interest of the individual and his or her need to avoid being destroyed by the self-interest of others. The overwhelming need of an anti-social species is to socialise, or it will destroy itself. Society proceeds not from the urge to communicate, to civilise, to love, but from the urge to survive at all costs. Communication, civilisation, love: these are compromises we have to make. In a society, even a global one, which exists by compromise, the concept of the 'general good' has a strong determining force on any developments. Not overriding, by any means; not always strong enough to be recognisable, easily missed, sometimes mistaken. In a society based on compromise expressed 'democratically' those in power will always come off best, and social change will be slow, the 'general good' a grey area. Utopia will never arrive because the mistakes made along the way will be too damaging; Utopia will be a compromise version. In other forms of society these compromises are enforced rather than negotiated; they are laid down as Law and are immutable; either they seek to empower as many as possible (pure communism) or as few as possible (pure fascism). In both cases the minority (paradoxically, the masses) are considered expendable as individuals; the 'greater good' is given too inflexible a definition. We cannot resort to fascism or communism. It seems we are lumbered with a compromise: democratic capitalism/democratic socialism. The 'middle way'. But the middle way has produced an awful mess, and we have no guarantee that it will not accidentally destroy us all. The answer must be: stop developing, until we have learned how to do it.

We are driving a car very fast but we have never had driving lessons; we are going to arrive, but we're knocking over an awful lot of pedestrians. We are coming up to a traffic light; green has turned to amber. We are in the split second of hesitation between braking and accelerating. Can we beat

154

the red light? Brake; gear-change down; stop; wait. The engine is still running, but it's under control. Which way do we want to go when the lights change again and we can go forward? How fast? To what destination?

If only. The trouble is, you are not driving the car, are you? You're in the back seat, and there are no safety-belts. You reach forward to draw the driver's attention to the changing light, but he has already put his foot down hard. As you start to speak he laughs a maniac laugh and slowly turns his head to grin at you. Whose face is it? Yours.

What on earth brought all this on? Newtown, an optimistic-sounding little dot on the map of Wales. Not a bad sort of place. No sense of imminent world destruction there. Firmly in the present, not half-trapped in the past like Montgomery. Not a bad compromise between a country town and an industrial town, between depopulation and development, between local people and newcomers, between history and progress, between beauty and function. Not bad, not bad at all, compared to some places. I mean *I* wouldn't want to live there, but . . . Sorry, what? Compared to where? Well, to Nantyglo, for instance. Never heard of it, eh?

There are two ways to get to Nantyglo. The quick way is by car. The other way is this: take a long wooded valley and cut down all the trees. Then dig a hole in the ground and extract whatever you find – coal, iron – and build a line of cottages on the hillside above the valley floor. Doesn't matter if it's on the cheap – they're only for workers, and the land is so unstable that they'll fall down however well-built they are. When you have dug out every last lump, go away. What you have left is Nantyglo.

Naturally enough I chose the quick way. This involved a long drive on a hot and very hazy afternoon through more mysteriously uninteresting upland scenery, and on a curiously empty road. Where was everyone? Upwards so gradually that only the sluggishness of the car and the popping of your ears indicate the gradient, into a rolling landscape – why aren't there any *things* in it? – like driving through a Henry Moore sculpture, feminine and sexy hills, smooth as green flesh. Somewhere near a place called Rock Chapel I passed one of the smallest inhabited houses I'd ever seen; one up, one down, alone in a sheep-field. On a high plain, a distant blue smudge of hills looms briefly out and back from the thick horizon. A stony river winding by the road, the Ithon on its way to the Wye.

Down to Llandrindod Wells, with the peeved air of a town whose heyday lasted only 30 years; apart from one or two mid-Victorian streets the whole place seems to have been built in about 1905. It looks a bit like the streets around Westminster Cathedral, in pale red and white brick. Later I check the guide-book; it was dead by 1939. Now it's like meeting a man who's still wiry and fit at 103, and tells you that the secret of a long life is spring water and regular bowels. But all his friends are dead. Someone has built a really nasty new estate on the southern side in brick the colour of dried blood. Why? Why that peculiarly repulsive colour, which finds no echo

155

whatsoever in the faded orange-brown town or the jewel-green fields? I passed a sign for Cwm Bach. Only if you pay me, I thought.

Builth Wells. Older than Llandrindod, more cottagey, with a vast quarry that has eaten an entire hill. No attempt to shield it or disguise it, but then would that be a good thing? Is it healthy to pretend that it isn't there? In Newburgh, where I live, is an enormous quarry for the extremely hard volcanic stone – the sort used in road surfaces and runways and under railway tracks. It has completely eaten away a hill called Clatchard Craig, but a tiny sliver of hillside only a few feet thick has been left standing so that from the village it looks as if the hill is intact. (After quarrying was well advanced, it turned out that Clatchard Craig was perhaps the most important Pictish settlement ever discovered; Fife retained its Pictish culture long after the Scots had muscled in elsewhere. It may even have been a royal site. Too late: it's been pulverised and is under the runway at Heathrow. The Picts, always a mystery, still are, thanks to someone's carelessness.) Quarries are so ugly that disguise, however cynical, is best.

Now into the Wye Valley, the loveliest lowland valley in Britain, but only by the skin of its teeth. Among its glorious wooded bluffs and meanders, new bungalows peek out, each with its own little view of the river, each carefully invisible from the next but visible to everyone else. Not quite enough to spoil it completely; just enough to make you sick. Am I completely paranoid or have the owners of these monuments to selfishness had a quiet word with the County Council about not building lay-bys on this road for the rest of us? There's only one, carefully sited so that you cannot see anything. Plenty of '20s and '30s houses along the road, built before the planning laws, so more excusable. But around every bend is a new patch scoured out of the woods with the concrete foundation laid in, or a brash plate-glass and crazy-paving ranch-style three-garage-and-solar-powered-barbecue job. I got angrier and angrier as I realised that I wasn't going to get to a stretch where this hasn't happened. Perhaps the government should introduce a Scenery Tax, designed to price such developments out of viability. Then they should compulsorily purchase all these places under a Naff Houses Bill, and make the owners demolish them with their own hands under the watchful gaze of armed Betjeman addicts.

Oddly, the Wye lies beneath Britain's ugliest mountains, the Black Mountains, which resemble a flattened coal-tip and look as though they were created by a cosmic JCB. They stand in stark contrast to the extraordinary Brecon Beacons, which come into sight shortly afterwards. Whereas the Black Mountains' strata are completely level for their entire length, the Beacons have been formed by the tilting of rocks almost vertically. From a distance they look like some kind of Art Deco building with two symmetrical towers.

Brecon itself is a curiously crowded little town, medieval dressed up as Georgian, and bearing the scars and the grubby look of a town which has

156

for years suffered from traffic congestion. This has now been eased by a huge bypass, but Brecon seems unsure what to do next. Ironically now that it has a new appeal due to the diversion of traffic, it is filling up again, this time with people who have come to see *it* rather than get stuck in the bottleneck on their way east or west. Most of the strollers seemed to be from the Valleys, but there was a party of Irish and another from Yorkshire. The newly-painted rows of houses along the main road were already stained from car exhausts. Like Denbigh, to which it bears a strong resemblance in terms of size and atmosphere, it has a little cinema, something now very rare in English towns this size. Among the pub names are The Sarah Siddons, so perhaps she was a native, and The Gremlin, the sign showing a small man on a toadstool, less explicably. It also has the very fine neo-classical Brecknock Museum, a structure of almost German severity and purity of form, completely at odds with the rest of the town. As I was wandering back to the car an aged man came pedalling down the street hailing all and sundry with a shout and a cheery wave, full of the joys of life. Look at me, I'm 106, mad as a coot, fit as a fiddle, still alive. Good to see.

The north side of the Beacons has a gigantic corrie, a huge bite out of the mountains scarred deeply by streams in a great fan of veins. You pass a hamlet with the unfortunate-sounding name of Libanus. Then the road begins to climb in a gigantic curve up Glyn Tarell – you can see the road for miles ahead lined with cars – and at the top you are suddenly tipped over the crest into a dessicated brown landscape, a shock after 200 miles of greenery. Miraculously, the traffic vanishes as five out of six drivers seem to want to use the public loos at the top of the pass. We bounced down the valley toward Merthyr, passing a series of reservoirs which were not well-managed or disguised but which nevertheless had attracted a good many parkers-and-knitters, folding furniture folk, boy fishermen and bird-watchers. A huge sill hangs on the mountainside at the top of the valley, presumably one of several for the road descends in a series of steep steps. Into Mid-Glamorgan and the Borough of Merthyr Tidfil, but it's at least four miles before the first urbanisation begins, at Cefn Coed.

Divided by thin, long hills like fingers, the valley towns are effectively one huge conurbation stretching 25 miles from Rhondda to Pontypool, though as with the Lancashire-Yorkshire conurbation they have never been managed as such. Across the head of the Valleys runs a big dual carriageway; I almost shot down it to Neath, but decided it was too far and instead settled for Nantyglo, which I had no idea how to pronounce.

'Merthyr Tidfil – Iron Heritage Town'. Difficult not to be cynical about it; when they close down your livelihood it becomes everyone else's Heritage. Why not 'Merthyr Tidfil – Cradle Of Industrial Exploitation', or 'Ebbw Vale – Silicosis Heritage Town'? I had a sudden, sharp case of *déjà vu* in Merthyr. I recognised several buildings I had never seen before, though I had a strong sense that I had travelled in the opposite direction along the road. Perhaps a subconscious memory of a tracking shot in a TV film? Perhaps, as they explain, an interruption in the blood-flow to part of the brain. It was quite alarming, powerful enough to make me doubt my own history and think carefully about whether I had in fact been there before.

The big road along the valley heads is bordered by new and not-so-new industrial estates and places where industrial estates might be and might have been; everything looks a bit piecemeal and desperate. A huge spoil-tip looking like Mount Fuji rears up on the left; in the valleys to the right are long housing schemes, each revealing in its layout the passing fads of town-planning: 1950s streets in long lines, 1960s with lines broken at 90°, 1970s with lots of little culs-de-sac and 1980s with 'villagey' grouping, but all unimaginative and grey and uniform. Valley after valley of cheap housing built on a massive scale over 40 years – one can only imagine what the places these houses replaced must have been like. At least up here there is clean air and the open mountainside across the dual carriageway, even if as mountainsides go it is pretty uninspiring, a tussocky, litter-strewn waste. The occasional farm is still huddled among the estates and factories, with chickens and goats and the ubiquitous shaggy pit-ponies people always hang on to after the mines have gone, matted and stumpy. Many of these farms are evidently very old and predate the industrialisation of the area; there is something moving about this. The Cumbrian coalfield towns had had them too; usually the last house in the street was a farmhouse, so that you could imagine them keeping the miners in fresh milk and eggs through the long, black years of Britain's satanic greatness. Now they have emerged into daylight once again, and the rubbish of the past 200 years is fading away, and the farms look as though they will still be there 500 years hence.

I turned off at Bryn Mawr, a tidy, respectable suburb of Victorian villas. Little old ladies tottered along the street to chapel under the cherry-blossom. A quarter of a mile beyond is Nantyglo, which welcomes careful drivers. I had never heard of it before that day; down the same valley a little way is Abertillery and across the hill in the next valley west is Ebbw Vale, if that helps. They are names which conjure up the grimmest of iron, steel and coal towns, a world of perpetual smog, black faces and wheezing coughs, smoking ground and ash-coloured lines of houses. Yet everything was pale and clean in the evening sunshine, at least from afar, almost intangible, like a Turner cityscape. Closer, it was tatty. That was the first word which sprang to mind; the adjectives got stronger the longer I looked. The valleysides were brown, not green. Nantyglo is basically one street built along the valleyside half-way up the west-facing slope. I drove along it and at the other end I stopped and wrote: 'Bungalows/terrible road surface/secondhand cars/Victorian terrace but not uniform/no building line/great craggy hillside opposite, bare, stony/Workman's Social Club and Inst./

Youths in beat-up saloons/new plastic factories below/broken glass/new redbrick flats fiery among ubiquitous white & pale grey pebbledash/atmosphere of quiet hopelessness.'

This was strange because Bryn Mawr, and indeed much of what I had seen coming across the valleys, had looked sad and a little dowdy, perhaps – but not particularly hopeless. Nantyglo struck me immediately, even from a cursory inspection from the driving seat, as utterly hopeless. I couldn't have put my finger on it then – the signs were too confused and impressionistic, but the town had a palpable air of desperation and of having the odds stacked against it. Back at the top end of the street my eye had been caught by a sign pointing to 'Nantyglo Round Towers', and I decided to investigate these first. They lie across the valley on the opposite hillside, next to an outlying farm, two squat turrets in massive stone, about 25 feet high, like miniature Martello towers. They were built in 1816 by the local Ironmaster, one Joseph Bailey, who was terrified that the ironworkers of Nantyglo would rise up and smash him and his family. The walls are four feet thick, with musket-slits with cast-iron sliding covers, and cast-iron fireplaces and fittings within. They were the last serious fortifications built in Britain between the Napoleonic struggles and the First World War. One is in ruins; the other was restored in the late 1980s as a local community project after the closure of the local pits and ironworks had left the descendents of those workers – how cruelly oppressed they must have been – with nothing. Ironic is the word.

From the towers the village looked innocuous enough, in a straggling line across the opposite slope; on the valley floor was a small new estate built on ground which had the tell-tale angularity of a reclaimed tip. Small factories and allotments are very thinly-spread along the new road on the bottom of the valley. Lots of tumbledown fences of scrap and corrugated iron; chickens, dogs, ponies; ramshackle smallholdings. Away down the valley towards Abertillery there is a denser huddle of new factories and sheds.

Back in the village I wait to use the phone while a teenage girl yaks interminably into it; a thin man in an ancient Cortina is also waiting. We exchange shrugs and eye-rolls; the girl has been talking for half an hour. I wander over and ask him how you pronounce the name of the place. 'I dunno,' he confesses, 'I'm from Pontypool, see. I just call it Bryn Mawr.' Later I discover from a Welsh colleague back in Perth that it's Nant-er-glo, with the 'o' half-way between 'glow' and 'ostler'. Eventually, when the valley is almost dark, I get through to Kate. For the first time I feel seriously, achingly homesick, but she is distracted by the children and the conversation is short and confused. My eldest daughter (aged four) pesters her for the phone, says 'Hi, Daddy' then is too shy or tired to answer my questions and only says 'Mm' and then 'bye'. Afterwards I drive down to the pub, feeling in need of company and warmth, but have a strange attack of panic as I look through the window at people laughing and talking and playing darts inside. For some reason I can't go in; I feel alien and self-conscious and afraid of these perfectly ordinary men and women having a Sunday-night drink. I stand there for what seems like ages, telling myself not to be a fool, remembering the pubs in Daviot and Gilsland and Llandudno and Montgomery and arguing with myself that this is no different, but for some reason it is. I even tell myself that it's my *duty* to go in and talk to them, to find out whatever I can about Nantyglo and redress the imbalance of my ignorance and prejudice. But it's no good; I get back in the car and drive away, despising myself, trying to rationalise my fear. But even now I can't explain it except perhaps as some kind of subconscious masochistic desire to wallow in and dramatise my self-pity. No, it was more than that. Partly it was undoubtedly the result of extreme fatigue and resultant depression; real depression is an irrational downward spiral like one of those chaotic geometrical computer-drawings. You want to break out but however hard your rational mind tries it cannot stop the maelstrom and spin it the other way, up and out. Having been through it before, I knew what to do in Nantyglo: sleep. So I drove out of town and up a long very steep hillside until I found a place to turn off behind a low bank which kept me out of sight of the traffic. It was an awful place, covered with litter and industrial debris and overlooking a huge opencast mine and the cramped valleyfull of chimneys and slate roofs. The sun went down like a blood orange. At night the valley looks fantastic, like something from *Close Encounters of the Third Kind*. I felt very keyed-up, every nerve buzzing, my brain a radio listening to the gibberish of a hundred dim foreign stations through the static of exhaustion. Gradually I quietened myself down; drowsiness hit me like a valium overdose. I became spastic, couldn't undress properly, simply curled up under a pile of sleeping bags, blankets and dirty clothes, and slept. I had driven almost 2,000 miles. Nothing was the same after that point in my journey.

This is what I wrote the next day, more or less verbatim:

'Cold windy night; slept well; woken at 6 by odd bleeping – dump-truck reversing in open-cast mine. Mist, chilly, gradually lifts to reveal huge estates below. Breakfast, pack up, teeth, shave, pee. Down to town. Of all places yet this most depressed and depressing, despite view of hillside opposite – looking one way you can pretend town isn't there and are in open country. Not having been to Valleys before, I'm unsure how typical it is. Parked on small area of waste ground near line of ramshackle garages and workshops. Opened car door to find pit bull terrier 2 feet away, no collar, no lead. Luckily poor old sod almost blind, waddled off. Walking up and down the main road I realised the untidy look of the place is due to the completely random height and front line of terraced Victorian cottages (perhaps some are earlier?) – all vary by a little. All are very small and most pretty decrepit – badly built in the first place and badly repaired. Asbestos

160

board on one end-wall instead of bricks, slates skewed. Scars where places fallen or been demolished. Several in terrible state or abandoned. 4 or 5 shops: the main village store, 2 other small grocers, an off-licence, a hairdresser who may or may not still be in business; she seems to have taken over premises of undertaker. 3 or 4 derelict shops. A small tatty car repair place. Chapels – 6 or 7: Bethel, Ebenezer, Berea, English Presbyterian, Wesleyan (demolished) and another, also demolished. The public toilet is indescribably smelly – chemicals have been poured in to compensate for there being no flush. Whole hillside obviously unstable, houses buckling. Graveyard behind where chapel was is very higgledy. Tombstones lean drunkenly, fallen flat, cracked, smashed. Lots of tombs of small children, 5 or 6 to a grave from the 1830s onwards – some too weathered to read – may be older. Until the 1880s the death rate was shocking; lots of teenagers and people in their 20s also. Some tombs are inscribed in Welsh, most in English: Jones, Roberts, Davies . . . Mary Ann, Mary Jane, Mary, Mary, aged 2, aged 3, 2, 3, 3, 5, 4, 3, 3 days, 6 months, 1, 4 . . . A plaque in the street commemorates a Chartist uprising in 1839. The valleyside opposite looks like infill; thin grass, unnatural contours. The pit was just south of town; earlier ironworks were nearby. Pit closed 15 years ago. Nantyglo does not have one decent building; chapels in disrepair are only 'architecture'. Otherwise it's completely mean and shoddy, or, in the new areas, banal and cheap. One exception: a small terraced house with nice art-nouveau cast-iron porch, someone's labour of love. There are two schools, a hospital, estates of featureless grey pebbledash. The Post Office is the dirtiest, gloomiest shop I've ever been in. The floor is filthy, the walls shored up with bits of wood where the plaster and brick is caving in. The shelves are falling off the walls, grubby cards, peeling wallpaper and lino, boxes of fading, cheap toys (a few) and bike parts literally rusting. Still the assistant gave me a friendly smile. Elsewhere there are 2 pubs: The Cog and Petal, and The Golden Lion, and a working men's club.'

It became a bright day with a chilly wind, but not bright enough to cheer it up. Nantyglo has evidently always been very poor. Even Harrington had some fine buildings. I heard a lot of Welsh spoken in the street and sometimes a mixture of English and Welsh in the same sentence; an unintelligible stream of gutturals followed by 'I said, "It's bloody terrible, boyo!" ' I felt very sad, chilled by it. Everywhere in the valley there were places being built or land laid out with roads waiting for factories which might or might not come, or where factories had been, or tips, or – who knows – houses worse than these. Everywhere it seemed, except Nantyglo itself, which is like the runt of the litter crying out, 'And me! and me!' and seeing all the goodies go elsewhere. Builders everywhere on the streets, patching, not building. There's nothing whole, nothing complete, old or new; they merely fill in empty spaces while other bits fall down, then fill in these new spaces. A woman in the shop tells me about the ironworks and the pits and says recently there have been lots of break-ins, car thefts and vandalism. She doesn't think it's local kids but won't say who, is very cagey. She complained that the 'bloody English' are buying up houses on the cheap. Why? Where the hell do they work? I asked what unemployment was like. She just said 'terrible'. I've never heard more bitterness in a voice.

Dismayed as I was by Nantyglo I had no idea whether it is typical of the Valleys. So I drove over to Ebbw as a comparison. On the way a sign read 'WE ARE WORKING TO RECLAIM LAND FOR NEW USE — BLAENAU GWENT BOROUGH COUNCIL'. It looks like an uphill struggle. Much has been knocked down, bulldozed, seeded with grass; not much has been built, or not enough. The scale of the redundant land is gigantic.

Ebbw Vale is a much darker valley. It looks narrower and is built up on both sides which gives it a more claustrophobic air. To my surprise, it was obvious that the houses in this valley were in a completely different class to those of Nantyglo. They are later, solidly-built Victorian terraces, some bay-fronted, though most not, with back yards and communal rear alleys, and they stand in immense lines. But they are well-built, well-maintained, far more spacious than their neighbours across the hill, their ashlar painted in bright colours, all looking scrupulously clean. Ebbw itself, though much bigger than Nantyglo, seems unfairly favoured with a welter of modern shops and facilities, a largely pedestrianised town centre, a new sports centre, new office-blocks; it could be any ex-industrial town, it could be Falkirk or Bingley. There are many new villas and flats, and many of the old terraces have been re-roofed, re-rendered, had double-glazing installed. A vast new multistorey serves the shopping centre. A little down the valley is what is left of the once all-powerful steelworks, now much reduced in capacity. It is still a mile long, and as the road comes off the hillside you look along the roofs of the sheds as if along a vast runway. Beyond, the coal yards and disused factories are being cleared away and the site landscaped in preparation for the 1992 Welsh Garden Festival. The soil is black with coal dust. Serpentine new tracks and paths are appearing in the long narrow festival site; shrubs and rose bushes stand shivering in the black soil under the gaze of the treeless terraced streets on the valleyside. It seemed that everything which could be demolished had been demolished, with one exception; here, as in Nantyglo, was a disused, boarded-up Methodist chapel.

Three days previously, in Chester, my godmother Audrey Wooldridge and I had been talking about the subject of Class. I had been saying that I found it both fascinating and depressing that the British remain so obsessed with class distinctions. We measure the social order with scrupulous attention to the minutiae of dress, speech, taste. Every material possession, every word and gesture is weighed up and filed. However much we are aware of this process, however much we resent it, we never escape it. The conversation drifted to and fro; had Thatcher really effected a permanent, fundamental shift in the class system? Why are the middle-classes so obsessed with the past, with nostalgia, with the rural, the traditional; or to be more exact the middle-middle and upper-middle classes? The lower-middle classes do not object to the modern, the convenient, the brand-new, but the intelligentsia, the bourgeoisie and the chattering classes do. Audrey confessed to having had qualms about moving to the quiet, safe modern estate on the outskirts of Chester. In retrospect, she was appalled at the strength of her prejudice against such places. What was more mysterious was that this prejudice was unspecific, vague, made up of received ideas and associations rather than based on knowledge or rationality. Yet much of her life as a vicar's wife had been spent in the most appalling slums; she knows that to judge people by their circumstances is a great mistake, a great evil even. We got on to the legacy of the industrial age and its continuing cultural stranglehold over this country; the idea that earned money is bad, manufacturing is no occupation for a gentleman, and so on, which persists although another aspect of the same historical process, working-class solidarity, is almost a thing of the past. She ventured that one of the key factors in the persistence of class distinction was Methodism; its doctrine of sobriety, obedience, temperence and familial integrity had effectively castrated revolutionary socialism in Britain. The curious amalgams of non-conformist Christianity and Marxism which arose as the result of the rapid and almost total acceptance of Wesleyanism by the rural and industrial working-class, and the middle-class Tawneyite Christian Socialism, and the mystic Christian Socialism of William Morris: all these peculiarly British compromises had ordained that state socialism of the kind which developed in France, Italy and elsewhere could never happen here, let alone full-blooded revolution. Am I right in thinking that it was only in areas where non-conformism did not have such a tight grip, such as on the Red Clyde, that a more full-blooded socialism flourished? Perhaps not. The last vestiges of this great historic partnership between materialism and mysticism are finally fading; Eric Heffer is dead, Scargill is broken; both ardent Christians. Has capitalism not so much triumphed as been let off the hook?

All over the Valleys, boarded-up, collapsed, weed-sprouting, the chapels where the oppressed begged forgiveness for the trespasses of their oppressors, sure in the knowledge of the life to come. The twin private fortresses overlooking Nantyglo where the Ironmaster sweated; 1816. The plaque marking the spot from where, under the leadership of Zephaniah Williams, landlord of the Royal Oak Inn, Nantyglo, Chartists from all over the county set out to march on Newport; 1839. After that, violence is abandoned; the Lamb lay down in Blaenau Gwent. And latterly the cruellest twist of all, that a lower-middle-class Methodist shopkeeper's daughter from Lincolnshire should take up the fervour of this revolutionary tradition and use it to lay waste the class which gave it birth.

I drove back up the new road along the valley floor beneath Nantyglo; to the south and the north of it the valley is lined with solid-looking new housing and well-built terraces of the kind found in Ebbw. Only Nantyglo, it seems, has this peculiarly shambolic wretchedness. From the road below it is almost invisible, marked chiefly by a scree of rubbish descending from the edge of the carpark where I had met the Bull Terrier. The few buildings which can be made out look uncannily like those of Soweto; indeed the whole area around the town has that broken, impermanent, wasted look. From this new road serving the redeveloping valley floor you would never know it was there. It would take a kind of socialist Professor Challenger to find it.

I drove out of the valleys singing at the top of my lungs – I was definitely cracking up, I thought to myself. In reality I was singing to drown out the possibility that I would find myself emotionally overwhelmed by what I had seen there. I was afraid to acknowledge my gut responses, fearful that in my ennervated state the trip would seem unfinishable, irrelevant, superficial. What those emotions were is easy to say: anger, sadness, a sense of betrayal not least by myself. Guilt. I was singing the greatest revolutionary hymn ever written, the poem which lies right at the root of the glorious failure of British Christian Socialism. The one that the Conservatives sing every year with shining eyes and voices trembling with patriotic fervour. Poor Blake! Poor mad, inspired, visionary, tender Blake. They have taken your sword and beaten it into electricity shares. They, who do not understand it – if they did, the words would choke them – have almost made it their own.

> Bring me my Bow of burning Gold!
> Bring me my Arrows of Desire!
> Bring me my Sword! O clouds unfold!
> Bring me my Chariot of Fire!
> I will not cease from mental fight,
> Nor shall my Sword sleep in my hand
> Till we have built Jerusalem . . .

Salem,
Bethel,
Ebenezer,
Berea . . .

Albion?

OXFORD

Open city?

The last of the valleys on the eastern side still have their trees clinging to the slopes, but many are dead, killed and apparently fossilised by the smoke of two centuries of heavy industry. Four miles beyond you are in open, rolling pasture land which has never been anything but rural and in which it is almost impossible to believe in the ecological degradation only an hour's walk west.

I tore out of South Wales, feeling an urgent need to put it behind me, hoping that a return to normality – my normality, at least – would enable me to look back at Nantyglo with a degree of disinterest. Alas, if you are seeking normality Oxford is not the place to go. But I was due a precious and much-needed rest-day and a *cri de coeur* from the phonebox in Nantyglo had gone out to an old friend with a flat on the Banbury Road. Oxford doesn't look too far from the Valleys on the map, but don't be fooled. It's a long way. Oxford is a long way from everywhere. I think it's actually in another universe altogether.

I kept mostly to the main roads; Blodwen seemed to relish the chance to pick her skirts up and let it all hang out. She'll cruise happily enough at 65 on level ground; anything over that and she gets over-excited, begins to quake and frisk. Downhill she has managed a screaming, clattering 74 mph, but this is close to disintegration-point; Warp Factor Ten. Even at 65 the engine noise fries your brain in an hour; it's like being rolled downhill in a dustbin full of wasps. I normally keep to 58, the point at which tolerable noise and tolerable speed are coincident. The problem is that everyone presumes this is flat out; lorries especially charge up behind her, swing out to overtake, and then find that the slightest gradient causes them to fall back, whereas Blodwen, with power to spare, sails up regardless. This makes motorway and multi-lane driving, well, entertaining. We tend to overtake quite a few embarrassed truckers on the inside.

Coming out of Wales I kept my foot down hard; I needed the adrenalin, the prolonged effort of concentration and stress, paradoxically, to blow away my blues. Speed is relative, I've found, not to the ground you cover but the vehicle you drive; 70 mph for ten miles in Blodwen is the physical equivalent of the Le Mans 24-Hour Endurance Race. Her narrow tyres scream and skitter across the concrete; her complete lack of aerodynamism allows the slightest breeze to blast her from one lane to the next; being passed by a juggernaut doing 85 is like being swamped by a tidal-wave on a surfboard. You *hang in there*. Luckily, despite her innate instability at anything over about 60, her steering is magnificently light and accurate, allowing you to compensate for the bludgeoning of the turbulence. Rear-end visibility is so poor you might as well forget about it; she's slow, she's blinding white, she's in the way; let 'em stack up behind – I'm having *fun*.

It was sunny again, cloudless but hazy and not too hot; perfect driving weather. I found a strange pub on a road now made redundant by a new highway, where I had a late lunch when hunger finally overcame desperate speed-need. It was a stained-oak-chintz-and-horse-brass job which might have been in Cobham or Rickmansworth rather than alone in the Welsh fields. I was the only customer; the landlady thoughtfully put on The Carpenters' *Greatest Hits* as I chewed my ham roll. Boy, did I chew fast after that.

Outside the last Welsh mountains, Mynydd Garnclochdy, Blorenge, Coity, were mere stains low in the sky. The hedgerows were bursting with new flowers, the trees looked so sappy you could almost hear them slurp. Birds yelled crazily from the branches, the red earth smelled like plum pudding. I burped good beer fumes, felt better, drove on.

I tried to review progress to date. Had I the right balance of towns, villages, cities, suburbs? How could I give the narrative shape? What was I looking at, thinking about, writing down? Why had I the feeling that I had met too few people and learned too little? Surely this was the result of the schedule, much more punishing than I had expected: too much driving and writing and sleeping and not enough exploring and interviewing. Yet I was certainly reflecting the modern experience of travel, if it can be called that. 'Travel' seems somehow redolent of Sir Richard Burton, Defoe, Boswell and Johnson, of leisurely, civilised, contemplative journeys. There ought to be a new word for getting from Point A to Point B in the modern way, which amounts to little more than getting into a lift or on to an escalator. Was I seeing what I wanted to see? In famous 'leisure' areas all roads seemed to be designed to lead you to particular points *and nowhere else*, to prevent you

166

from making your own journey, finding your own point of view. Here again the question of 'choice' and 'freedom' rears its ugly head. Susan Sontag wrote somewhere that modern tourism is geared to the 'possession' of places, and the tourist collects them as a lepidopterist captures and pins down butterflies. In order to 'possess' a place you have to get out of your car and photograph it; that is the only real demand made upon you. The photograph has become a substitute for real knowledge and understanding, a shorthand guided tour, a token signifying experience which is never experienced, as if you were to photograph a meal rather than eat it. Management of leisure = management of traffic. Stop now. Eat. Enjoy. Move on. Have a Nice Day. This way. Stop. Photograph. Move on.

Unwittingly, despite the fact that most of my destinations were outside the field of tourism, I seemed to some extent to have fallen into this trap. This feeling was exacerbated by the dash from South Wales to the South Midlands, with the big new dual-cariageway A40 scooping me up at Raglan and hurling me eastward. Raglan Castle looks like Camelot, the countryside looks wonderful, but there's no way to stop once you are on this road; I had a strong sensation, as in the Wye Valley, that 'they' don't want you to stop. Private. Trespassers Will Be Prosecuted. No Overnight Parking. No Turning. Move, move.

I found myself, looking at this verdant but seemingly untouchable country, wondering what somebody brought up in Armadale in the era before TV would have made of it. Unbelievably fertile, gentle land, saturated with moisture, full of huge trees – trees with bright green broad leaves, trees full of flowers – grass as smooth as velvet, soil like red flour. Hedges – living walls. Where are the rocks, the long tumbled walls, the broken houses? Could that mansion be a mere farm? Where are the snapped ploughs and rust-solid tractors, the heaps of rubble and twisted wire? Where has the wind gone?

This stretch of road is 100 yards wide; I can see a mile ahead. It carries four cars. An awful road, but there's no choice if you want to get across country fast. Half the time seems to be spent in cuttings with nothing to see except rye grass. Why don't they seed these banks with wild flowers? Potentially we have a nature reserve of millions of acres, where nobody can stop and do damage, protected by a lethal wall of hurtling metal. So simple, but beyond us. A road built for people obsessed with speed, deadlines, time-management, efficiency. A road to nowhere – all the places are *off* the road.

When at last there was an exit – to Monmouth – I took it more as a matter of principle than out of a desire to see the town. I noticed that here someone had taken the trouble to plant the verges and banks. Why not do the same in South Wales, Harrington, South Yorkshire? Because this is an area of 'outstanding natural beauty', and they aren't? What kind of logic is that? Monmouth, like Brecon, is punch-drunk from decades of being a bottleneck; now it is bypassed. Also like Brecon it is medieval pretending to be Georgian, but spread much further over an undulating plain and up into steep wooded hills, where more exclusive houses stake their claims to the view. At the top of the hill a little gleaming white folly, like a politer version of the Nantyglo towers, perhaps built by the local MP after the introduction of the Poll Tax.

There was, as far as I could see, no sign marking the border between Wales and England. My attention was, however, taken up with a sudden massive increase in traffic. I fought artics up the road to Ross, and with the lorries came a deterioration in both the road surface and in traffic manners; one bastard came past at about 80, barely in control, fishtailing across both lanes, leaving me on the hard shoulder dodging burst tyre fragments.

I've never seen soil of the colour they have there; it's almost rose pink in places, with patches of crimson where it is shaded and damp. The underlying sandstone is also deep pinkish-red, very frangible and almost useless for buildings; the barns look as if they're made of wafers. Much of the landscape I managed to glance at seems to have been planted with trees to enhance the views; one magnificent hillside was a symphony of mature trees, the work of an artist – oak, beech, birch, hornbeam, whitebeam, aspen, holly, horse-chestnut . . . why can't I stop, dammit?

The road follows the Wye at a discreet distance, curving up and around the Forest of Dean toward Ross. The Wye is a most freakish river. It begins high up on Plynlimon Fawr, from which the Severn also flows. The Severn starts off north-eastwards towards the Midlands and then curves in a long sedate clockwise arc until it spills into the Bristol Channel, by that time flowing south-west. But the Wye, beginning only two miles from its big sister, starts south-west to Rhayader then joins the Ithon near Llandrindod and carries on quite sensibly for another 20 miles or so before suddenly losing its head and turning in the opposite direction completely, north-east to Hay and then east to Hereford. Below Hereford lies an area of lowland and by rights the Wye should turn this way and flow south-west down the valleys of the Usk and the Monmow. Instead, it scorns this easy option and moves south in a tortuous series of huge meanders through increasingly steep hills and finally a gorge, before spilling into the tidal mud at Chepstow, just below the Severn Bridge. It is as if the hills have been put there just to provide scenery for the river to flow through – I don't know another river where the surrounding land gets steeper as the river gets nearer the sea. As a result the lower Wye is justly famous and in danger of becoming seriously overwhelmed by visitors. Ross-on-Wye was a huddle of steep roofs, a great spire in the golden haze, and a long straggle of new estates on both sides of the dual carriageway which is about to meet the motorway. I couldn't take any more sound and fury and escaped on a more minor road toward Cheltenham, one of those roads which became a main route but was actually just a series of country lanes strung together, full of craziness and humorous lethal bends. Another hazard; suddenly I come upon a vast field of polythene sheets all mirroring the sun, which almost made me put both hands over my eyes. I suggest that roadside warning signs should be installed near such fields: 'DANGER – SHRINK-WRAPPED FOOD'.

Gloucestershire: the landscape of ostentation. All my worst prejudices come to the boil there, not least because I am jealous. But less so now than ten years ago, and perhaps not at all soon, for before long it will be ruined enough for me not to care anymore. Too much money, not enough scenery to go round, and an architectural heritage which is too easy to mimic and impossible to equal. In Gloucestershire they seem to have decided that to stick pieces of 'Cotswold Stone' on to any piece of prefabricated crap will render it lovely, blend it into the scenery and add £30,000 to its market value. Only the last of these is actually true, unfortunately. The remaining countryside is wonderful but the villages make my flesh creep; the genuinely old and beautiful buildings are over-restored, like Mae West at 80, and sit smugly inside rings of what would be perfectly decent modern houses if they hadn't had 'Olde Worlde' written all over them in stone-cladding and carriage-lamps and plaster-eagle gateposts. In many villages there are no shops, no cheerful dilapidated country garages. Nowhere is there a scruffy little factory making pork scratchings to add a sense of balance. Little stone toadstools serve as traffic bollards to keep your tyres off the impossibly smooth grass. I suppose they aspire to the condition of a Miss Marple set, but if that redoubtable lady were living here she would be investigating tax-frauds, thefts of Mercedes, circumnavigation of the planning laws and breaches of good taste.

It grew increasingly hot; large insects began to splatter yellow smears on the windscreen. At Lea I passed a line of cars illegally parked by mums picking up their offspring from school: Saab, Volvo, Saab, Range Rover, Audi, Volvo . . . and I thought of the cars that had passed while I was waiting to use the phone at Nantyglo: Cortina, Fiesta, Cherry, Mini, Escort . . . Yes, I know that's too pat. I tried to rationalise my distaste. This is pretty countryside, fertile, productive, good farming land. People work hard to get enough money to live here, to escape as I would from urban dreariness into a version of the rural idyll. Why not? I couldn't answer then and I can't now, although I can interject an anecdote which seems to me to amplify, if not actually confirm, my misgivings. Recently a very bad author, resident in Salop, came to our shop to sign copies of his book. We got talking about Shropshire and its marvels. 'Yes, it is lovely,' he said, 'though of course we've got Telford now, the New Town. It's full of people *you and I* don't want there . . . Liverpudlians.' Far be it from me to tar the entire upper-middle class with the same brush, but I do detect among a number of them the conviction that a certain type of English countryside – the rolling-hills-and-villages-half-as-old-as-time sort – is theirs by right, and furthermore that they are somehow the *real* English, some sort of naturally (or super-naturally) superior race. I think my eyes must have popped a bit at his remark, because he sidled off rather abruptly, like an animal which finds it has been trying to mate with the wrong species.

Past a sign for May Hill, the huge hump crested with a Mohican of trees which is visible for miles up the Severn, and which is a famous area for psychedelic mushrooms and people who think Hawkwind are far out: then Huntley, where one of the houses was painted dark green, a big mistake but a sure sign that English individualism is alive and well. And then Birdwood, where I chanced to glance at the mileometer and found that I had come exactly 2,000 miles.

Birdwood is unprepossessing, but I pulled over in front of an attractive farmhouse and took a celebratory photograph of Blodwen. On the other side of the road I found a most curious chapel, shaped like an ordinary house, but with a porch stuck to one end and round-arched windows only on one side, the other walls blank. So I photographed that, too.

Come back all I said about the upper-middles. I have evidence that they may not entirely be to blame. Emerging at the bottom of a particularly steep hill and series of bends, and thinking how pleasant the trees looked in their full blossom, I spied a cottage, quaint and charming. On its gatepost a poker-work nameplate: 'GRUMPYVILLE'. No *Telegraph* reader would ever perpetrate such a thing.

Gloucester has the reputation of being a rough town on a Saturday night. It is more heavily industrialised than any other southern cathedral city I know, and looks from a distance like Rugby or Doncaster. The traffic around it was very snarled-up; I decided to press on to Cheltenham, and as a result noticed that the ring of factories I remembered is now itself surrounded by an enormous series of new housing estates. I very much hope that this doubtless well-deserved success is not allowed to encroach too far into the mysterious floodplain of the lower Severn, a country of enormous atmosphere and curiosity. A little north of there, near Tewkesbury, is one of the most bizarre stretches of land I've found in Britain. It consists of a few square miles of fen where, in high summer, one can walk through gigantic reedbeds like sugar-cane plantations, and from which one can occasionally see both the Cotswolds on the eastern side and the Malverns on the western, giving a most curious sensation of being outside normal space, tucked away in a hidden fold of the eiderdown of fields and hills.

I once spent part of a summer helping my brother, who was then at Oxford, measure hillsides with a curious and ungainly piece of equipment called a pantograph. This has nothing to do with *Jack and the Beanstalk*; it determines the angle of the slope. We worked on a series of Cotswold escarpments near Gotherington. Despite the tiring and tedious business of recording one metre of hill at a time from bottom to top, it was a wonderful experience, for there is nothing quite like the sensation of standing on those hills and looking out over the broad floodplain of the Severn to the Malverns, May Hill, the Herefordshire marches and the dim Black Mountains of Wales. It is arguably the view which comes closest to the ideal of the imagery of Britain which has served so well over the years in advertisements for Nuclear Power, cake, any political party you care to name, beer, the Army (recruitment posters in both wars showed strapping young patriots against this sort of background), and anything which might remotely be described as being 'Traditional', 'Natural', or 'Full of Country Goodness'. The power of this archetype in British advertising can be demonstrated by the fact that Patrick and I set new world records that summer for the consumption of Wadworth's 6X Bitter and Mr Kipling's Cherry Slices.

But it is a sad fact that when I remember this awe-inspiring view (it is perhaps best from Bredon Hill, beloved of UFOlogists) I don't recall the distant whirr of a tractor or the bleating of sheep. Nor, sadly, does the internal gramophone cue Elgar or Vaughan Williams. From the top of the Cotswolds the noise of the M5 in the valley bellow sounds like an oncoming tank regiment. Lead and carbon dioxide are not the only pollutants for which the internal combustion engine is responsible. If you close your eyes up there you might be standing on the Willesden flyover.

Gloucester runs on into Cheltenham, or 'Regency Cheltenham' as it proclaims itself on a Tourist Information board in a lay-by a couple of miles out of town. There is a useful map to prevent you from parking somewhere unsightly when you get there. Hands up all those whose worst suspicions were confirmed when the Cheltenham Tories had that bloodletting over the 'selection' of a black candidate. Strangely Cheltenham too, for all its mythological status as the Baden-Baden of Britain, is not a place where one hangs around alone when the pubs close. I must confess to disliking Regency architecture in large quantities; it somehow manages to be both airy-fairy and Germanically strait-laced. For a famously gay and naughty era it is remarkably anaemic. Much more interesting are the series of mid–20th century flats one passes on the ring-road, not that you'll believe me. They show just how successful modern mass housing can be; they are 'traditional' in the sense of referring to but not apeing the past – they look modern, not old, but at ease with their older surroundings. They are well-built, laid out in communal gardens, have ample parking off the street, and as a result they are unvandalised, clean, attractive and, one hopes, safe. They derive from the English Arts-and-Crafts movement which produced, or influenced, both the cottagey style of Ashbee and the 'Georgian' style of Lutyens. Both these developments contributed immensely to the outstanding success of much early twentieth-century British housing: Letchworth and Hampstead Garden Villages, Bournville, and the council estates of Norwich, which delegates from cities all over Europe came to admire. Yet this tradition was abandoned for an inappropriate fake modernism and has not been returned to since, although there are hopeful signs. Well, it is Cheltenham, I suppose; you wouldn't expect it to look like Brixton. But that only shows how badly betrayed our inner cities have been; *mens sana in civitate sana*.

Ahead was Cleeve Cloud, the thousand-foot Cotswold scarp which overlooks Cheltenham. Housing has run riot along the lower slopes northward to Bishop's Cleeve, trying to rise a few feet up in order to get a view across the Severn, straining a few more feet to see over the roof of the last house, and so on . . . I swung along the escarpment looking for a turn to Winchcombe, for there more than anywhere I would be able to judge how the Cotswolds have fared since I had last visited them. I remembered Winchcombe, a little town in a steep valley, as being almost perfect: a Saxon burgh still full of medieval and later splendours, all in the honey-coloured limestone which perhaps more than any other material has come to symbolise the English ideal of rural buildings completely in harmony with their setting. Winchcombe, alas, is now full of ostentation, flashiness and snobbery – 'Exclusive' developments, art-dealers, estate-agents, brash advertising signs and ersatz rusticity. I got out and strolled around, remembering a sleepy place where a dog might lie all day in the road and only get run over once or twice. It's not easy for someone of my political sentiments to like a place which has a Conservative Working Men's Club, but ten years ago I was seduced by its beauty and quietness and integrity . . . its *rightness* if you'll forgive the pun. Now it's gone. Is it inevitable that such places must be destroyed by people who love them, like corny romantic heroines? Isn't it possible to leave somewhere alone, to understand that a place can only take so much before it becomes something else? Compromise here has meant not a compromise between development and conservation, which might have been a success, but the compromise of values, of responsibilities. Why should a town not be counted a work of art like anything else? If five people, or five hundred, jointly own a Van Gogh, do they have to cut it into little pieces in order to share it? Is one of them allowed to paint out his little square and insert an advertisement in its place? Winchcombe is no different in its decline from a hundred others. Everywhere there are villages which time and chance have brought to some kind of wholeness but which are now 'spoiled' – they have been changed out of character, and the new character is not as good.

I don't believe that history produces ideals, or permanences, or that history's happy chances should be pickled for all time. But if chance has arrived at a work of art, we should at least do our best to ensure that what we change we change artfully.

The Cotswolds are famous because of their villages, not because of the hills themselves. In fact the hills, for hundreds of years sheep-grazed but now almost entirely under the plough, are bare, cold and tedious. All the villages lie in the narrow valleys along the clear streams which flow east into the Thames basin; there's no water higher up.

Going to Oxford was a mistake. My motives were sound; in the first place the contrast with the Valleys could hardly be starker, and in the second the lure of a flat, heating, a bath and good company was irresistible. But Oxford is not easily compared with anywhere, even Cambridge. It is a lunatic lucky dip of arcane tradition, architectural splendour, industrial workhorse and tourist trap. After the apparent simplicities of Wales and the Cotswolds it was too much to grasp. Was it a city or a confection? Being a stranger in Oxford is like looking at a wedding-cake without being able to eat it.

Mysteries everywhere: why was that American woman making a video of her husband entering the Edinburgh Wool Shop? What was that wildly gesticulating French schoolteacher saying to the horde of nose-picking, snogging teenagers who blocked the entrance to Christ Church? Why is Oxford so full of (a) beautiful women and (b) winos? Were my eyes deceiving me or was it ludicrously easy to distinguish Town from Gown?

I wandered around at a loss, taking photographs in the hope that somehow everything would gel and I would be able to seize Oxford, reduce it to a neat parcel of words and pictures and spirit it away in the car. There is much less to all this than meets the eye, I told myself, but the eye is bamboozled by all the finery and frippery and felicitous falderal. But I couldn't penetrate it. It is a poetic city, suggestive rather than blunt; poetic not in the dreaming-spires way but because it harbours oddities, quirks, incidents whose meaning may only be guessed at rather than understood. Where else would you find a man waiting at a bus stop with a bucket of ice? Oxford is mysterious in a way that few British cities manage; mysterious in the way that Paris is, melancholy and enigmatic. The air of secrecy and exclusion is overwhelming; there are enormous, ornate, *closed* doors everywhere. So much ornament and dignity and formality must, one feels, have been designed to deflect attention from what lies beyond. The battling crowds and groaning traffic do not break this spell, indeed they accentuate it, for when you turn off St Giles's or Cornmarket into some maze of quiet alleys it is like stepping out of a party into a room which is empty except for three people in the far corner who were whispering together until the moment you entered. And if you are English then you feel that the party is in your house, yet you cannot identify these conspiratorial guests. It is the perfect city for detective fiction, though strangely the televised *Morse* uses the colleges as pretty backdrops rather than psychological amplifiers. It would be possible, I felt, to make a film in Oxford in which the crime was solved by reading the buildings and tasting the air instead of interviewing the suspects.

It is, however, a schizophrenic place in which the centre (almost entirely academic and commercial) and the suburbs (almost entirely industrial and residential) are continually at odds. It is possible to stand at Carfax and imagine that you are watching a battle between the academics all trying to go one way towards the Senior Common Room or the Bodleian, and the townies all trying to go the other, to BHS and the bingo, and each side resolutely refusing to acknowledge the existence of the other. The duality of the city is fractured again; each side has territorial rights in the others' half; the centre has the shops and the suburbs house the dons as well as the workers of the Rover plant. How wise were those planners of the 1950s and 1960s who decided to place the new universities of Lancaster, Canterbury, Warwick and Colchester *outside* their host cities. There was a good deal of pressure to go for city centre sites, which it was believed would help integrate the academic and the indigenous communities. This has never happened in 800 years in Oxford or in Cambridge.

The hapless tourists stand in this battleground getting in the way of both sides, getting their toes trodden on and their ankles flayed by bicycle pedals. They mingle and meander with the other slower element in the flow, the down-and-outs. I've often wondered why Oxford has such a high proportion of matt-haired, muttering bin-grubbers. Somebody once told me that Oxford was a historic crossroads for the traditional men of the road, a sort of bagperson's convention-centre. Someone else explained that London down-and-outs have a sort of summer break there; it's only a three-days' walk away. Yet another theory, which took into consideration the very high proportion of Scots amongst the vagrant populace, was that they were largely refugees from the redundant coalfield of Corby, in Northamptonshire, which had a largely Scottish workforce. I myself fancy that a good many of them were working on PhDs in quantum physics and cracked under the strain; a lot of them have the frightening visages of high intelligence tipped over the edge into mental instability, like Biblical prophets, wild-eyed and seeing in four dimensions.

There seemed to be more homeless people than ever, and more Irish and Scouse than formerly, though still lots of Scots. Maybe it is simply the scent of money which attracts them, the thousands of biddable tourists crammed into the small city centre; easier pickings than the unruly scowling hordes of Londoners. I counted 35 bagpeople in two hours. One was standing between two parked cars at the edge of St Giles's staring into space; he was still in exactly the same place two hours later, though the cars had changed. All the vagrants I saw were male, mostly in early middle-age, with a few old-timers and a smattering of youths. The latter were distinguished by their sociability, sitting in little huddles in churchyards and shop doorways, though apparently with little to say to each other. They may have been postgraduate students doing serious research into the effects of glue fumes and huge amounts of Cyprus Sherry, but I doubt it.

I wandered purposelessly the length and breadth of the city centre, gently as this was supposed to be a rest day, photographing passing traffic, architectural ornament and closed doors. I climbed the narrow iron staircase up Carfax Tower and dutifully photographed the view, watched the groups of people below fragment and coalesce. I pushed along Cornmarket and sneaked – no, snuck – down alleys, watching for the miraculous. Oxford's atmosphere of poetic enigma manifested itself from time to time in sights which seemed bizarre only because of their setting: lovers under a bridge; a pallid, wisp-haired face at a high garret window; a gowned figure running from one doorway and vanishing into another. But Oxford like any academic centre has its out-and-out wackos, like the portly man with side-whiskers bicycling in an ulster, wellingtons and a yellow beret. The tourists in fluorescent shell-suits seemed not to notice anything unusual, flowing in and out of shops and quads with an air of polite boredom, or sitting on cold steps scoffing hamburgers. Perhaps at that very moment, beyond the door they have their backs to, some secret deal is being struck; biotechnological or nuclear research in exchange for a safe house in Tripoli or Moscow. Or certain photographs are being redeemed for cash; Oxford is incredibly sexy because in the British psyche, sex is so strongly associated with secrecy and guilt. It must be the perfect city for sex in the afternoon, hidden away in a quiet room above the crowds, safe behind the barriers of class, convention and élitism. No need for a 'Do Not Disturb' sign here: Oxford has the words written all over it.

A city of gurus, lovers, madmen and tramps. And who's to say that one may not become another, if it's convenient? In an open city full of closed doors, a city which thrives on paradox, the millions of watching eyes guarantee that invisibility is possible, privacy assured. For the eyes are watching the face and not the hands. A lovely face, the face of a beautiful spy.

PERRY BARR

Property, postmodern precinct, polytechnic

It was difficult to leave Oxford. My friend's flat, a tiny and expensive breeze-block box, had seemed palatial, her sofa a bed of down. Good talk, good food, reminiscences, plans . . . so easy to slip out of a journey too far and find yourself at rest.

I headed north to Banbury, a town where as a child I had been able easily enough to picture the fine lady upon her white horse, and had been delighted to find the place covered with custard powder from the Birds factory. The opening up in the late '80s of the so-called Banbury Corridor by the new M40 has put paid to its charm: now it is an ultra-modern little town, gleaming with steel and mirrored glass, a miniature Milton Keynes. Big new estates, and a new black and Asian population have completed Banbury's transformation from a sleepy market town.

As I crossed the new motorway, a heavy black cloud blew up and released a violent sleet shower. By the time it had blown over I found that somehow I had taken the wrong road, heading north-east to Coventry rather than north-west toward Stratford and Birmingham. I cut across country through Warmington, which has a massive green surrounded by prosperous-looking houses of various dates; they have the sleek look of country houses inhabited by city folk. Then up a sharp little escarpment, one of many cutting across this country, part of the geological complex of Edge Hill. The steep climb led on to a very flat plateau of rich red soil and crumbly sandstone. The road was stained rose-pink by the dust. Suddenly it swerves sharply and runs along the top of the Edge itself. I got out and crossed the road to the spinney which hangs on the lip of the escarpment. The land which stretches away below is totally flat, giving you the impression of being much higher up than you really are, a dizzying sensation like being in a hot air balloon. The billiard table of the Midlands, sprinkled with farms, small factories and a barracks among the fields, looks so completely different to the land through which I had come, that I felt I had accidentally stumbled upon something more significant than a mere hillside. It seemed to be the boundary between one domain and another, as at Montgomery; a place where the change in the land must, one feels, give rise to changes in temperament and culture. The geographers of Victorian times made a whole pseudo-science out of the influence upon temperament of topography and climate; it is an appealing 'common-sense' notion, like phrenology or physiognomy. Edge Hill is also a place where one can very easily imagine gazing down on Royalist and Parliamentarian troops locked in indecisive bloodshed.

Edgehill village has a most extraordinary pub, the Castle Inn, a tall folly built to resemble a graceful medieval tower. The road becomes increasingly bumpy; there are frequent 'Risk of Grounding' signs, presumably due to the frangible nature of the underlying rock. Where this is quarried, the freshly-cut damp rock is a vibrant orange-pink, almost day-glo. It must be mined for building-sand, as one can break the stone between one's fingers.

Coming down off Edge Hill into the rolling countryside of Warwickshire, the sky once again turned black and in the eerie light the pinkish sand on the road turned blue-mauve. I felt as if I had taken some pleasant psychedelic drug; Blodwen turned yellow and the green trees reddish-brown. I was expecting another sleet shower, or perhaps a sudden hailstorm; instead it began to snow gently. Even after the cloud had passed the occasional flake would drift down miraculously out of a clear blue sky. As I came over the last little scarp beneath Edge Hill the land opened up to the south-west, and again I had the feeling of entering another realm, or re-entering it, for this is once again the fringes of the Cotswolds. It seems that Edge Hill is the nexus of three discrete territories; from it you are led away into the Midlands, or down into the Thames basin, or south-west to the Severn. The road became a tiny, rutted track covered with loose stones, manure and mud as I came down through Winderton, a steep little place which is more a collection of farms than a village, with the road blurring between one farmyard and the next under the muck.

The next village, Brailes, was where my father's parents retired to. My grandfather was a Methodist priest, and the house they retired to is a converted Methodist chapel in the middle of the village. It was built on a Quaker burial ground; when they were moving in a figure in a wide-brimmed black hat and a black frock coat walked through the living-room and out into the garden, where he vanished. He never troubled them again; just checking them out, I suppose. As a child I never sensed anything uneasy about the place. The little motte called Castle Hill, however, felt thoroughly magical, as if it might harbour sleeping knights. It still does.

Brailes church is magnificent, a sign of long-vanished prosperity, as are the many fine houses round about. Alas, today the village has a faintly desperate scruffiness; I wonder if the Banbury bubble has burst. It might well be Ambridge, I suppose, a working Warwickshire village rather than a Birmingham dormitory. Above the village (really two, Upper and Lower Brailes joined in a straggle a couple of miles long) is Brailes Hill, like Bredon a lone outlier adrift from its mother range, and similarly exhilarating to stand on. (Since the journey I have discovered that in the opinion of David Icke, the New Age visionary and apologist, Brailes Hill is one of the three 'Chakras' or key energy-points of the British Isles, the others being the Needles and, I think, Lindisfarne. Persons wishing to unblock the energy-channels and thus free Britain from a multitude of unpleasant symptoms of materialism such as the desire to build motorways and nuclear power-stations are invited to climb Brailes Hill and do various inexplicable things with rocks, dowsing-sticks and themselves. If I thought it might help prevent the spread of shell-suits, gambling-machines in pubs, and half-digested esoteric lore I myself would be up there in a flash.)

Four miles further up the road, Shipston-on-Stour, unlike Brailes, is definitely on the up. Traffic crawls through its tiny but very smart-looking medieval streets, and there are bright new showhouses and a mill converted into flats on the outskirts. Brailes lies between Shipston and Banbury but seems to have missed out, but then perhaps the success of the two towns is unrelated.

Across the Foss Way, the greatest Roman Road in Britain, stretching form the Dorset coast to Lincoln, and part of which I was to travel down a few days later in Somerset. And so to Stratford-upon-Avon, which has never had any difficulty turning a bob or two.

I suppose rape is not too strong a word for what has been done to Stratford, although its location on flat marshy ground can never have been very exciting. I cannot think of anywhere, however, which manages to combine world fame and sheer dullness in quite the same way. Most of it resembles an airport: the same vast expanses of tarmac and low-slung rectangular modern buildings, flagpoles, scurrying coaches and shops full of garbage. The remaining older buildings in the centre, which do not amount to much, sprout these days from acres of paved precinct so that they look like reconstructions in a theme-park (Bardsville, perhaps). The hotels, doubtless entirely necessary due to the fantastic volume of unsuspecting Americans and Japanese who are bussed in, might look fine as car-factories in Latvia but are completely inappropriate in a small Warwickshire market-town, and the theatre, surely the one building above all which ought to be distinctive and memorable, looks like a branch of ASDA.

Shakespeare's birthplace itself can only be reached via a Visitor's Centre housing an exhibition of plastic armour and similar stuff from BBC productions; the house itself, complete with rusty burglar alarm, is tatty on the outside and uninteresting within. Bemused Japanese wander around outside among the shop displays of Union Jack boxer shorts and Ann Hathaway tea-towels. Having been belched out of the far end of the Shakespearience they stand clutching their pewter maquettes of the bearded Bard contemplating the difficult choice between the Coriolanus Fish Bar and Mistress Quickly's Olde Englishe Bun Shoppe. (Why not 'bunne'?)

In the name of Culture the place has been turned into a cross between Great Yarmouth sea-front and Slough. It's like going to a zoo and finding that all the animals are inside their dens; there is absolutely nothing to see. It is purely and simply a trap, a monstrous slot-machine based on the promise of cultural glamour but delivering only Spud-U-Like and Kylie Minogue T-shirts. For God's sake, they might at least have the decency to flog Gielgud T-shirts, or knickers imprinted with Judi Dench. William Shakespeare's ghost has, I'm sure, long since fled screaming to somewhere more civilised.

I went north into the Forest of Arden and then through Henley-in-Arden, a town which has one of the finest main streets I've ever seen, a wonderful range of the best of British architecture from Elizabethan to Victorian, and entered the Birmingham commuter belt. The first of the city's high-rise blocks soon came into view almost among the fields. They looked all right, but I wonder if they have the shops and services which such dwellings were originally intended to complement and which have so rarely been provided in developments of this kind. Without them, being stuck seven miles from central Birmingham at Druid's Heath must be thoroughly miserable, in spite of the greenfield location.

There is no factory belt as one approaches Birmingham from this angle, no lorry parks or waste ground waiting for development. Indeed the southern side of the city is about the most pleasant stretch of suburbia a major conurbation could wish for. Feeling that I might be biased because I was born there, I tried to be critical, but all seemed very green and pleasant. A few miles away the giant Longbridge car plant admittedly looks like a giant car plant, but otherwise a succession of quiet suburbs and swallowed-up villages, full of parks and trees and well-served by arterial roads and suburban rail lines takes one right into the city centre.

I went to look at the house I was born in, at Bournville, the model suburb built by the Cadbury family for the workers of the chocolate factory. It is a remarkable place, a great advertisement for benevolent capitalism. Leafy, cottagey, hushed ... a little dull, perhaps, but built to exacting standards and jealously preserved ever since. So out-of-key is Bournville now with the run of British suburbs that it is difficult to believe that it was built for, and to an extent still houses, ordinary working people. The atmosphere is identical to an exclusive estate. Indeed Bournville is so pleasant that one wonders why any other type of housing was ever contemplated, particularly since this was the result of private rather than public enterprise. It has schools, libraries, a swimming pool, sports facilities, parks, a boating lake, a hospital, even a Greek Orthodox church, incongruously built in Byzantine style but in the same orangey-red brick as the rest of the suburb. As for the house I was born in, one of the earliest on the estate and a thoroughly ordinary semi, stare at it as I might I could dredge up no memories of it whatsoever.

Compared with the social housing of the 1960s and 1970s, Bournville is a miracle; the cost must have been immense, yet presumably the Cadburys regarded it as money well spent. They were no fools. They wouldn't part with their money simply to ease their consciences, but in order to provide a healthy, well-educated, contented workforce. Yet if someone was to copy their example today they would be accused of mimicking Japanese rather than British capitalism. Today the factory, itself well ahead of its time in terms of provision for its employees (still ahead, if truth be told) also houses the visitor's centre 'Cadbury World', a sort of Willy Wonka in Brum. Ploughing private profit back into local communities is today one of the lynchpins of Green politics. It makes sense, but you don't need the historic example of Cadbury's or Kawasaki's to prove that. Everywhere the people who worked in the powerhouses of industrial Britain, however poorly housed and shabbily treated, demonstrated real affection for and pride in the factories at the heart of their communities, whether in Jarrow or Clydeside, Cumbria or South Wales. How much stronger those emotional ties would be then if the workplace provided not just the wages but other fruits of labour: houses, hospitals, schools, community centres. It's easy to be cynical about the idea on paper – the Company owning you body and soul – and it's quite possible to find examples where there are less pleasant aspects to the system. But it's difficult and churlish to find fault with Bournville, given the many tragedies which litter Great Britain – Moss Side, Brixton, Handsworth and the like.

I backtracked a couple of miles to Northfield, where we moved when I was a toddler, to find it much as I remembered, including the incredibly ugly house we inhabited. Northfield is a swallowed-up village which is hidden among crowded roads and dense Victorian suburbs. It still feels very removed from the city.

I shot a roll of film – behaving like a tourist in my own history – and fought my way into central Brum, happy that the stage of my very ordinary childhood dramas remained intact, but unable to decide why I felt this relief.

Negotiating the bizarre maze of the city centre was an experience which left me feeling as if I had gone ten rounds with an anaconda. Birmingham is quite hilly; the Victorian buildings around Corporation Street and New Street form steep chasms, still utterly black in places, though enormous chunks were bombed to smithereens and a great part of the centre may justifiably be described as concrete jungle. Only Coventry, as I remember it from thankfully brief experience, is uglier and more totally under the rule of the internal combustion engine. New roads triumph over everything here; they smash through old districts, or tunnel under them or are carried above them on stilts. The Bull Ring is perhaps the most notorious example in Britain of how not to improve a city centre, a filmset for *Death Race 1965*. The citizens take refuge on spindly, windswept walkways and bridges or in dank subways, or up immense towers of flats. I can't imagine that Birmingham has much of a problem with vandalism. How would you decide where to start?

It was 6.15 when I hit downtown Perry Barr, in the north of the city near Aston. The streets seemed to be deserted, though when I got out in a lay-by at the side of the dual carriageway a small black boy somehow wove through the traffic to ask what I was taking photographs of.

'Everything,' I replied. 'The whole lot.'

'What for?'

'Fun.' I couldn't think of a sensible reply. He seemed satisfied with this and scooted off.

First impressions through tired eyes: not a place at all, a mere area. Old and new factories, old and new houses, old and new shops all jumbled up every which way and divided into irregular islands by gigantic roads, flyovers and underpasses. Next to the railway station a shopping precinct which looked to have been built in the early 1970s, now abandoned and ready for the ball and chain. On the other side a brand-new shopping precinct in blue-painted steel girders and glass looking like the Snowdon Aviary crossed with the Palm House at Kew. High-rise, mid-rise and old terraced houses. A vast brutalist block which proved to be Birmingham Polytechnic. A dog track. Allotments. A sign next to a pedestrian crossing singing the praises of the City Council, erected by the City Council and mentioning in passing that Birmingham is now the home of the English National Opera and Simon Rattle. I wonder if he lives in Perry Barr, I thought, and went in search of accommodation.

Instead of having the gumption to ask directions to the nearest B&B zone, I decided to drive north along the main road and try the first place I came to. Unfortunately, this proved to be in Lichfield, 25 miles away. I drove for almost an hour through the endless semis of Kingstanding and Sutton Coldfield and then decided, after a brief spin around Lichfield, that perhaps after all I would kip in the back of the van, and spent another 40 minutes searching the area for a suitable lay-by, to no avail. Finally as it was growing dark I found the Tourist Information Centre and blessed them for sticking a list of local guesthouses on their door. The fourth one had a room, and I was very glad to be in it, for it was to be a ferociously cold night. For reasons best known to themselves none of the guesthouses had signs outside; I expect I had passed dozens on the way to Lichfield without realising it. But then it's that kind of area; on the way, I had passed a sign outside a pub which read 'MOTORCYCLISTS BY APPOINTMENT ONLY'. It brought to mind the unlikely picture of a gang of Hell's Angels all heading for the nearest phonebox to book in.

Two curious coincidences at the guesthouse: the owners' daughter was dyslexic, which gave rise to a long conversation about the difficulty of diagnosis – not until the age of 14 in this case; much too late. She had nevertheless just passed her secretarial exams, but this was small compensation for years of traipsing around specialists who were apparently unaware of the symptoms and schools who were sometimes sympathetic but just as often convinced that the girl was dim-witted. Secondly, the landlady's sister ran the campsite at Applecross. Was it raining when you were there, they asked. You bet, I replied, and they nodded sagely.

I ate an excellent Indian meal in a deserted restaurant in the city centre, despite the attentions of about 14 waiters who took it in turns to come and ask if everything was all right between each mouthful. In the morning I felt duty bound to go and see the cathedral, which is not particularly large but so purely Gothic that it is tremendously impressive; so many English cathedrals are in a mess of consecutive architectural styles that it is refreshing to see one which has come out more or less as the architect intended. In the town, which is oddly untouched by the proximity of Birmingham's industrial might (the cathedral alone is sooty-black), large coaching inns and fine Georgian houses give a properly Johnsonian atmosphere to the place. It is the civic equivalent of steak-and-kidney pudding, dumplings and ale. The good Doctor's solemn face is everywhere, naturally.

Back through the smug, dissembling villas of Sutton Coldfield into the raw mess of northern Birmingham. I parked in the shadow of a small power-station next to some allotments, a workshop making office furniture and the Ansells Brewery Social Club. They drink the beer they make, you'll be pleased to hear. Glad somebody does.

Once more in Perry Barr I went into the new One-Stop Shopping Mall. As these places go it isn't unpleasant, being tall, light and airy and still new enough to be thoroughly clean. Apart from the usual chainstore jewellers and shoeshops there is a 'covered market' of fruit and veg, knitting wools, sweets and so on. Many of the larger units were as yet unoccupied. The ubiquitous weeping fig trees tried hard not to look plastic; the piped muzak was surprisingly good, Robert Cray's classy svelte blues if I'm not mistaken. Although it might be utter hell on a busy day, at this early hour with the sari-clad or beturbanned stallholders laying out their wares it was painless enough. I felt I might easily find myself wandering through in it in a daze, giving my credit card here and there to people with nice teeth; the ambience does as it is supposed to and lulls you into wanting to buy things, which is why I don't have a credit card.

It is difficult to imagine that the One-Stop will go the same way as the

Newtown Centre, the grim pre-stressed concrete fortress abandoned a few yards down the road. For a start, the steel and glass architecture of post-modernism looks a good deal more difficult to vandalise, but also the building is far more pleasant. Another difference is that the One-Stop appears to be being promoted as a city amenity rather than a local one: there is an enormous carpark and a purpose built bus-terminus (with decent shelters for once) and the railway station across the forecourt. At the back of the precinct are several huge superstores, Halfords and ASDA and Texas and so on, so it looks to have a better chance of success than the Newtown, which was altogether less ambitious. Still, it is extraordinary that such a vast construction as the Newtown Centre should have had such a short life and have failed so utterly. The One-Stop has transformed Perry Barr, which beforehand must have been exceptionally dowdy. As it is, apart from the giant Lego polytechnic, the One-Stop is just about all Perry Barr has to offer. The oldest rows of Victorian shops are mostly abandoned, apparently held together by flyposted rock concert ads; the later ones look to be in the process of being superseded by the new 'covered market'.

I sat in the weak sunshine outside the One-Stop and watched the Polytechnic students emerging from the station and weaving through the subways and bridges across the Walsall road; an equal mix of Asians, Caucasians and Blacks. Some of them bade farewell to their friends and headed off into the surrounding terraced streets, which gave me an idea. In the row of shops by the station was an estate agent's; I moseyed in and glanced around the advertisements, then collared a member of staff and grilled him on the local property market. As you might expect, the man was fairly cagey even though he knew I had no vested interest, no axe to grind; I suppose one gets into the habit of referring to a dump as an 'ideal starter home'. According to him the area was a 'good mix', which confirmed the visual impression I had gained that it was a patternless jumble. There certainly seemed to be a lot of property for sale in both up- and down-market areas. Apart from Perry Barr itself, which is largely very late Victorian and of fairly roomy terraces, the agency covered Witton, with a high concentration of smaller, older terraces and post-war council flats, Handsworth, still largely an Afro-Caribbean enclave but according to my source 'definitely on the up' (I wonder if he meant that the population was changing or prospering), Handsworth Wood, a middle-class ghetto of quiet 1930s semis, and parts of Kingstanding and Great Barr, two gigantic regions of inter-war ribbon and speculative housing. Prices start at about £29,000 for an unimproved two-bedroomed terrace in Witton or Handsworth, though an end-terrace with all mod. cons. in the latter might cost £50,000. To some extent this is due to the benign influence of the Polytechnic, with lecturers and technicians attracted to areas which are cheap, convenient and 'ideologically sound'; croissantification is in progress. At the top of the market, a five-bedroomed detached villa in Handsworth Wood might be £140,000.

Over the area as a whole the average was on the low side at £60,000. A good mix? It rather depends, I suppose, on whether it is a mix at all, or a series of mutually-exclusive islands. One area in Perry Barr is actually known as 'The Island'; it is completely cut off by huge dual carriageways, and prices are low there because getting off it, especially after dark, requires stamina and bravery if one is to negotiate the labyrinth of subways.

To complete my in-depth analysis I went to the library across the main road in the Birchfield Institute – Birchfield being another name for this part of Perry Barr, confusingly, as it also seemed to be part of Witton. I wandered past the sections on Romantic Fiction, Westerns, Urdu Literature and 'Self-Help' to the Local History shelves, but the only thing on Perry Barr was a little mimeographed pamphlet written in the early '80s. Still, I learned that 'Pirie' (Saxon) and 'Barre' (Celtic) were originally two separate manors which came under single ownership around 1090. There had been a prehistoric fortified camp in the area and Ryknild Street, the Roman military highway, passed through and is or was still visible in the local park. A local area called 'Halfway House' may dimly echo this route as it stands exactly midway between two major garrisons on the road, and would have had a fortlet or staging-post. Industry came very late to the area compared with most of the Birmingham conurbation; until the 1880s it was over-whelmingly rural with small cottage industries such as charcoal-burning, tanning, smithies and brick-making. Unusually, the railway arrived before the canals, in the 1830s, but no serious industry got under way until the turn of the century; there was a new 'model' dairy farm on the site of what is now the greyhound stadium as late as 1900; its farmhouse was demolished in 1981. The only exceptional turn of events in the area's long history was the development of Kingstanding, a paradigm of 1930s speculative development which, by the end of the Second World War, had a population of 65,000 – but with no shops, no cinemas, schools or hospitals and only seven pubs. The market-force run riot – yet people are still suspicious of town planning.

So Perry/Barr, dualistic from the first and until very recently no more than a scattering of hamlets and farms, has never been a place in the true sense at all. I was very struck with this apparent confirmation of my initial impression. Nobody has ever given it a focus, a centre; the One-Stop and the Polytechnic do not provide one because their populations are transient and diurnal and from outwith the area. It developed bit by bit, an unhappy amalgam of competing interests: transport, industry housing, shopping and education. In another place these might coexist perfectly harmoniously, but this can only happen if they are all there for the same reason – to serve the community which is also there. In Perry Barr these elements are not only geared to outside interests but the local population is also highly fractured and stratified wood an overall 'community' does not exist.

Not as drab as Kearsley, not as sad as Harrington, not as desperate as

Nantyglo, Perry Barr is a sort of post-modern place, a series of references to other things, a rabble without a cause. The first three places might inspire devotion or even pride. Perry Barr never could.

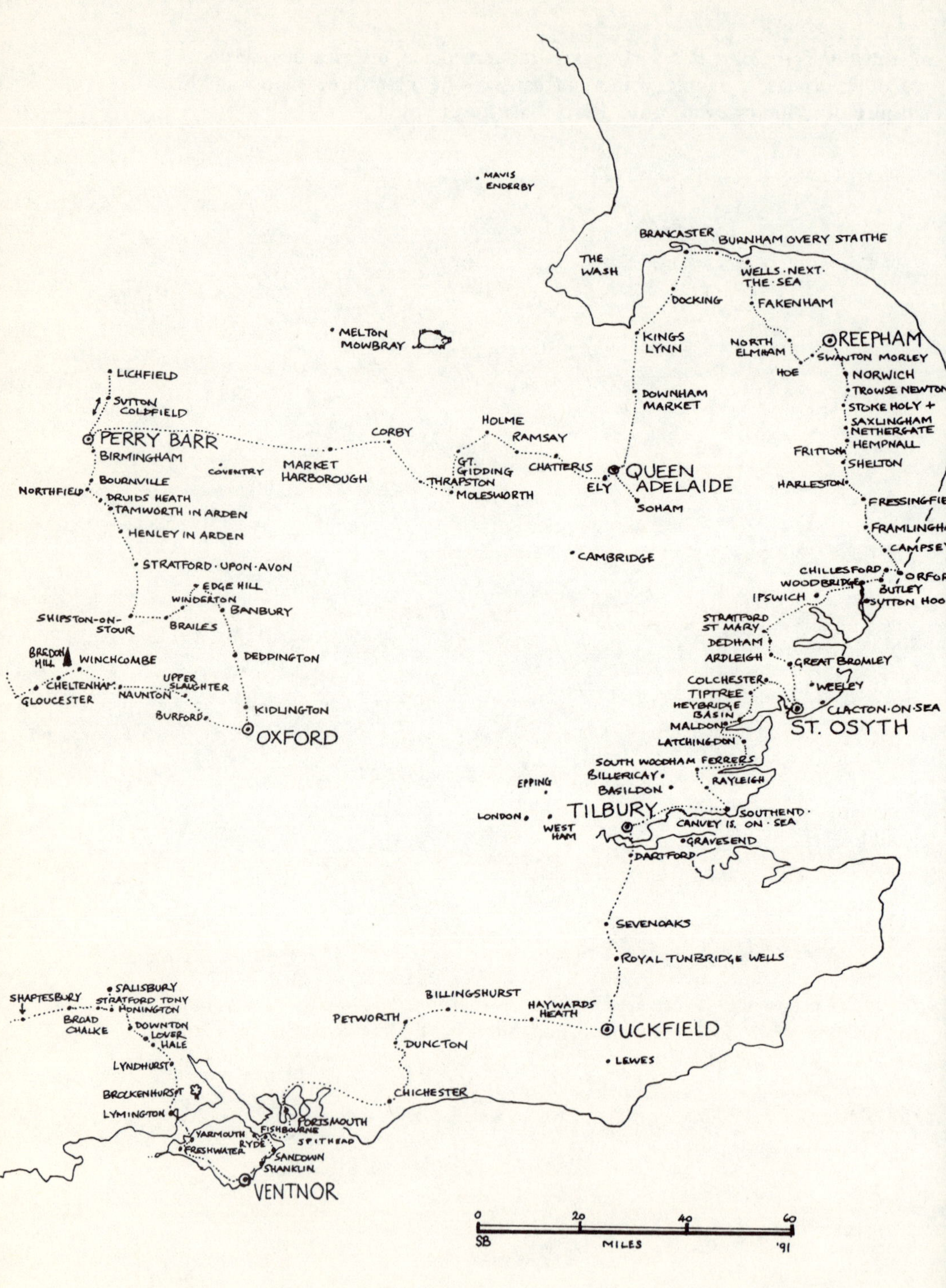

MAVIS ENDERBY
BRANCASTER
BURNHAM OVERY STAITHE
THE WASH
WELLS · NEXT · THE · SEA
DOCKING
FAKENHAM
KINGS LYNN
NORTH ELMHAM
REEPHAM
SWANTON MORLEY
HOE
NORWICH
TROWSE NEWTON
DOWNHAM MARKET
STOKE HOLY +
SAXLINGHAM NETHERGATE
HEMPNALL
FRITTON
SHELTON
MELTON MOWBRAY
LICHFIELD
SUTTON COLDFIELD
CORBY
HOLME
RAMSAY
HARLESTON
PERRY BARR
BIRMINGHAM
COVENTRY
MARKET HARBOROUGH
GT. GIDDING
THRAPSTON
CHATTERIS
QUEEN ADELAIDE
ELY
FRESSINGFIELD
FRAMLINGHAM
CAMPSEY
BOURNVILLE
NORTHFIELD
DRUIDS HEATH
TAMWORTH IN ARDEN
MOLESWORTH
SOHAM
HENLEY IN ARDEN
CAMBRIDGE
CHILLESFORD
ORFORD
WOODBRIDGE
BUTLEY
STRATFORD · UPON · AVON
IPSWICH
SUTTON HOO
EDGE HILL
WINDERTON
BANBURY
SHIPSTON-ON-STOUR
BRAILES
STRATFORD ST MARY
DEDHAM
ARDLEIGH
GREAT BROMLEY
BREDON HILL
WINCHCOMBE
DEDDINGTON
COLCHESTER
TIPTREE
WEELEY
CHELTENHAM
UPPER SLAUGHTER
HEYBRIDGE BASIN
NAUNTON
MALDON
CLACTON·ON·SEA
GLOUCESTER
BURFORD
KIDLINGTON
LATCHINGDON
ST. OSYTH
OXFORD
SOUTH WOODHAM FERRERS
BILLERICAY
BASILDON
RAYLEIGH
EPPING
LONDON
TILBURY
SOUTHEND
WEST HAM
CANVEY IS. ON · SEA
GRAVESEND
DARTFORD
SEVENOAKS
ROYAL TUNBRIDGE WELLS
SHAFTESBURY
SALISBURY
STRATFORD TONY
BILLINGSHURST
HAYWARDS HEATH
BROAD CHALKE
HONINGTON
DOWNTON
PETWORTH
LOVER
HALE
DUNCTON
UCKFIELD
LYNDHURST
LEWES
BROCKENHURST
CHICHESTER
LYMINGTON
YARMOUTH
FISHBOURNE
PORTSMOUTH
RYDE
SPITHEAD
FRESHWATER
SANDOWN
SHANKLIN
VENTNOR
0   20   40   60
SB   MILES   '91

QUEEN ADELAIDE

Quiet. Well, quite quiet

The motorway took me east from Birmingham in torrential rain, high winds and an unruly battalion of HGVs. I had had little difficulty in choosing my Q; apart from the charm of the name, I wanted to get round East Anglia before heading south and west again. Quadring in Lincolnshire was a possibility but a little too far north; Quidenham in Norfolk too distant; Quorndon in Leicestershire too near. I headed for Cambridgeshire.

The sheer torture of the wild and wet M6 prevented me noticing anything except the number of times I came close to death; only when I came off it near Lutterworth and the sun simultaneously appeared did I begin to look at anything other than the road ahead and the rear-view mirrors. The bland, green East Midlands gradually unrolled – very gradually, since east-west links are notoriously poor in this area. It is forgettable scenically, though the villages and towns look prosperous and seem to have been so always; the grand assurance of eighteenth-century success continuing through to the bland assurance of the present. Market Harborough typifies this region, the ultimate smug little shire town, inhabited by 40,000 variations on *Terry and June*. I had lunch there: a pork pie, since that is what the area is famous for. The pie was from Melton Mowbray. It didn't travel well.

Blodwen began to make odd noises – weird croaking sounds from somewhere in the rear – and my blood pressure rose accordingly. When I got out I saw that she was listing to starboard; the rear suspension had cracked somewhere on the bumpy country road. I decided to press on regardless and, apart from a sound like a ship breaking up whenever I took a sharp turn there seemed to be no cause for alarm. (Three months later there still isn't, except her impending MOT.)

'NORTHAMPTONSHIRE: ROSE OF THE SHIRES' boasted a roadside sign. I almost crashed the car laughing. Corby was next, unrecognisable as the depressed pit-town I had last seen in 1976. Now Corby is spruced up, with new offices and road systems, green and cheerful-looking. It even has a Tourist Information Centre – presumably redundant industry repackaged as 'Heritage' once more. I pottered along to Thrapston, on the Nene, which has become a centre for holiday boating and for fishing in the many flooded gravel pits round about. Northamptonshire's chief glory is its sacred architecture; as one progresses eastward the spires and towers of the churches vie to outdo each other in height and gracefulness. But the countryside, though easy on the eye, is curiously uninteresting, not least because it tends to roll just enough to bring the horizon to within half a mile or so of wherever you are standing. The farms are highly mechanised, with few remaining hedges or trees amongst the huge fields, and across every horizon seems to trundle a procession of heavy lorries on their way to or from the East Anglian ports.

Since the road on which I was travelling has been much widened and improved over the past 20 years there is little to see; it bypasses everything except the odd rabbit, which it pulps. I grew bored and turned off on to a section of the old main road running parallel to the new one, hoping to swing north and then cross eastwards to the Fens on country roads. The last few donkey-jacketed men were still tinkering with the junction; unfortunately they had not yet got round to replacing all the road signs, which were lying flat next to their post-holes. Thus I approached an unmarked 90° left-hand bend at around 50 mph, saw it too late, and at the last moment indicated right and shot straight on up a rough farm track, bouncing and skidding to a halt just short of a heap of excavated mud. This was the first of many excruciating corners in East Anglia, but I negotiated all the others with more decorum. After a long rest and a cigarette I reversed gingerly out and continued. Molesworth on the left, scene of so much passionate defiance, is a long, menacing collection of squat grey buildings covering up the end of the world. Now that it looks as if the world may end not with a bang but under the weight of discarded McDonald's wrappers, how distant those evil days of the early 1980s seem: a succession of more-or-less dead Soviet premiers, a United States president who could barely grasp the jokes on *Sesame Street*, and a spiteful megalomaniac British prime minister surrounded by thugs and spineless sycophants. The Falklands, Nicaragua, the Miners' Strike, Grenada . . . a strong feeling of teetering on the brink. Remember *Protect and Survive*? *Red Dawn*? *The Day After*? *When The Wind Blows*? Madness and malevolence everywhere; dark days. I remember a succession of news stories of families slaughtered by the mother or the father, convinced that they were only hastening the inevitable by a few months. Now, standing near the chain-link and razor-wire fence at RAF Molesworth, it is difficult to grasp the reasons for that perilous flirtation with Armageddon. Did they really believe that the end of the world was a price worth paying for sovereignty, democracy, capitalism or communism? The base looks inexplicable, extra-terrestrial. I turned away and stared at the gentle Cambridgeshire farmland, feeling that I ought to be weeping or shouting for joy. Were we all saved by the chance accession of a sane man, Gorbachev? What if he had failed? What if he fails yet? The mind cannot live with such thoughts for very long. I went away.

Cambridgeshire, though flatter than Northants, is more interesting to look at because the horizons have broadened out. Raised in the East, I felt a sudden hard twinge of regret at having left this vast simplicity. The new wheat rippled in the wind; the huge sky raced eastward. On a little strip of tarmac between the fields with no hedge or ditch I stopped the engine and listened. It was probably the quietest place I had been; no tumbling water, complaining sheep, undertone of distant traffic, just the exhalation of the wind and a skylark, invisible and all-pervading.

By far the most dangerous and hair-raising point in the entire journey came as I tried to cross the A1; ten minutes of sheer terror as I waited to pounce through four lanes of seamless high-speed traffic. A rise and a bend in either direction limited visibility to less than 200 yards, so that I had about a second in which to decide whether I could get as far as the central reservation, where I had to wait for another five minutes. Blodwen is not much good at pouncing. She can lurch or galumph, but needs plenty of time to think about a pounce.

One hundred yards beyond the far carriageway the soil abruptly turned jet black and I was in the Fens. Simultaneously the wind picked up and the road began to hump and curl at the edges like a British Rail sandwich. The fen peat contracts as it is drained, drying into a sort of fibrous compressed cake, and thus roads and buildings constructed a few years ago tilt and buckle as improved drainage gradually shrinks the ground beneath them. Fen roads are doubly treacherous, for though invitingly straight, they are often so corrugated as to practically tip you into the ditch which always runs alongside, and periodically they turn at right angles for no very good reason, a fact which the local council seems to assume you will be prepared for and so will not require advance warning of. Most roads are carried on embankments, the fields on either side having shrunk as they dried, so a mistake can either drown you or throw you 12 feet down into the beetroots.

The road into Ramsey flirts with the edge of the fen, and from time to time lifts a few feet off the peat on to the lip of the clay which overlies its rim. This elevation of no more than four or five feet is enough to give one a tremendous view over the levels northward, there being nothing in the way of hedges or fences and only the occasional line of poplars or birches as a windbreak. Not that these seem particularly effective; the wind had come round to the north-east and was ripping across the Fens from the Wash, shrieking through the crazily-leaning telegraph poles and bending the trees like rubber toys. Where the top-soil is dried out by the wind it turns a deep crimson. As the road nips on to the clay and back on to the peat it is extraordinary how everything changes: buildings, flowers, trees, the road itself.

Ramsey has everything I expected of the Fens: a magnificent tall church, houses with barely a right-angle between them, in the Dutch style with gables, lots of new bungalows, wrecked cars, decrepit sheds and a scrapyard. The Fens, like the extreme north of Scotland, is one of those places where nothing seems ever to be thrown away; things simply lie where they died. It is not unusual to see a small bungalow with a typically generous plot of land neatly sown with vegetables, a rickety chicken-run, a couple of geese and six or seven rusty wheel-less cars serving as hen-houses or simply scattered sculpturally around the garden. Ramsey is largely built in yellow Victorian brick; older buildings are comparatively rare as the ground has tended to weaken them irreparably. There is also a ruined abbey – the Fens seem to have attracted the more macho strain of early Christian, and there are many monastic foundations and ruins throughout the area.

Beyond Ramsey I followed the road along the Forty-Foot Drain, also known as Vermuden's Drain after the Dutch engineer who was largely responsible for bringing these swamps into cultivation. The sheer scale of the drainage work, involving the most minute judgments of gradient and sometimes the complete diversion of rivers for many miles, is breathtaking. I think the Fens are one of the wonders of Britain. The landscape is immensely powerful, riven by the huge perspectives of the canals and roads, a brute assertion of mankind's dominance over the forces of nature. Graham Swift's novel *Waterland* captures its atmosphere perfectly; what at first seems utterly simple, laid out as serenely as a chessboard, gradually invades the mind until its nakedness and titanic scale become weirdly oppressive. It is as if one is under a microscope, or indeed is a pawn on the board: there's nowhere to hide. Fenland people, I felt, must keep their eyes to the ground and concentrate on the unending vigil against the tricksy water. If you keep your head up to the horizon and the immense sky you will inevitably go mad. Not surprisingly, the Fens do have unusually high rates of suicide, mental illness, alcoholism, incest and retardation. They are lonelier than any mountain range.

I bypassed Chatteris, and crossed the Hundred-Foot Drain at Mepal, where there is what can only be described as a hill, about 30 feet high. Many fen villages have the word 'hill' in their names, but usually they are built on dead flat ground, often below sea-level: 'hill' means 'island' in this context. But from this genuine hill between Mepal and Sutton the most famous rise in the Fenland landscape was visible for the first time: the

190

extraordinary and tiny city of Ely crowned with its vast cathedral, a Fenland Avalon.

Ely Cathedral dominates the Fenland landscape for many miles in every direction, hovering in the sky in mute miraculous rebuke to the ungodly. The ground at the foot of its octagonal lantern tower is 85 feet above sea-level; its towers add a couple of hundred feet to that. In an area where buildings seem to cower from the incessant wind, where canal-side cottages may be lower down than the embanked surface of the water flowing past them, the effect is as awe-inspiring as its masons intended. The city itself is a compact collection of houses clinging to the steep hillside, now gradually extending on to the surrounding peat along the railways and roads, and with the traditional Cathedral Close and monastic buildings as weirdly disproportionate to the surrounding streets as the church itself. Despite the tiny hill, barely a mile across, the church managed until recently to preserve a large area of greensward and meadow near the summit. Financial pressure has forced the Dean and Chapter to sell off part of this for housing in the last few years; thus the order of 900 years is broken by the parsimony and philistinism of a 'conservative' government.

Queen Adelaide lies at the north-eastern foot of the hill. The road down to it meanders through scattered bungalows and light-industrial sheds, and the village itself proved to be a single street lined with Victorian villas and bungalows on both sides for about half a mile. Four railway lines come through the village; you cross the first by a bridge and the next three by level-crossings. Finally the road crosses the Great Ouse, here canalised and pencil-straight, and continues out of the village to Prickwillow. That, at first glance, was all there was to it, and at second glance too.

I was expecting to have to find accommodation in Ely, but a B&B sign beckoned at the roadside half-way along the street in Queen Adelaide itself. They had a room, the largest and one of most comfortable of the trip, with such unheard-of luxuries as a washbasin, double-glazing, a wardrobe and a wastepaper bin. The only other guest was a small wiry mysterious man in his 30s. He looked rather like the jockey John Francombe and spoke with the same twangy burr. He was slight enough to have been a jockey, but made his living entirely from betting, moving from one guesthouse to another around the racecourses of Britain. So far this year he was down £600; last year he had made £9,000. He did not much want to talk about it; he was superstitious about discussing his luck or his method. The £600 didn't worry him – he could win three times as much in an afternoon. In his best year he had made over twenty grand and he had never failed to break even. He studied the form with the ease which comes from complete familiarity. All the wisdom he would vouchsafe was this: the trick is to know when to stop. He had caught a cold in the rain at Newmarket the day before, and thought it might turn into flu. Just like anyone else this meant a few days off work.

The landlady recommended a pub in Soham for my evening meal. Thankfully the road was a wide, smooth, new one, for the wind was gusting over 60 mph and throwing the van about like a skateboard. It was worth the ten-mile drive, however: home-made steak-and-kidney pie with three vegetables, washed down with a pint of Ruddles County, for about £4. No jukebox. No fake horse-brasses. A friendly unsuspicious smile, and a log fire.

In the morning the gale was, if anything, stronger. Over breakfast I asked the landlady (a Londoner originally) who Queen Adelaide had been. 'I've always meant to find out,' she replied, 'I think she's something to do with Hereward the Wake . . . there's a lot of stories about him in these parts.' It turns out she was the wife of William IV, which dates the settlement, like Adelaide, Australia, to the 1830s. As for Hereward the Wake, he is indeed the chief hero of these parts, a minor Saxon landowner from Lincolnshire who led a series of guerilla campaigns against the Normans – the last Englishman to resist with any degree of success. He was also a bigamist and not averse to robbing churches.*

I put on a T-shirt, a lumberjack shirt, two sweaters and a windcheater in preparation for my investigation of this unremarkable little hamlet, and thus clad was able to remain outside for at least five minutes at a time. Whilst writing up my notes that morning I had serious doubts as to whether I would be able to find anything beginning with Q; the area is not noted for its Quince production, and if there were any queens other than the eponymous Addy they remained firmly in their closets. It was difficult to walk either into the wind or with it behind you. One side of my face became completely numb going one way and the other followed suit as I returned. In vain I searched for any remaining patches of Quagmire, but the area was thoroughly drained. There were no houses of Questionable Quality so far as I could see. At least it was quiet, I thought, standing in the middle of the level crossing to see how long it would be before either a train or a car showed up. Just then an ice-cream van, of all things, came along the street. Instead of a tinkling rendition of *Oranges and Lemons* or *Popeye The Sailor Man*, it used one of those car horns which plays part of a tune over and over again – in this case the first few bars of *Colonel Bogey* no less than 11 times in succession. Not surprisingly nobody wanted an ice-cream, and the van departed in the direction of Prickwillow, renowned for its tropical climate.

I suppose Queen Adelaide was laid out originally as a wharf on the Ouse from which heavy goods could be carted up to Ely, for the hill is at its gentlest on this side. Apart from a couple of small factories which give no clue from the outside as to their business, and a Wesleyan chapel, rather

* For the best account of the real Hereward see *Folk Heroes of Britain*, Charles Kightly, Thames & Hudson 1982, now sadly out of print

192

a pretty one, converted into a house, there is absolutely nothing unusual or interesting about it beyond the way it is cut into slices by the railway. Except, that is, for the experience of being in the Fens, in itself a very curious sensation. The uneasy angles of buildings, the crazily-leaning willows and poles, the constant hammering wind and the broken road surface all conspire to give an uneasy sense of impermanence. If global warming follows the gloomiest of current predictions Ely will once more be an inaccessible island, and Queen Adelaide will be washed away by the Ouse as it breaks its earthen bonds.

I drove up to Ely to look at the cathedral. The precincts were periodically criss-crossed by crocodiles of well-scrubbed children from Cathedral School, whose classrooms are scattered about the close in several beautiful old buildings. As for the cathedral itself, it gives the impression of being not so much a church, but as with the Ark of the Covenant in *Raiders of the Lost Ark*, a machine for talking to God. One can barely imagine the strength of motivation of those who built it, nor the colossal wealth they must have commanded. Christian faith as strong and militant as the faith of the most fervent Shia Muslim today produced this masterpiece of stone in a land of reeds and silt. Those descendents of its craftsmen who can be bothered to enter today are begged to give a few pounds to stop it falling down and are politely reminded what a cathedral is.

REEPHAM

Redundant railways, regeneration and renovation

I travelled north along, or rather below, the Ouse towards King's Lynn, into the teeth of the gale, barely managing 45 mph. I crossed into Norfolk at Brandon Creek and passed Southery (Blow-the-Wind-Southery) and Hilgay, crossed the Wissey and left the Fens, for the land climbs gradually toward Downham Market and the road skirts this eastern side just as the Ramsey road plays with the southern edge of the peat, allowing you to see an immense distance westward. Immediately substantial oaks and other trees appear and, for the first time in many miles, large country houses, for none could be built on the spongy fen.

Most of the buildings here (as in the Fens) are of red brick, very fine in texture and with a tendency to flake rather than crumble with age, leaving frontages with thousands of concave facets. But here and there are rubble-stone constructions, presumably limestone imported by boat via the Fenland waterways. Lynn itself is a mixture of flint and brick, an impressive little port with many magnificent buildings, some of great age. The outskirts are thoroughly industrial, but the town centre is laid out around an enormous market square fringed with opulent mercantile buildings and banks. The Dutch influence is striking; the orangey brick gives the place the look of a painting by de Hoogh, and the town's windy perch on the edge of the Wash gives the place the gleaming clear light of those Dutch townscapes, the buildings scrubbed-looking and sharp-edged. But the frequent use of knapped flints as ornament is thoroughly English; West Norfolk is chalky and flints are abundant. They have a strong dark-blue tinge in bright sunlight. It is fairly miraculous that so much of the town has survived, for severe floods are frequent here; several buildings have marks on their walls commemorating the high water-levels of particularly bad years. There are a dozen or so lines between one and five feet above ground level. The almost cathedral-sized church (really two churches together) has a lengthy dedication as befits such a huge and fine building – St Margaret of Antioch with St Nicholas and All the Virgin Saints. It also has two towers side-by-side and a Norman west end with walls which lean outwards at an alarming angle. Lynn has fine buildings from every century between the 11th and the 20th; although its chief glories are 17th and 18th-century, even the modern redevelopment of the shopping area is in keeping with its surroundings, and the state of preservation of, for instance, the large 13th-century timber house near the church is unbelievable. It also wears its success with a jaunty nautical air; many of the buildings are positively playful. Lynn never seems to have fallen on hard times; it is the only substantial port between Boston and Yarmouth and a natural staging-post for traffic between Norwich and the Midlands.

I had lunch in a coffee-and-bakery place, taking my time, glad to be out of the wind, although the sky was now completely clear. It was wonderful to hear real Norfolk voices again; the interrogative rise in every phrase and the long, relaxed vowels. 'Is that right?' is the typical Norfolk phrase, on three rising notes, the rhetorical answer to any imparted information. 'That's a bootiful day but that was raining when oi left the house.' 'Is that right?' And the Norfolk greeting, 'Are you all right?' – pronounced 'Aahy'awroit?' – only means 'hello'; if you answer 'Yes, thanks, how are you?' they look puzzled. The correct answer is 'Are you all right?' Two women were nattering away at the next table about their holidays: 'Hev yew got your foo-ty-graafs beck then moi dare?'

'Oi hev – Oi shoe them to you, dint oi?'

But don't make the mistake of presuming that the accent means that these are slow country folk – they're as sharp as knives and their architecture proves it.

Norfolk has the lowest highest point of any English county – barely 300 feet – though Coward was wrong about it being 'very flat'. I crossed the chalky, undulating and almost waterless countryside north-eastwards and emerged on the north Norfolk coast at Brancaster in the blinding white light unique to that shore. The westernmost part of north Norfolk is extremely depopulated, with villages often 12 or 15 miles apart, and the highly-mechanised denuded fields add considerably to the feeling that one is crossing a desert. The coast, however, has become an increasingly trendy resort and has been considerably gentrified: little galleries and craft shops abound and the smallest flint hamlet is likely to contain a delicatessen. This process is also measurable by the extraordinary cost of basic goods in many of the shops: at Wells-next-the-Sea a can of Coke cost me 55p. Here and there the semblance of traditional pursuits survives; there are still fishing boats hauled up on the shingle, herds of cows meandering along the seafront roads and across the dunes, and at Wells the odd coaster ties up next to the amusement arcade and the artists' supplies shop. Even the men of the soil seem to be caught up in the excitement of the social climb – I passed at least two asparagus farms.

Just as in the Cotswolds, where the sticking-on of pieces of limestone is thought to give credibility to shoe-box architecture, so here the addition of beach-flints in panels on the brick walls gives equally pathetic results. Actually, what little new development there has been goes almost unnoticed, and to be fair this is as much because of the generally thoughtful addition of new buildings as because of the sparseness of settlement in general.

On a sharp bend in the village of Burnham Overy Staithe I almost ran into a herd of Jersey cows being nudged along the road by a limping labrador – no humans were in sight. Damn good dog, I thought, if it can be trusted to bring in the cows along the public highway . . . can this be legal? But then all was revealed: a cow shot out of the doorway of the mill at the road-side, followed by a puffed and sheepishly-grinning farmer.

The wind off the sea (the road is separated from the shore by half a mile of dunes) was so fierce that every time I passed a gap or gateway in the hedge I almost lost control of the van as it lurched sideways. Intermittently it snowed, but for most of the time the sun shone brightly. I passed a pub called The Hero at Burnham, with a portrait of Nelson, a local lad. Long lines of pines trail down to the shore at Holkham, almost, it seems, into the sea, for the beach here is huge, about a mile wide when the tide is out. I remembered a friend at university telling me that they had once been about to take off all their clothes on this beach (even in summer it can accommodate a few thousand people and look deserted) when they were startled by the sudden appearance over a dune of a man in a grey raincoat and sunglasses and city shoes, followed shortly by a woman in a headscarf and quilted jacket surrounded by corgis. Sandringham is a short drive away.

A cream-coloured Morris Minor van passes in the other direction – hoot, flash, wave.

At Wells a solitary Chinese crewman was painting the bows of a small red coaster on an otherwise deserted quay. The channel dredged beside the mile-long harbour-bar through the shifting mud and sand had about six inches of water in it at low tide, so that the ship appeared to have flown inland. The town had the appearance of a Dalí dreamscape under the cerulean sky, with the same beached boats at odd angles on the flat sand. I bought the world's most expensive Coke and drank it in the car and watched the street for 20 minutes or so; one car passed, and three people. It was Friday lunchtime . . . had I missed something? Had Saddam Hussein dropped the Bomb? The Chinese sailor put down his pot of paint and hopped back on board, to reappear a minute later wearing a cap with fur-lined earmuffs. It was either too cold, or the sound of his paintbrush was driving him nuts.

. I realised that for once I had time to kill and could afford a detour to use up a couple of hours. So I drove south to Brisley, past Fakenham, where there is an unenclosed common which looks exactly like a Cotman landscape, and on to North Elmham to look at the cathedral.

I suppose, since it has a cathedral, North Elmham must be a city, though perhaps that rule doesn't apply if the cathedral is defunct. In this case the collection of flint-and-mortar stumps and foundations was actually thought for a long time to be a castle, its original function completely forgotten. Only when it was excavated in 1900 was it realised that this was the Saxon church which had been the seat of the early Bishops of East Anglia. The see was transferred to Thetford, however, shortly after completion and the church fell rapidly into disuse. One Henry le Despenser, Bishop of Norwich between 1370 and 1407, had the temerity to take over what was left of it and use it as his hunting lodge, which annoyed the godfearing populace considerably (doubtless they still considered themselves Saxons). To make matters worse, 'hunting lodge' seems to have been a euphemism and there were accusations of debauchery and general naughtiness. Finally le Despenser, who used a great deal of church money in upgrading his little weekend hidey-hole, started building extra rooms on to it, which involved the summary exhumation of bodies from sacred ground. He was left in no doubt of the unpopularity of this move and was driven out, after which the cathedral rotted away, becoming in popular fancy 'North Elmham Castle', perhaps a folk-memory of the bad Bishop's alternative use. Today it is interesting chiefly because it is unusual; large Saxon churches are as rare as hen's teeth, since those which survived were almost entirely rebuilt by later and more ambitious generations. It was built rather late in the Saxon period, in about 1010, and was a good deal more complex than any Saxon church known before the excavation, much closer to the Norman style than had been thought possible.

For the rest of the afternoon I pottered around the leafy countryside of mid-Norfolk, letting Blodwen decide which turns to take. In this serendipitous manner I found the tiny village of Hoe with a towerless church like a long flint barn, a place so lost and quiet it might not have changed at all in a hundred years. The church gate seemed to be held shut by ivy, like something from a fairy-tale. It was the sort of place where one wouldn't be surprised to find a completely mad upper-class family living in a cobwebbed house with no electricity and kept alive by the villagers leaving the odd packet of Ritz Crackers on the doorstep.

I followed the valley of the fledgeling Wensum through Swanton Morley and discovered there an extraordinary bungalow with an amazing carved porch which had twirly wooden pillars. Crossing the Wensum I realised that I had hardly seen a stream all day; I checked the map and found that

I had in fact crossed only four in the past 50 miles. In a 50-mile stretch of western Scotland I would have crossed something like 100, perhaps 150. This is not a sign of imminent ecological catastrophe; the water flows underground here. But a few miles short of Reepham I found myself stopping to check the atlas once again. I had come along a road which had substantial woods on both sides. At first I couldn't work out what was unusual about it; then I realised that although I had come *past* woods often enough it was some time since I had come *through* one. I thought back . . . the Forest of Arden had had well-spaced trees and copses rather than woods. Near Huntingdon there had been a pretty plantation of mixed woodland but only on one side of the road. Nothing in the Fens, certainly, and nothing filling more than a few hundred yards in the Cotswolds. I traced my route backwards across page after page. There had been plantations of conifers on both sides of the road in the valley above Merthyr Tydfil . . . did they count? If not, the last large natural wood had been in the Vale of Conwy in North Wales – *1,000 miles* back along my tortuous route. All right then. The City of Fields.

Reepham proved to be a fine little market-town with many lovely buildings, but its immediate appeal was distinctly more exotic – there was a peacock sitting on the roof of the Ladies' lavatory. Perhaps it's waiting for the peahen to come out, I thought. It turned out that Reepham has a feral population of these elegant but incredibly noisy and stupid birds. What it lacks in avifaunal brain-cells, however, Reepham (Reefam, now, but properly pronounced Reffam) makes up in highly-developed human cerebra, for it is evident that its residents have taken great care to preserve it. It has a number of little hi-tech businesses ('Computer Services', whatever they are) and craft workshops housed in old buildings, and its shops have kept their Victorian and Edwardian frontages. There is no suggestion of tweeness in this, however; nothing has been tarted up or 'reconstructed'. If a building is attractive and serviceable, it has been left alone. How rare that is. In the centre of the town stand two churches joined, as a local guidebook puts it, as delicately as two butterflies: the corner of the nave of one is attached to the corner of the nave of the other, with their respective towers at opposite ends. Originally there was a third church within the same churchyard, which is the meeting-point of three parish boundaries, but it was burnt down in the 1600s.

On either side of the market square stand two enormous inns, both fine buildings: the whole of the centre, though not by any means exceptional, consists of good, straightforward country buildings which have somehow avoided the attentions of developers. This is extraordinary given that by the early 1960s Reepham was almost a ghost-town, with a dwindling and ageing population, its two railway stations both closed, and the market – once one of the most important in the county – reduced to the odd gypsy horse-trader and stick-in-the-mud cattle-farmer. The market is long gone; it was moved out of the square on to a new site which is itself now a carpark. What saved Reepham from the awful fate of a hundred other Norfolk villages which have become bungaloid Norwich dormitories was its designation as a conservation area by a council which was willing to put its money where its mouth was and a community which was determined to resist unnecessary change. For this they both deserve great credit, for Reepham has since become a success once again, retaining a proper community who work, sleep and shop there *and* a number of commuters to the offices, factories and the university at Norwich. The new development that has been allowed has been carefully placed on the periphery in land which has retained as far as possible the shrubs and mature trees which were there beforehand. On the southern side a small inter-war council estate is no great handicap; indeed, without it the place would not seem genuine at all.

One unpredicted but very substantial benefit to the town has been its great popularity as a setting for period television dramas and, indeed, contemporary stories which require pleasant rural backgrounds; Reepham can easily double as either. No less than five television crews used the place during 1990. Film scenes are also shot there on occasion. The benefit to the local economy must be fairly considerable, especially in the current recession; in King's Lynn a local newspaper poster bore the grim headline: 750 CHASE 35 JOBS IN LYNN.

In the evening I went down to Norwich to stay with some old friends from my university days. It is significant that as at Exeter, a very high proportion of former students of the University of East Anglia choose to stay in the area after graduation. In two recent surveys of the quality of life in European cities, Norwich and Exeter headed the British contingent. The surveys took account of a wide variety of factors including local services, shops, traffic systems and employment prospects as well as the standard of housing, both public and private. An indication of just how pleasant Norwich is can be glimpsed by the fact that despite a notoriously poor level of public sports facilities (no sports centre or modern swimming pool) the city came 14th in a survey of European towns with a population of over 100,000, with no other British names in the top 20. (Frankfurt headed the list; London was 200th.)

Norwich was busier and, sad to say, tattier than I remembered it, an impression not helped by a temporary but extremely large hole in the ground by the castle, where a new underground shopping mall is being built on the site of the old cattle market. Once the building is finished the surface is to become a large city-centre park, an indication of how enlightened modern town-planning can still be. But Norwich has always been a law unto itself, and its citizens famously independent and proud. A local saw, 'We Do Different', has been adopted as the motto of the university.

> So all sufficient in her selfe, and so complete is she
> That if need were, of all the Realme the mistresse shee might bee

So wrote John Johnston, quoted in Camden's *Brittanica* of 1610, and 60 years later Thomas Fuller remarked that Norwich:

> is (as you please) either a city in an orchard or an orchard in a city,
> so equally are the houses and trees blended in it; so that the pleasure
> of the country and the populousness of the city meet here together.
> Yet, in this mixture, the inhabitants participate nothing of the
> rusticalness of the one, but altogether of the urbanity and civility of
> the other.

For a time Norwich was in fact the second city of the realm behind only London and, in the days of an agricultural economy, usually extremely wealthy. It became a centre for the manufacture of iron and leather goods, particularly shoes, but its enormous catchment area always guaranteed an agricultural underpinning to its economy. Between the wars Norwich was blessed with a particularly enlightened Labour council, whose programme of public housing, which continued after the ravages of the Blitz and the so-called 'Baedecker Raids', provided the citizens with an unrivalled standard of housing. I cannot think of another city in which the council estates can be said actually to add to the pleasantness of the city as a whole. There has been virtually no high-rise building, and remarkably few brutal office developments. Much of the worst of the medieval slum-dwellings which cluttered around the market-place was cleared away, leaving the city centre (which isn't large for a city of that size) unusually open, with a sensible balance of broad main roads and narrow, pedestrianised medieval alleys. One result of this (and an embarrassment to the Conservative Party for decades) has been the overwhelming continued dominance of local government by the Labour Party. Even during the lowest troughs of left-wing fortune the city has returned over 80 per cent of Labour candidates in local wards. This is remarkable in a place which at face value is the quintessential southern shire town. After the boundary changes (which were surely of questionable impartiality) the city was for a time in the ludicrous position of being represented by two Tory MPs, while the City Council was made up of over 30 Labour councillors and no more than five from the other main parties put together. Labour has since recaptured one of the Parliamentary constituencies. There can only be one explanation for this in a city which has modernised and developed as much as (though with a good deal more grace and tact than) any equivalent. The evidence is all around: the people of Norwich like what they see.

There are signs, however, that Norwich is at last succumbing to the sheer weight of traffic which is being put upon it. The inner ring-road is hopelessly out of date after only a few years; the outer one is little better, and a new circuit several miles out of the city is to cut through much of the green belt. Despite the architectural finery it was not a particularly pleasant experience to walk around the main shopping area on a Saturday afternoon, though hopefully the new Castle Mall will relieve this. Nevertheless, Norwich remains by a considerable distance the most attractive British city of its size I know, and it is still possible to echo Thomas Fuller and say that, while Norwich no longer resembles an orchard it does manage to combine the atmosphere of a country town and the civility and sophistication of a city in a unique way. It is an ambience which must be jealously guarded. Provided they continue to do different I see no reason for pessimism in that regard.

ST OSYTH

Sorcery, subterranean secrets and a supernatural serpent

Despite the overwhelming hospitality I had enjoyed in Norwich and the pleasure of meeting old friends in such salubrious surroundings, my mood as I made my way southwards by country roads through the East Anglian heartlands was little improved. The edge had been taken off the depression which had been building ever since Nantyglo, but even the sybaritic day I had spent in Mustard City had not entirely cleared it. I continued in a sort of haze, going through the motions but feeling no real involvement with the scenes passing by. Admittedly the green desert of South Norfolk, in places the most dramatic illustration of what has gone amiss with modern farming, are not calculated to inspire any traveller to prodigious flights of Nobel-standard prose. Yet even here, particularly in the shallow river valleys such as that of the Tas, there remain patches of countryside which might have been cobbled together from Constable landscapes, and as in Cambridgeshire and the Fens, even the most denuded stretches of plateau can be attractive in their very simplicity and tremendous scale.

My first stop was about four miles out of Norwich at Caistor St Edmund, the site of the Roman settlement of Venta Icenorum, which is still visible as a large square on the gentle slope of the valley. Venta was built to house the remains of the Iceni tribe after the suppression of their famous revolt in AD 60–61 under the redoubtable Budicca or Boadicea. The Iceni gave the Roman authorities a major scare, completely razing Colchester and St Albans and coming within an ace of capturing London itself. As a punishment they were re-settled not within their traditional homelands in the Brecklands of the Norfolk/Suffolk border but at Caistor, within a tight, easily guarded area which was better garrisoned and more accessible; just, in fact, as some of the American Indians and tribespeople of South Africa were treated. Later in the Roman occupation, with much of the Roman Army proper recalled to the European mainland to fend off barbarian invaders, Venta was garrisoned by Germanic mercenaries on the Romans' behalf. There is archaeological evidence that these soldiers slaughtered the (by then entirely peaceful) Britons and burned and looted the town. Today the site is simply an earthen bank around a field, in one corner of which is a pretty little medieval church.

This part of Norfolk has some of the best village names: Stoke Holy Cross, Saxlingham Nethergate and Newton Flotman being prime examples. Mostly they are Norwich commuter places now, with barely a shop or a pub between them and deserted during the day; burglar alarms are everywhere. The lovely old clinker-built watermill at Stoke is now a restaurant; another at Trowse Newton on the edge of the city has become an executive dwelling. Only when one is more than 20 miles or so out of Norwich do the villages begin to show any signs of independent life. The larger villages and small towns which are scattered in the area between Norwich and Ipswich do manage to retain some of the atmosphere of self-sufficiency which they have enjoyed for centuries; affluent, contented places such as Beccles, Bungay, Framlingham and Harleston were once lynchpins of the British economy when wool was to this country what oil is today. Some, like Stowmarket and Diss, have developed apace, and are now surrounded, as with the rural centres of Aberdeenshire like Keith and Huntly, with shiny new factories; indeed, the countryside of Norfolk and Suffolk shows more than a passing resemblance to that of the North-east of Scotland, though it rises and falls far more gently, if at all. Another recent development, aided by the electrification of the London to Norwich line, is a boom in property prices in what were formerly pretty remote areas. The present recession has temporarily slowed this, but for a time in the mid- and late-'80s the prettiest places, such as the coastal town of Southwold, were ludicrously overpriced; a beach-hut at Southwold was offered at £65,000, and there were plans, thankfully resisted, to develop the marshes between Southwold and Walberswick with an estate which would have been topped off by a plastic windmill.

Much of the southern part of Norfolk, mid-Suffolk and northern Essex consists of a clay plateau into which streams have cut steep wooded valleys. In places this usually undulating clay gives way to entirely flat areas of very light sandy soil; these are raised beaches, left inland as the coast has progressively built up. The clay overlies huge amounts of sand and gravel formed in this way or deposited by the melting glaciers of the Ice Age, and aggregate quarrying is widespread.

These diggings when allowed to flood form just about the only surface water throughout much of the region other than the occasional village pond, and most places require wells and huge water towers to keep them refreshed. These towers form one of the most notable features of the East Anglian landscape, for they are often built where a slight rise in the ground aids the action of gravity in emptying the tank, and so they are visible for many miles. Many are of splendidly futuristic design, and stand sentinel over the fields like invaders (or their craft) from outer space. It is rare to find an East Anglian landscape which isn't given a focus by one tall structure or another – if not a water-tower then a television mast, radar installation, silo or church tower. Many of the latter, particularly in Norfolk, are immense. Given that so often the foreground is dull, with most of the hedges and woodlands gone and often the crops running right up to the edge of the road with no space for wild flowers or trees, these various human embellishments compensate to some extent by adding interest to the broader view. Nevertheless, there are substantial areas where the mechanisation and clearance of the old farm landscape has been so total that one might almost be standing on a prairie in Canada or the mid-western USA. One can only hope that eventually the economic incentives to ravage the land in this way will abate and allow back a degree of the variety necessary not only to the ecology of the area but also to recreation within it.

At Fritton, after some time driving through monocultural tedium, there was a small but encouraging sign that all is not lost. The village has retained its common, about a square mile of rough pasture, unfenced and scattered with shrubs and small trees, with the first wild flowers of the season in bloom and the ponds laden with spawn. Travelling through East Anglia, it is quite easy to forget the scale of transformation which has afflicted most of the land. Possibly its lack of topographical variety leads us into believing that it has always looked more or less as it does today. Areas like Fritton Common demonstrate that, on the contrary, much of the landscape must only a few decades ago have resembled the present scenery about as much as Hyde Park resembles Oxford Street. Although in ecological terms the changes have been very fast indeed, they nevertheless have been gradual enough to have gone almost unnoticed in some respects. Even in the three years I have been away from East Anglia I could see in places I knew well how yet more trees and hedges had been grubbed up, sometimes with bewildering results, altering the entire atmosphere. Dutch Elm disease in the 1970s had similarly startling effects, but actually worked largely to the benefit of farmers interested in increasing the productivity and accessibility of their fields, so little was done to replace the lost trees. But over a period of five or ten years, if you live permanently in a place, the series of small changes which gradually amount to the total transformation of a landscape may not seem in themselves particularly significant, and it requires the jolt of a clear memory of a specific view, or the memorandum of a photograph, to bring home what in many cases has proved to be a disastrous and barbaric process. I stood at the roadside in the fields outside the village of Shelton in South Norfolk and remembered a passage in Kerouac's *On The Road* where he and his buddy are stuck in the town of Shelton, Nebraska, in the middle of the plains. Today, perhaps, there is less difference between the two than ever before, except that the Nebraska town quite possibly has more trees. And yet a few miles away at Starston, set in a tiny stream-valley no more than 10 or 15 feet below the boulder-clay prairie, you might be in a different country, certainly a different century. The furrow seems to be as stuffed full of trees, shrubs and hedges, meadows and flowers as possible.

Over the Waveney into Suffolk at Harleston, which has a pretentious little minaret of a clock-tower decorated in wrought-iron on what must be the Town Hall, a strangely frivolous addition to the stolid brick sobriety of the rest of the place. Fressingfield Church for some reason was flying the Cross of St George at half-mast – perhaps it simply got stuck – and The Fox and Goose pub there had a sign showing a weedy fox being carried in the beak of a huge macho goose. Even on this sunny and relatively calm day the wind howled across the fields and carried along puffs of dust. A high veil of cloud came over and gave everything the look of being lit by strip-lights, very typically East Anglian – after a while your face muscles begin to ache because without realising it you have had your eyes screwed up.

Somewhere I passed another recent development, the cottage painted an exotic colour, in this case crimson; later I also saw canary yellow, various greens, turquoise and a range of pinks. A slightly orangey-pink is in fact, with white, the traditional colour of external plaster in East Anglia; wooden houses were generally tarred black. Since plaster is not a permanent covering the effect of a magenta cottage shoved into *The Haywain* is not necessarily permanent; much more foolish is the tendency to paint brick without rendering it first, since the original effect is then impossible to restore. Thatch is definitely making a comeback here, after almost dying out as a craft in the late 1960s and 1970s, and so is pargetting, the art of decorating plaster with ornamental designs and mouldings. In some cases this has been taken to ludicrous extremes, with houses ending up looking like exhibits at a Bavarian festival of cake-icing, but this has some historical precedents, such as the extraordinary Pococks' house at Coggeshall in Essex.

I stopped for lunch at Framlingham, a rather posh little town with an enormous but uninteresting flint keep and a minor public school, which is presumably the source of the obsession of local grafittists with bondage, buggery and caning. The walls of the public loo were a forest of invitations to do or be done to; one lone scribe had written 'Why is this toilet full of poofs? Because it's in England. I am a Scottish man and like women.' The curious clumsiness of this message led me to conclude that it was not in fact of Caledonian origin; surely no Scot would refer to a 'Scottish man'? I think I detect a faint air of German syntax about it. The town centre was full of horribly twee little galleries selling loathsome effete watercolours in the manner of Beningfield and Crawshaw but without their slick skills. There were also a number of chi-chi restaurants and antiqueries, one of which is called, for no explicable reason, Teapots and Quail, which almost made me bring up my lunch. It was all rather anaemic, and the outskirts are dull and tatty.

Further evidence, perhaps, of the decline of red-bloodedness in the Shires came at Hacheston, where what appeared to be a wicker-and-straw shooting-butt had been erected at the edge of a small pond in an orchard. On the pond, which was no more than 12 feet across, swam one duck, obviously preternaturally foolish even by duckish standards. If the modern idea of good sport in Suffolk is to atomise ducks from a range of about seven feet things have come to a pretty pass, and ought to be thoroughly aired in the correspondence columns of *The Telegraph*, *The Field*, *Country Life*, the *Ball-Bearing and Shot Manufacturers' Gazette* and the *Journal of the Association of Rustic Swains and Bumpkins*.

At Campsey Ashe, north-east of Ipswich, you come on to the very light soil – almost pure sand in places – which runs down the Suffolk coast from the Alde estuary to that of the Stour. Until very recently this land, unless forested, was useless for anything except rough grazing, but large tracts of it have now been brought under cultivation, presumably by the application of huge amounts of chemical fertilisers and constant irrigation. For most of this century, however, the area was chiefly notable for the enormous conifer plantations of the Tunstall and Rendlesham Forests. I was expecting a long drive through tall mature pine trees, but I had forgotten, or under-estimated the effect of, the great gale of October 1987. The area has been utterly devastated; of literally millions of trees perhaps a couple of hundred still stand. The ground has since been partially cleared, leaving broken stumps, piles of sawdust and discarded branches bulldozed into long rows like the defences of some strange battleground. Mostly, however, the trees still lie where they fell, all pointing in the same direction, one of the weirdest things I have ever seen. The risk of fire is evident, with millions of tons of tinder-dry dead pinewood covering many miles of flat land. Many will not lament the passing of what was in any case not a great ecological asset to the area, but it is nevertheless a dispiriting and awe-inspiring experience to go through what most closely resembles the aftermath of a nuclear explosion; the same completely uniform direction of blast, the same total and indiscriminate laying-waste.

More grievous was the damage done to the area of ancient oak forest which adjoined the modern plantation near Butley. I remember walking through those woods on a moonlit summer night 15 years ago; the forest was so dense that the path was actually a tunnel. I suppose it was as close as it is now possible to get to the kind of forest which covered medieval England. It consisted of venerable stag-headed oaks, some of them truly gigantic, between which had grown up an impenetrable mass of shrubs and lesser trees as solid as a wall. Now, although most of the great tree-boles are still standing, the crowns, many of which must in any case have been dead for decades, have without exception been removed as if with a huge mechanised scythe. The floor of the wood is simply a layer of dead branches five or six feet thick. Here and there in the forests there are isolated cottages and houses. What the residents experienced during The Hurricane can only be guessed at; they are lucky to be alive, I suppose. At least East Suffolk has got firewood to last about six generations now; they won't be selling many oil-fired central heating systems in these parts for a while.

For no very good reason I ended up at Orford, a curious little town on the coast with a dinky castle, a slender fairytale keep. Here, too, all the trees have gone, leaving the Dutch-style brick houses as naked as if they were beside some polder 70 miles to the east. The main street of Orford is extremely wide – 60 or 70 feet, and with the afternoon now turning chilly and misty it was a bleak place.

Chillesford had a pub called The Froize Inn, which had a picture of a monk; Friar's Inn, presumably, rendered into local speech. Beyond, the road suddenly filled up with huge cars; there are two major American airbases nearby, RAF Woodbridge and RAF Bentwaters. Stories of fear and loathing, of strange and inexplicable sights and sounds in the night, abound in these parts, most of which I suspect can be accounted for by the enormous quantities of marijuana consumed by these nuclear-armed guardians of peace and freedom. I remember a village shopkeeper near Bentwaters telling me that once a week the same group of airmen come in to purchase a *carton* of cigarette papers each . . . a carton contains 144 packets, or enough for a joint the size of an F-lll. I also remember a local band invited out to do a gig at one of these bases. At the gate a large black sergeant in mirror shades strolled up to the van. 'Hi,' said the driver, 'we're Russian spies and we've come to blow up your base.' The guard nodded. 'Drive on, man!' he drawled.

Woodbridge has changed almost beyond recognition since I last saw it ten years ago. It was formerly a slightly decrepit little boatyard town, apparently sinking sleepily into the mud of the Deben estuary, the sort of place where trains sometimes forgot to stop. Now it appears almost totally new, with lots of expensive-looking flats, smart supermarkets, restaurants, three bookshops and a record shop as well as innumerable businesses connected with boats and a sprinkling of small electronics industries. It also supports an independent theatre on the waterfront, with a very chic restaurant attached, the sort of place where they do Chekhov rather than variations on *No Sex Please, We're British*. This proves conclusively that Woodbridge is not near Ipswich at all, but a suburb of Hampstead. Most of the new development is good, as these things go – variations on the local vernacular which stop short of silly mimicry: flats which remind one of, rather than pretend to be, old mills and maltings. Not that this matters all that much, for the quayside, as in all really successful boating towns, is an utter shambles.

I hate boats, but I do like boatyards and boating people. They tend to be individualists with a low regard for authority. Boat people divide into three types in England, and all were immediately visible here: (a) the portly, rolling, bearded type who potter from poop to pub and are always having their bottoms scraped; (b) the thin, desperate-looking, cardigan-clad sort who got clobbered for alimony or sought refuge on a houseboat from the rates and the rat-race and then got caught by the Poll Tax (lots of For Sale signs); and (c) the kind who wear fluorescent clothes and sunglasses and bottled sun-tan and are accompanied by pale boys in T-shirts and very short shorts. These three types, I should stress, are *boating* people, not yachting folk. A boat place is entirely different from a yacht place. There's no credibility in being smart in a place like Woodbridge – in fact it's probably social death. Moneyed, yes, but definitely not showy. On the other hand, your average Woodbridgian, were he to be shipwrecked at Cowes or Lymington, would probably be treated like a leper. Interestingly, serious yachtsmen and women, as far as I can gather – the round-the-world types – tend to come from boat places like Woodbridge or Brightlingsea, not the world of Martini-ads and powerboats run on aftershave.

It was pleasant out of the wind down in the boatyard, eating buns purchased from a caravan on blocks (you'd never get that at Cowes) and listening to the tinkle of marlinspike against belaying-pin. Up on the valley-side across the estuary overlooking the town was once a much greater ship than any here. It was hauled up from the river, a sleek, mean-lined single-sailed longboat, to take the dead High King of the Angles and Saxons on his voyage to the afterworld. It was discovered in the 1930s at Sutton Hoo, beneath one of a collection of earth mounds in a sandy field. On excavation in 1936 it proved to be laden with golden treasure beyond the dreams of avarice – easily the most important Dark-Age burial site ever excavated in Britain. The lines of the ship, every nail and plank, had been imprinted into the hardened sand; even, perhaps, the cremated remains of the King himself, laid in a gigantic silver dish, survived as a result of the stable, acid, well-drained soil. Legend has it that when the great dish, buckled by the collapse of the 'cabin' amidships, was uncovered, a gust of wind blew away the ash which it contained, and it is not clear whether it was a human cremation or a sacrificial animal. The Sutton Hoo jewels, fabulously-worked creations in gold, silver and garnets (from Afghanistan) are in the British Museum. Amazingly, much of the rest of the cemetery has yet to be excavated, despite the fact that this was obviously the burial-ground of a royal dynasty whose palace, we know from Bede, was at Rendlesham. The ship-burial is likely to have been that of Raedwald, who died in the 620s, or one of his sons. They stand at the darkest and most mysterious point of post-Roman British history, in the faint pre-dawn glimmer which came before the establishment of monastic Christianity. Every time I go there my feet itch as I think about what else may lie beneath.

There is a less romantic side to this story. Although it was long known that the court of this dynasty was at Rendlesham, the palace was lost. The buildings would probably have been wooden and long since rotted away. Eventually, however, aerial photography revealed what was almost certainly the site, half-covered by forestry plantations but certainly substantially visible. Preparations were made for a preservation order to be placed on the site. Just before it came into effect, the landowner deliberately deep-ploughed the field to destroy all traces of the palace. The loss to archaeology, perhaps, was incalculable; no written history and precious little in the way of solid artifacts survive from the fifth to seventh centuries. The Sutton Hoo treasure reveals that the Germanic ancestry of ours were almost unbelievably skilled in the art of metalwork and possessed a highly sophisticated culture far above the image of Dark-Age barbarism promulgated by historians for a thousand years.

About 4.30 it was evident that the sun would not show its face again and a procession of BMWs, Mercedes and Rollers headed out of town towards the A12 and London, accompanied by a white Morris-Minor van. I bypassed Ipswich, chugging along in the wake of a motor-cruiser being towed by a Range Rover, and musing on whether, when he finally Crossed the Bar, the friends of Quentin, interior designer from Barnet, would place his cremated remains inside *Lone Wolf II*, lug it up a hill and bury it. Even better, as in Beowulf, set fire to it and push it out to sea. What a way to go.

I was woken from this reverie on the Ipswich orbital. It may well be that whoever decided to build this bypass had a good look at the rest of the A12 and decided that a little more wanton destruction would probably go unnoticed. It is a pig of a road, both to drive on and to look at. A few miles south of Ipswich its designer thought for some reason that it would be a good idea to run four lanes of concrete through the middle of Stratford St Mary, in the heart of Dedham Vale, lopping off the church from the rest of the village. Legend has it that if you stand at the spot where John Constable stood to paint one of his views across the valley you will be squashed by the traffic. This is not true, since none of the views are real, being based on Dedam Vale in spirit rather than fact, and painted for the most part in a studio in London. Nonetheless, it ought to be true. The traffic screams down the hill into the Stour valley and across the meadows outside Dedham. There was absolutely no need for the road to be put there; to the east are vast swathes of incredibly dull Essex countryside and an existing main road which could have been upgraded; after crossing the Stour lower down, the road could have connected with the main Harwich road and saved a lot of money and scenery. Meat-heads.

Dedham is unfortunate enough to have been associated with two well-known painters; one was the greatest landscape artist Britain has ever produced and the other a tedious old hack who painted horses. Unjustly, there is a Sir Alfred Munnings Museum there but precious little of John Constable beyond ashtrays decorated with Will Lot's Cottage. Munnings once produced a canvas entitled *My House, My Horse and My Wife*, which strikes me as being in order of preference, apart from sounding insufferably vain. Of all the British painters of this century perhaps only William Russell Flint deserved success less. Constable, on the other hand, was an artist of revolutionary genius and, in my opinion, one of only three painters of world stature – the others being Reynolds and Turner – this country has ever produced. He was the first British painter to influence significantly the development of European art as a whole. His legacy in the Stour Valley, however, consists largely of a severe traffic problem and a lot of people under the misguided impression that photographing Flatford Mill is a worthwhile activity. It is, after all, just a mill. But Constable's *Flatford Mill* is not just a painting of Flatford Mill.

Even on this chilly April evening Dedham was stuffed with people. It is a tiny place, ill-equipped to cope with the tonnage of pilgrims and, apart from two superb old pubs, offers very little except the usual tea-shops, antique dealers and similar gubbins. Most of the fringe is carpark.

I meandered down through North Essex, across another raised beach at Ardleigh, of billiard-table flatness, and through a succession of the kind of scruffy, elongated villages for which Essex is unremarkable: Great Bromley, Aingers Green, Kirby-le-Soken. They tend to have a core of old cottages tarted up with fake bottleglass and bay windows, a dingy array of inter-war pebbledash semis, and a pub with live Country and Western on Saturday nights. I don't know why Essex should be blighted with so many of these curiously centreless, etiolated places. Many, like Weeley, are of immense age but have become either drab or tawdry or both. Still, for some unfathomable reason, I like them. They mirror the tedious fields around them; at least they are unpretentious. Occasionally they are interrupted by somewhere attractive and interesting, and St Osyth is such a place.

The first thing that should be said about St Osyth is how to pronounce it: 'Toosey'. Toosey (if you don't believe me, look it up in the *Oxford Dictionary of English Place-Names*) is now no more than a nickname used by people in the immediate vicinity, but was once the usual pronunciation. Nowadays the most common pronunciation is 'Saint Oh-zith'. In Essex vernacular this would have been 'Oozith', hence ''t oosy'. Actually the original nickname was 'Chich', but this died out by the 19th century. The Saxon name was Cic Saint Osgyd, the Church of St Osyth.

I had two very good reasons for choosing Toosey as my letter S. One is that I lived there for years and my father still does, which guaranteed me at least a pint of Adnams and a bed. The other is that it is a fascinating place.

Osyth was born in the eighth century, the daughter of a Mercian king, and she is the patron saint of Aylesbury in Buckinghamshire. A marriage was arranged for political reasons with a son of the royal house of the East Saxons, which Osyth agreed to only on condition that it was never consummated and that she live out her days as a nun. This was accepted and a nunnery was built for her. Apparently a woman of singular holiness, legend has it that Osyth was martyred by an band of Danish pirates out for a bit of rape and pillage. When their leader lopped off her head, a spring flowed up at the spot where it hit the ground; the redoubtable lady then picked it up, tucked it under her arm and walked to the village church where presumably she was finally overcome by the loss of this useful appendage. The nunnery eventually became a priory occupied by Austin friars and, after the Dissolution, a private house. It has a famous Elizabethan gatehouse (Elizabeth spent a night at St Osyth and was kept awake by a thunderstorm) and a tremendous medieval tithe barn, as well as various other buildings and remains dating from the 12th to the 19th century. Substantial parts are Jacobean and Georgian. Like all good country houses it is haunted – not only does St Osyth still carry her head to the church door but a White Lady or nun prowls around from time to time. It is surrounded by a deer park and other land five miles in circumference, which contains several further ruins of monastic buildings including a sort of pump-house, and a couple of ruined 19th-century summerhouses, one of which is encrusted with seashells. The remains of a Roman villa are also on the site; the straight edge of the deer park looks tantalisingly like a Roman field boundary. There was also an ornamental Victorian water-garden, now overgrown.

One of the most interesting questions about the foundation of the priory is why the site was chosen at all. Until the surrounding marshes were drained in the 17th and 18th centuries, the village was surrounded by malarial swamp. Sixteenth-century sources remark that it was a singularly damp and foggy spot, famous for its agues and rheumatics. Of course, it was regarded as a sign of holiness in the Middle Ages to live in awful places, such as Ely or the Abbey of St Benet on the Norfolk Broads. But it is tempting to speculate that it was chosen because the Roman villa, which had a small wharf on the creek below the village, was still a workable – or even working – estate. There are plenty of examples of villas remaining productive after the effective end of Roman rule in the late 400s; indeed, there are signs in places that the Romano-British or Saxon inheritors of these estates more or less camped in the ruins even when the original buildings fell down. It may be that the foundation of the nunnery on this land was a generous, rather than an ascetic gesture. What is certain, however, is that at St Osyth we have an area of several square miles which was originally endowed by at least one royal family and probably two; which has been occupied continuously since the late 700s and quite possibly since the second or third centuries AD; which was a site of medieval pilgrimage and a foundation of considerable wealth (as is attested by the magnificence of buildings such as the gatehouse and the so-called Abbot's Tower); which contains the remnants of a Roman villa which, although overgrown, has never been built over; but which has never been archaeologically investigated.

The priory was recently sold for several million pounds. The vendor, one Somerset de Chair, had always resisted archaeological overtures, and instead flirted with development of the 'commercial potential' of the grounds. He applied to build houses on part of the deer park and also to open up gravel pits, moves sensibly squashed by the local council. Now, rumours abound that the priory is to become a hotel or conference centre, a golf-course, a theme-park . . . you name it. So far no firm plans have emerged. What we have at St Osyth is an illustration of the almost total lack of inclination or strategy by successive governments to identify and protect important historic sites. While the priory remains in private hands there is always the risk of the site being despoiled either deliberately or through negligence. Ironically, due to the chronic underfunding of investigative archaeology in this country, private ownership may also be the best bet, if a faint hope, if the site is ever to be thoroughly examined. It is to be hoped that the priory is not overtaken by the same fate as the palace at Rendlesham, for it is entirely possible that St Osyth is a place of similar importance.

This place has more than one other connection with the supernatural. In the early 1300s the village was attacked by a dragon. You may scoff, but this is a very curious incident well-attested by apparently genuine contemporary documents. It seems that the serpent, breathing fire and smoke in the traditional manner, hung around for several days, amusing itself by setting fire to the roofs of thatched cottages and causing the villagers to lock up their daughters. A knight was sent for to come and deal with the beast. Since he had to come from Epping, two or three days journey away, this may be taken as an indication of the seriousness of their predicament. Whether or not he killed the dragon or chased it away is not recorded.

What on earth, provided that this is not an entire fabrication, can lie at the root of this tale? After all, having your home attacked by a sizeable winged lizard is not something you can easily mistake, particularly if it is intent on barbecueing you. Even if the rural inhabitants of 14th-century Essex were as superstitious as we tend to suppose, there would seem to be few natural phenomena which could worry them enough to hire a Saint George from the other end of the county. Without the knight the story might be easily dismissed as an old wives' tale; with him, and the interesting detail that he came from Epping, it looks as if something occurred which was thoroughly out of the ordinary.

Something of this air of inexplicable panic reappears a few centuries later, by which time St Osyth was a very prosperous centre of the woollen trade. The village was one of the centres of the extraordinary bouts of moral and religious hysteria about witchcraft which blighted England and Scotland between the reigns of Henry VIII and James I. (And which seem to be reappearing today.)

Today the chief business of St Osyth is the holiday trade. There is a thriving little boatyard (there has been one since the 1200s) and a Nature Reserve on the marshes behind the priory. The priory itself is the chief attraction, though on the seashore a mile or two east of the village are a number of chalet and caravan parks complete with amusement arcades, pubs, nightclubs and so forth. Most of the residents are commuters to Colchester, Clacton or London; apart from the village shops and the local farms there is little employment within the village, which has a population of a couple of thousand. Within or near the village are seven or eight pubs not counting those in the holiday parks, which implies a very high degree of civilisation.

The town's accessibility from East London means that like nearby Clacton and Southend down the coast, St Osyth has long been popular with Cockneys. It is rumoured that the Kray brothers bought their mother a chalet at St Osyth beach. I can certainly remember a day on which the village suddenly filled up with scores of policemen, and a police helicopter hovered over the sea-front. Although not technically in the area which has recently become known as the home of 'Essex Man' (a sort of monied lager-lout invented by the middle-brow press) there is certainly a rising Essex Man presence during the summer, when muscular young men in XR3is descend on the village in order to water-ski on the mile-long millpond. There is also a rising tide of petty crime, burglary and so on, and not-so-petty crime. There have been one or two particularly nasty incidents of violence and a bit of suspected arson, as well as rumours of drug-smuggling using a local airstrip. A prominent local citizen is a London Irishman who drives a Rolls with a personalised number-plate, wears a camelhair coat and chunky jewellery and whose fingers are in more pies than Mr Kipling's. He is a charming man who is good to his mother.

I spent a happy evening catching up on the local gossip and sampling several pints of Adnams falling-down water just to make sure it was as efficacious as ever. My father filled me in on the tittle-tattle, which varied from the usual illegitimate pregnancies and traditional agues and rheumatics to alarming incidents of grievous bodily harm, back-room politicking and speculation as to the new owner of the priory. I nodded across the pub to an old acquaintance, a man of about six-foot five or six, who has shed about seven stone to weigh in at a sylph-like 16 or 17. He used to ride a bike to work, which was invisible beneath his bulk, giving the impression that a large bear was flying down the road. ' —— has been told to cut down on the booze,' my father whispered. 'He's got diabetes.'

'He's certainly shed some weight.' I remarked.

'Yes – he's down to 10 pints of lager a night instead of 15.'

Personally I find that half such a heroic intake is beyond me. Nevertheless the nectar of the Southwold Brewery worked its old magic and a modest three pints, after a month of almost total abstinence, was, I regret to report, enough to send me on my way next morning with a head like a lead balloon.

TILBURY

Terrible terminal

I went to school in Colchester, then a quiet market town bedecked with Roman and Norman finery. In the late 1970s and 1980s the town boomed – it was the fastest-growing town in the country for a while – and became almost unbearably busy, a tangled cock-up of concrete and cars. So now I approached it with caution, only to find that since I last saw it something has clicked and it has become positively pleasant once again.

Colchester boasts that it is Britain's oldest recorded town, the pre-Roman capital of the Trinovantes. They, however, were conquered by the Catuvellauni, the fiercest of the Belgae tribes who occupied south-eastern England at the time of the Roman invasions. The conquerors wore their hair in spikes gelled with lime, fought their battles naked, and collected the heads of their enemies. Two of the leaders of the Catuvellauni were Cunobelinus (Shakespeare's Cymbeline) and Caratacus, the greatest resistance-fighter of all apart from Budicca. The Romans, having quelled the tribes as best they could, establish their greatest garrison at Camulodunum/ Colchester, symbolising their supremacy over the most powerful of the natives. Later the Normans built their largest keep at the town; now 80 feet high, it was once twice as tall and Colchester has been a garrison town ever since. Yet unless you go looking for it, you would never guess that Colchester has a military presence. The barracks occupy a large chunk of the southern outskirts, but apart from the occasional jeep the town centre itself is completely civilian.

There is usually some kind of excavation going on in the town somewhere; in a fast-growing place of such antiquity there are often fierce battles

215

between developers and historians. The developers usually come out on top, literally. A few years ago a very famous supermarket chain applied for permission to build a new store in St John's Street, near the centre of the old Roman town. Local archaeologists objected; the new building would bury a previously unexplored site in several feet of concrete, from which evidence would be irretrievable. After much petitioning and bickering, permission was granted for an emergency dig before the builders moved in. It proved to be one of the most productive excavations ever undertaken in Colchester but there was no time to do more than a basic, hurried job. The supermarket was built, destroying whatever remained beneath. Less than five years later the company abandoned the shop.

For a town which boasts of its heritage Colchester has had a very high number of such grim incidents. Over the past 15 years much of the town centre has been completely redeveloped, a ring-road installed, and a large number of office-blocks and multi-storey carparks now encircle the old citadel. Nevertheless, it must be admitted that in terms of convenience to the inhabitants this exercise has been a great success. The traffic congestion has been eased significantly, and two large pedestrianised shopping precincts (one of which is rather dour, though the other is singularly pleasant) allow the townspeople to enjoy spending their money without being run over, crushed to death by bargain-hunters or poisoned by exhaust fumes. Whether or not a town so uniquely important to British history should have been subjected to such an orgy of free-market development is another question.

South of Colchester the countryside becomes increasingly tedious, though the really appalling stuff doesn't begin for 20 miles or so, when the Badlands of Essex's London fringe transform the atmosphere utterly. Between Colchester and Tiptree the land is merely dull and Tiptree itself is the dullest town I can remember. Around Maldon, on the Blackwater estuary, there are a number of pleasant little ex-maritime villages, now very upmarket, such as Goldhanger and Heybridge Basin. I had lunch by the lock-gate at Heybridge Basin amongst a forest of yacht-masts, a couple of decaying old Thames sailing-barges, and a swarm of French schoolchildren who I could have sworn were the very same lot I had run into in Oxford. Mind you, one Gallic oscular technique looks much like another. Maldon is another boating town, scruffy and slightly seedy on an amazingly steep hill above the muddy estuary, where the Anglo-Saxons slugged it out with the Vikings in 991. South of Maldon you leave Britain altogether and enter a sort of nightmare country designed by an American Nazi with the brain of a pit bull terrier. The land flattens out and becomes dusty and bedraggled, like Paris, Texas: this is the driest place in England. There is a marked increase in the number of flashy ranch-style houses. The road fills up with sports saloons such as XR3is, SRis, Jaguars and BMWs, driven by very young men with unnecessarily violent haircuts. There are a disturbing number of gun clubs and shooting-ranges. The flat, bright light gives everything an edge of paranoia and the sides of the main roads are littered with bits of mechanical wreckage. There are no pubs, only fast-food places bedecked with flashing coloured lights, and 'roadhouses' where Tuesday is 'Heavy Metal Night', Wednesday is 'Ladies Nite' and so on. In between this grisly, patchy, urban ugliness are either completely flat fields of fine dust in which nothing has apparently been planted or expanses of stinking tidal mud streaked with oil; the Canvey oil refinery glowers on the horizon.

The towns are the heartland of Thatcherite hard-right conservatism. This is the land of the self-made, the home of such luminaries as Teresa Gorman and the editor of the *Sunday Sport*, David Sullivan. Ian Dury spotted this trend and identified Essex Man ten years before the papers picked him up:

> I ain't a bleedin' thickie
> I'm Billericay Dickie
> An' I'm doing very well.

I accidentally went into South Woodham Ferrers, a 'New Village' built on the Crouch estuary in the late '70s and '80s. It is a good deal more attractive than its older sisters, Basildon and Rayleigh, but somehow utterly dispiriting all the same. Built in a style which is supposed to resemble the traditional waterside buildings of the Essex coast, it looks instead like some kind of isolation hospital. Every single building is in the same material and the same style, whether it is a house, a block of flats, a supermarket or a church. Trying to drive through it as rapidly as was decent I discovered that this is not possible as all roads lead, spider-web-like, to a central carpark outside an enormous hypermarket (with a little clock-tower, of course). The only recourse is to retrace your route. What kind of a mentality produces a 'village' around a branch of ASDA?

Still, even I would admit that South Woodham Ferrers (even the name sounds like a firm of property developers) is a paradise compared to my next destination, Southend-on-Sea. Unless you have actually been there it is hard to understand just how utterly charmless it is. Briefly, from the front backwards, it consists of (a) a view of the oil refineries and power stations of North Kent; (b) either the Thames, which is the colour of liquid mud, or a mile of mud beach, depending on the tide; (c) a dual carriageway along the esplanade; (d) a line of fast-food joints, and betting-shops and amusement arcades which have given up any pretence of family entertainment, and are inhabited by hordes of youths who beat the crap out of any machine which doesn't give them a replay; (e) a 'Town Centre' resembling the basement of a Manhattan carpark; and (f) several miles of shoddy Victorian terraces which have in places fallen down and been superseded by used-car lots. The town seems to be the used-car capital of Europe:

Daleyville. Most British seaside resorts are tatty, but some are cheerfully vulgar, and almost all contain an element of rictus-faced jollity. Southend, so tatty as to be positively decomposed, has the air of a place which exists by grabbing people by the lapels and demanding money. There is about as much fun in the air as at the Nuremburg Rally. Worst of all, once you are in it it takes ages to get out of. I spent about an hour there, mostly because I couldn't face driving any further for a while. The French schoolchildren were on the pier. (Were they following me? Was Le Tour de la Grande Bretagne Alphabétique à Blodwen the talk of Paris? What on earth did they make of this piece of *Merde-sur-Mer?*) It then took me the best part of an hour and a half to cover the 20 miles to Tilbury.

At Tilbury I finally cracked. I flunked. I copped out. I lost my bottle. Tilbury at the end of a long day's drive through the arsehole of England was more than I could bear. I drove around the streets for ten minutes, across the tracks to the dock gates and back, eyeing the ugly blocks of flats and tumbledown shops, the corrugated-iron backstreet workshops, the scrapyards and sooty gin-palaces. Then I fled, first to Thurrock, where I ate an awful meal in a motorway service station, and then through the Dartford Tunnel into the Kentish hills.

UCKFIELD

Utopia?

I think I had some vague idea that Tunbridge Wells might replace Tilbury as my letter T, but by the time I reached that famously disgusted town it was getting dark and the streets were deserted; expecting somewhere rather posh I was surprised to find it a very ordinary, rather drab place with few architectural pretentions. So I abandoned the letter T and struck south for Uckfield in Sussex. The motorway south of the Dartford Tunnel had brought me across the North Downs in the dusk, with little to see except the basic undulations of the ground and contrasting patches of woodland and open field. The Weald too seemed extremely well-wooded after the emptiness of South Essex. About 10 o'clock I found a wide grass verge in a lane just east of Uckfield, brewed a cup of tea, stretched out on the back seat while it cooled and awoke, chilled to the bone, at three in the morning to find the mug still balanced precariously above my head on the back of the seat, full to the brim. I wriggled into the sleeping bags, drank the tea cold and slept until 6.30.

After the usual couple of hours getting the kinks out of my spine, eating, writing and rearranging the interior of the van I ventured into town. Situated on a steep slope with the main street running straight up the hill, Uckfield now consists almost entirely of modern estates of '50s to '70s villas with open-plan gardens. The shopping street is neo-Georgian, perhaps 1935 or so, with a few medieval and other buildings higher up. The railway station lies at the bottom of the hill; a new road runs down to it from the bypass, and on this access road a light-industrial estate and a supermarket (with a little clock tower) have been built. That, in essence, is it.

It struck me immediately as the quintessence of the bland, conformist, modestly well-to-do Southern town, the sort of place in which the impossibly healthy, well-scrubbed, untraumatised nuclear families who act out little dramas concerning detergent or stock-cubes are supposed to reside – where Mum does the Window Test while little Kevin helps Dad mend the fence and Sharon plays with about £600 worth of My Little Pony accessories.

The housing seemed to be either fairly expensive (the modern three-bedroom stuff), very expensive (anything vaguely 'period') or unbelievably expensive (anything remotely 'rural'). The price range was from around £60,000, with a median of 75 to 85,000, rising to £650,000, which would buy you a 13th-century mill with a lake and a few acres of mature woodland. The town was very clean, with little grafitti or litter, and apart from the usual run of shops has a small cinema, the Picture House, founded in 1912. There is also a bookshop, Potter's, into which I went. For a town the size of Uckfield to support a bookshop is unusual; I would guess that the place has no more than 15,000 inhabitants, but they must have a high disposable income. Inside the shop I asked for a copy of *The Bookseller* ('The Organ of the Book Trade') and pointed out to the woman at the counter a small paragraph referring to my endeavour. When asked to provide a brief summary of the delights of Uckfield neither the woman nor another who joined her shortly could think of anything to recommend it other than that Lord Lucan used to live there (which might explain a lot) and that the woman who wanders around Norfolk surrounded by corgis disturbing nudists has been known to stay up the road with her husband's private secretary. Presumably Philip knows about this.

'Oh, and there was a murder, just before we moved here . . .'

'When was that?'

'Oh . . . 18 years ago, now.'

Most of the working population commute to London or to Gatwick. Those unfortunate enough to be out of work have recently suffered the indignity of having their Job Centre closed down and now have to get a bus to Lewes. The biggest problem was that there was nothing for the kids to do in the evenings, they said, echoing what I had heard in Harrington, Kearsley, Montgomery, Nantyglo, and several places in between. Strange, no one brings up this subject in places like Armadale or St Osyth, perhaps because there aren't enough kids to block the pavement on a Saturday night. It was a well-stocked little bookshop and considering that I am employed by a company they probably regard as their arch-enemy, the staff of Potter's were very polite and forthcoming, not that there was much to forthcome about. Even the reading habits of the townspeople were predictable: local history, Jeffrey Archer, thrillers and romances. Wasn't there anyone collecting the works of the Marquis de Sade, or classics of Serbo-

Croat literature? It seems not. I bet they say the Round Table is very active, I thought.

'The Round Table is very active,' one of them said. 'And the Rotarians,' the other added, to show that there was no class prejudice. Were there any Asian or West Indian immigrants? Not that they had noticed.

It was interesting that both women were faintly disparaging as they discussed the town, as if apologising for its extreme ordinariness. I had been careful not to prejudice their answers by saying something like 'My God, how can you stand living in the architectural equivalent of John Major?', but perhaps, nevertheless, they sensed that I would not be convinced by a paean of praise. I said that for want of something more obvious beginning with the letter U I had been thinking about a little conceit about Uckfield as a kind of Utopia, an apparently untroubled, contented, ordered, not-too-big, wash-the-Sierra-on-Sunday-morning Home Counties paradise. They looked at me rather oddly and one of them said something about the sports centre. I didn't pursue the remark and having thanked them went for a wander around the town. What should I find at the top of the hill but the Utopia Sports Centre. Either these people are insufferably conceited or somewhere in the Recreation Department is someone with a very droll sense of humour.

VENTNOR

Victorian vacations and vacancies

Away to Haywards Heath, a larger version of Uckfield. It's not surprising, I thought, that Southerners have the impression that anything north of Watford is on a cultural par with Pago-Pago. This countryside is so tame, so benevolent, and the succession of small towns as I headed due west towards Billingshurst, so bland and self-assured, that it must be all too easy to slip into a sort of late-Imperial haze, to come to believe that the Sussex countryside is a kind of Canaan to which civilised people everywhere aspire. Not that there is any real countryside there. The whole county seems to be a sort of park. Between the extensive patches of woodland are meadows and paddocks but rarely anything which looks as if it is productive. Indeed, there is very little even in the towns which smacks of trade. It's a sort of Betjemanesque dream-world, where it is always tea-time, there is always a cricket-match going on and sturdy athletic girls hack around on barrel-bellied ponies. The lanes are littered with posters advertising point-to-points and whist drives, and policed by ramrod-backed matrons walking labradors. Most telling of all, it is impossible to drive a quarter of a mile without passing a house; the land is too densely populated to be rural, but built up with just few enough houses to prevent one having any neighbours. It has the look of the countryside with none of its drawbacks, such as peasants or gigantic overspill estates.

It is more than 40 miles between Uckfield and the first town which offers any variation on this theme, Petworth. All along the road I was expecting some kind of interruption, a new development of small factories, an ordinary pebble-dashed council estate, or a densely-packed rash of neo-vernacular executive dwellings. But there was not the slightest variation in the pattern of stockbroker-belt detached houses with tennis-courts and paddocks, copses and fields of horses or cows. Considering the overpopulation of this tight little island, the fantastic intensity of farm production in much of Britain, the eating-up of swathes of green-belt by new roads and houses, it is obvious that the residents of Mid-Sussex lead a charmed existence. In order to fend off these pressures they must have two things in abundance: money and influence. It is the home, in both fact and spirit, of the ruling class – not the aristocracy nor necessarily the actual rulers (though there must be more senior civil servants per acre than anywhere else), but in large part the upper-middle class, public-school-educated, 'natural' conservatives from which the upper echelons of government, diplomatic corps, and city business have traditionally arisen. We are always being told that this old order is in terminal flux but the lanes of Sussex give that the lie.* There are no yuppies here, or not enough to matter. These trees are bedded in a rich mulch of old money.

Petworth breaks the monotony (I almost said monopoly) at last. A hilltop village in limestone on the edge of the Rother Valley, across which the South Downs rise steeply, Petworth can only really be done justice to by one adjective: bijou. It stands up from the brick-and-timber Pony Belt as if further to refine the already rarefied atmosphere, improbably pretty and impossibly expensive, full of the chic and chi-chi: delicatessens, wineries, bistros and the kind of antique shops which display only one choice item at a time. People who meet on the streets scream 'DAHLING!' and kiss the air a hygienic six inches from each cheek. It's all in such good taste as to be dangerously close to vulgar ostentation. There's new money here all right, I thought; they probably wash the Porsche with handfuls of it. A very good friend of mine lives there (she was out, or she might have persuaded me that all is not as it seems). Apologies go to her – this may just be envy.

The South Downs are as different from the valley below as could be. Now almost totally under the plough, these narrow chalk hills once supported a unique ecosystem of birds, animals and wild flowers which were totally dependent on the ancient tradition of sheep-grazing on the downs. This fragile and delicate upland world survives only in tiny strips and squares, for the most part the hillsides are as flayed as anything in Norfolk or Essex. Why should nearly all the fertile lowland behind be pasture and woodland while nearly all the dry, acidic downland be forced to produce cereals? It is utterly crazy. As a result of this ludicrous inversion the Downs are now no more than a tedious series of bumps and bends rather than somewhere to idle in.

It had been a misty, muggy morning in the central valley but as I came

* This impression was later borne out by Jeremy Paxman's *Friends in High Places* (Penguin 1990), a fascinating and scrupulous analysis of the vested interests who haunted my journey.

over the crest the sea-breeze blew away the haze and ushered in the most pleasant weather of the journey, with a clear blue sky and sunshine verging on hot. This cheered me no end, and no doubt greatly improved the impression I gained of Chichester, for I found myself thoroughly liking a city which to all intents and purposes is no less mollycoddled than any other Sussex town I had passed through. Perhaps I am wrong and even on a day of lashing rain and fog Chichester's air of cheerful, unforced civility would have shone through.

For a start, everybody there looked ridiculously healthy. Even the old-age pensioners resembled either the Queen Mother or Captain Birdseye, positively glowing and twinkling. It is a bright little city with an elegant toy cathedral, well-preserved Georgian houses and rows of pretty terraced cottages with the unmistakable freshness of style that nautical history gives to domestic architecture. Nothing looks restored; it all seems simply to be well-preserved. It has a generous number of parks and gardens and a wide, calm pedestrianised main shopping street leading up to the Old Cross and the Cathedral Close.

An hour later I was in Portsmouth, which gives Tilbury a lesson in how to be a successful historic port and still remain fit for humans to live in. It is, of course, very much larger and wealthier than the Essex town, and shifts more people and cars than containers.

V was a tricky letter. There is one in Essex, Vange, part of Basildon, but it sounds suspiciously like a disease of the gums. Then there is Venn Ottery, near Exeter, but that was too far away, and two in Sussex, Vinehall Street and Vines Cross, but I had done Sussex. Vobster, in Somerset, was also a bit of a stretch, although it sounds terrific, like a 1940s motorcycle. So I was left with no choice but to take the Isle of Wight Ferry (at a cost which almost made me faint) and descend on Ventnor, which sounds like a patent Victorian enema:

> THE 'VENTNOR'
> Dr Clutterbuck's Patent Hydraulic Appliance
> – Guaranteed Relief From Inner Stress –
> Gold Medal Winner at the Surgical Exhibition,
> Baden-Baden, 1888
> Gastric Irrigation – The Key To Vitality

I spent most of the crossing on deck. There were hardly any other passengers and the Solent was calm. A great number of aged cargo vessels were laid up at the mouth of Southampton Water, like the floating corpses of dinosaurs; yachts picked at them like birds. The ferry loops around, taking three-quarters of an hour to traverse the six miles to Fishbourne, and passing three of the massive circular sea-forts which guard Spithead. A month later I was leafing through an old copy of *Country Life* in a dentist's waiting-room and discovered that one of these forts has been converted into a private house, complete with powerboat and helicopter-pad. It was on the market at an undisclosed price, with the slogan 'For the Millionaire Who Has Everything'. Surely that should be 'Who Wants Everything'?

It didn't take more than half a mile's journey to convince me that the Isle of Wight has the worst road surfaces anywhere in Britain. Blodwen, already leaning rather drunkenly, groaned and squawked along and there were a couple of unnerving cracks on particularly corrugated stretches. Later examination revealed that her rear suspension had begun to disintegrate. Driving through the steep maze of Ryde and the tedious suburbia which stretches from that town southwards through Sandown and Shanklin was like being dragged across volcanic rocks on the seat of my pants. Every wart and cavity in the tarmac seemed to imprint on my gluteus maximus. I suppose there are two reasons for this degenerate transport system: one is that seaside towns have the most appalling drains and the road is constantly being dug up and repatched. The other is that being chalk, the ground underneath subsides.

The strongest impression on entering the island is that it is completely unlike the Sussex and Hampshire countryside you have just left. It looks much more like Dorset – pale, windswept and dessicated. The eastern resorts were now crowded but almost everyone visible seemed to be over 70. Neither elegant nor dowdy, these are middle-rank Victorian resorts whose one concession to their recreational purpose is a bit of wrought-iron frippery here and there. You can almost smell the mothballs and the lily-of-the-valley talc; you fancy you glimpse blue-rinsed matrons ironing antimacassars in the front parlours. The sunshine had persuaded a few under-dressed pensioners to venture on to the prom to begin the summer-long process of turning lobster-pink.

As you proceed south the number of sub-tropical shrubs and palms increases until the resorts have the faintly raffish air of a British enclave overseas. Riviera-style villas and bungalows, all whitewash and plate glass, begin to occupy the best clifftop nooks, some of them only accessible by Alpine driveways. The countryside becomes an odd mixture of bare chalk downland and sudden green-packed little valleys, but the road continued to be so dangerously out of condition that I didn't have a chance to take in much.

Finally the road runs along levelly half-way up a hillside almost steep enough to be a cliff, with the calm aquamarine carpet so nearly below you as to make you dizzy, and just as the first houses of Ventnor begin, you plunge down into the town, which is built on a ridiculously steep slope.

Ventnor was laid out in the 1860s, at the height of the island's popularity as a holiday resort, when the bourgeoisie who could not afford the Grand Tour or the Riviera aped their Queen and their Poet Laureate by settling for the balmy almost-overseas atmosphere of Wight. The town has the unmistakeable atmosphere of a sanatorium; space for it was quite literally dug out of the cliffs of this south-eastern corner so that the houses would catch the maximum sunshine and yet be sheltered from the fierce westerlies which race up the Channel. It has the architecture and the hushed air of a Victorian hospital. The climate allows the most lush vegetation to smooth its corners, and at the foot of the cliff a cosy little shingle beach is backed by a miniature promenade and pricked by a delicate iron pier, now in a dangerous condition and closed. I found the whole place absolutely delightful.

For the rest of the afternoon I wandered its steep slopes, savouring the atmosphere of polite desperation. The town is not as decrepit as most of the residents but nevertheless there is hardly a building which doesn't show signs of the strain of clinging to a crumbling chalk cliff for 130 years. The buildings are mostly very large, and almost every one of them is decorated by a wrought-iron balcony, adding further to its faint exoticism. There are several very large hotels, all of which looked, and later proved to be, almost entirely empty, and innumerable small ones, ditto. The prom has a couple of small arcades, a tiny longshoreman's museum, a few burger bars and shops selling seashells and glass weights: nothing flashy. Most striking of all was the almost church-like hush; I half expected to find sawdust laid on the roads to prevent the noise of Hansoms disturbing the dying.

I picked a guest-house after carefully examining about ten; I suspected that any of them would have rooms to spare. The one I chose, about a hundred yards behind and a hundred feet above the beach, had rooms with tall French windows opening on to a covered verandah overlooking the sea. In the hallway a sagacious-looking African Grey parrot eyed me as I carried in my bags, muttered ''Ere we go' and screamed so piercingly that my ears rang. A notice on the cage read 'My Name is Henry and I Bite'. The scream brought the landlady out to greet me; yes, they had a room. It was tall and airy and the floor was about 20 degrees out of true. I opened the French windows and made myself a cup of tea. The sound of the sea politely washing the pebbles and the late afternoon sun were wonderfully relaxing. I felt, for the first time in ages, contentedly alone and also vaguely expectant, like a character at the beginning of a short story. Henry James, perhaps, or Anita Brookner.

In the evening I went to The Spyglass Inn at the end of the prom. I had an interesting conversation with the amiable landlord about the town and the holiday trade in general. The new business rate and VAT increases have hit hard an already teetering business; Ventnor is much quieter than it was ten years ago. Most hoteliers' hopes are pinned, ironically, on the recession: rising unemployment may mean that an increasing number of families will no longer be able to afford to take their holidays in Spain or Greece. It seems a faint hope, particularly since the ferry fare alone amounts to about a quarter of the price of a cheap flight to Alicante. Two rooms in

226

the cheapest Bed & Breakfast would cost about £140 for a week, with lunch, evening meals, fares and admission fees to add. Still, if anybody is thinking about a change from Benidorm I can unhesitatingly recommend Ventnor along with Llandudno, particularly if you are the quiet type. In fact, if you happen to be a terminally-ill hermit I'd say it would be ideal.

The Spyglass Inn was as likeable as its owner. Done up with nautical bric-à-brac but not overstated, the beer was excellent and the food was delicious and cheap. There was the additional pleasure of a live Trad Jazz band, the Unity Stompers, who provide a rather stolid but merry variety of New Orleans purism. The landlord told me they were from the mainland, amateurs who played strictly for fun. They looked like accountants, and sang like them too.

Over breakfast the next morning (the breakfast room could seat 34 but I was the only eater), I talked to the landlady about my trip. Strangely, she too had a dyslexic child, like my hosts in Lichfield. Once again, the problem had been ignored, pooh-poohed or misdiagnosed until the boy was 14 years old. At one point he was almost certified deaf. He was sent back from secondary school to attend with the juniors twice, once because they thought he was stupid and again because they decided he was lazy. This was in London; the Isle of Wight authorities are 'quite good' in their services to the dyslexic and he now attends a special class in Ventnor once a week (that's *good?*) having left school, not surprisingly, with a deep suspicion of education and no qualifications at all.

The morning was dull and misty with a hint of rain, but it had been lovely to fall asleep listening to the sound of the sea and I had slept more deeply than for many nights. I went for a walk on the beach after breakfast, aware that the ferry would slow down my day's journey but unwilling to shake off Ventnor's pleasant spell too soon. There were only two people on the beach, an angler apparently asleep under his umbrella and a woman jogging in a coral tracksuit. Even up on the main street (it was about ten o'clock on a Wednesday morning) one would think it was a Sunday in February. Ventnor seemed to be in a coma; the landlord of The Spyglass had ruefully remarked that the average age of the town council was 105. I wandered slowly back to the car, passing Blakes Boating and Bathing Hut (established 1830), and a closed-up nightclub with railings along the front wrought like a musical stave scattered with quavers. In the end it is a gently, genteelly sad place, apparently determined to resist the 20th century with the kind of stiff-upper lip that General Gordon displayed at Khartoum. Not until every last man-jack of 'em is dead will anything give. Ventnor cannot last; it would rather slip quietly into the sea than change.

WELLS

The witch of Wookey Hole

The protected eastern side of the Isle of Wight is warm and verdant; the western and southern coasts are bleak and windswept. After a drive along the tortuous road out of Ventnor through what appeared to be tropical rainforest, I emerged suddenly into a landscape which reminded me powerfully of north-west Scotland. There is the same unceasing gale, the same twisted little thorn trees grow, and the same uncomfortable-looking sheep wander at will in the middle of the road. Only the boulders are missing. Shortly afterwards it became clear that the sheep were an anachronism: as with the Sussex Downs almost everything has been ploughed up. The main road follows the coast closely and there are no villages on it after Niton, back in the Temperate Zone, until you reach Freshwater Bay just below the Needles at the westerly tip. On a cool April morning this stretch of road was merely boring; on a winter's day it must be positively antarctic.

Freshwater is a dull little place, terribly jammed-up with traffic, where I once spent a summer holiday with a school chum which was enlivened by two factors. Firstly I kissed a girl for the first time with something approaching sexual passion (an event for which I would forgive Freshwater looking like Smethwick) and secondly my friend's older brother, a tall, thin young man of about 26 (we were 13) with a two-inch beard growing out of his Adam's Apple who collected moths, suddenly stood up in the middle of afternoon tea, shouted, 'This bloody family makes me sick!' and stormed out of the room. For a long minute everyone was as silent as they had been for the long minute before his outburst, then his mother offered me a Rich Tea biscuit as if nothing had happened. It was my first encounter with the strange ways of the English upper-middle classes. Eventually he reappeared and offered to show me a moth he had discovered. It was about two millimetres across and pure white. I tried hard to look impressed, but I couldn't take my eyes off his beard. When he talked it waggled up and down, as if some small creature stranded halfway up his giraffe-like neck was trying to attract my attention by waving a red towel.

I had to wait half an hour for the ferry from Yarmouth to Lymington, a painless enough delay since it's a pretty little place with a little naval fort and a number of picturesque red brick buildings grouped around the quay. I made a cup of tea and wrote postcards. In my schooldays the ferry here was a battered old Second World War tank landing craft which rolled like a rubber duck. Now it is an unlikely looking contraption, like a stack of Portakabins balanced on a mattress, and certainly oughtn't to float. On board an Orwellian voice gave an interminable safety talk in tones which suggested it was talking to a valium-soaked three-year-old; 'The life-boats are po-si-tioned to-wards the rear of the pa-ssen-ger deck on ei-ther side. If you he-ar an alarm bell ring-ing con-tin-u-ously . . .' and so on. Then seamlessly the same pre-recorded voice launched into an invitation to buy re-fresh-ments, tea, coff-ee and bev-er-ag-es in the sa-loon. Luckily most of it was inaudible due to a frenzied attack on a nearby slot-machine meted out by a mild-looking young man – obviously a genius who rode the ferries every day solely in order to empty the machines of as much money as possible in the half-hour it takes to hop the Solent. I watched open-mouthed as the thing virtually lay on its back and said take me, take me. He won, by my count, £60.

Lymington is a yacht-place. They may call them 'boats' but only in the same self-deprecating manner that a Rolls-Royce owner refers to 'my saloon car'. For about a mile as the ferry chugs into the Lymington River it passes floating pieces of conspicuous wealth lined up along the quay with scarcely a cocktail-stick's length between them. Gleaming, phallic and lean, they belong to the mysterious world where to sail does not simply mean to cross the water, but to utilise as much equipment as possible in doing so. They bristle with radar and aerials, anemometers and satellite dishes. Some of them are big enough for the racehorses to come along too. Lymington itself is a sedate little town where even the women behind the till in the bakery seem to have taken elocution lessons. Everyone I encountered had a sort of strangulated lock-jawed delivery which made Elizabeth Windsor sound like Barbara Windsor. I passed a headscarfed woman attached to a dalmation which was sniffing the bum of a black labrador attached to another headscar-fed woman.

'Rarely, dahling, hye offl!' exclaimed Mrs Dalmatian.

'Yers, isn't it?' replied Mrs Labrador, 'nye, hev you got time for larnch?'

'Nay, aim afraid not, ai've got to do Molly's flars. Hye abyte Teeoosdy?'

I drove out before I started to talk like Prince Charles and plunged into the New Forest. At first it is largely heathland, but then you drive for several miles under mature oaks. There seemed to be considerably less storm damage here than in East Suffolk, unless they've made a much better job of tidying up. The oaks were just coming into leaf, mustardy green. The New Forest Ponies wander around with haughty contempt for traffic. There are signs everywhere: 'HIGH RISK ROAD FOR ANIMAL DEATHS – STAY UNDER 40 MPH'. So I stayed under 40 mph – not difficult – and was promptly overtaken by a succession of cars whose drivers gave me you-stupid-bastard stares as they passed. Through Brockenhurst and Lyndhurst to Brook, a lovely village with a huge roadsign: 'ANIMALS ON ROAD DAY AND NIGHT'. I suppose it is possible that there may be people who think that all the ponies go home at 5.30 to watch *Telly Addicts*?

I left the forest at Hale and crossed the Avon at Downton, where the river is divided into three parallel streams. I wanted to see Salisbury but I was pressed for time and the city proved to be inaccessible in any case. I think it was Salisbury because in the distance I could see a very tall spire, or what might have been a spire, covered with scaffolding. Is there a single cathedral in the land which is not permanently encased in steel poles and plastic sheeting? They weren't all built at the same time, so why are they all falling down at the same time? At any rate, I found myself zipping around an enormous concrete moat, from which periodically I ventured on to various sliproads only to find that they were cul-de-sacs or led me smartly back on to the bypass. Eventually I gave up and went west along the valley of the Ebble.

This little chalk stream runs almost straight along a furrow in the Wiltshire Downs, for 20 miles or so. The road which runs alongside, like the river itself, gradually gets narrower and narrower as one proceeds until at the western extremity it is little more than a muddy track between steep banks with scarcely room for a bee to pass the van on either side. Along the way are a line of famously pretty villages: Stratford Tony, Bishopstone, Broad Chalke, Ebbesbourne Wake, Alvediston and Berwick St John. Oddly, these all lie across the river from the road and are reached by bridges. Even when the road itself crosses the river the next village, Alvediston, is on the opposite shore. The valley is shallow and the sides are bare, but the riverside is of untouched watermeadows and stands of willow and broad-leaved trees. Broad Chalke was for many years the home of Cecil Beaton, and his house, as elegant and fey as he was, is one of the most delicate Georgian houses I've ever seen. The valley is as charming as anything in the Cotswolds but receives far less attention; I passed no cars at all along its entire length.

It was now late afternoon and the sky was like cloth-of-gold. The lane ran across a patch of heath which might have formed the opening scene of a Hardy novel, down a hill and then up into Shaftesbury, a town whose reputation rests on one street, the impossibly steep Gold Hill. This cobbled lane, so precipitous that the lower storey of one thatched cottage abuts the

230

upper storey of the next, is blocked at the top end by a medieval building with an arched lower part so that pedestrians can fall down the hill but not horses and carts. I found Shaftesbury a workaday little market town (there is still a market, though housed in a new factory-like shed on the outskirts) with an air of sleepy Dickensian contentment, where one expects the price of a bushel of barley to be the chief topic of conversation over pewter pot and churchwarden. But in fact the extortionate cost of new tyres for the Range-Rover proved to be the chief source of grievance in the pub. I ordered a pint of fresh iced orange juice, which got me plenty of funny looks and cost me a fortune, but it was worth it.

Gillingham, the next village, was as ugly as Shaftesbury had been attractive, and the entire main street was being dug up, so that it took about 40 minutes to travel two miles. I was by now pretty exhausted, though still cheerful, and since the evening promised to be a long, light one I kept my speed down and stopped fairly often to peer around. I was still some way from Wells and over 30 miles from my sister's house in Bristol where I had scrounged a bed for the night, but I was encouraged by the growing feeling of light at the end of the tunnel and, strangely, this made me acutely conscious of my good luck in being free to roam the countryside and determined to enjoy my last few days of liberty. It is not difficult to enjoy rural Dorset on a fine spring evening, particularly when you know there is good company and a proper bed waiting at the end of the day.

On a hill overlooking Bruton I found a ruined dovecote, once part of a priory but now the only trace of it, standing like a broken and mysterious watchtower guarding the quiet valley below. Inside, someone had sprayed the words 'Hip Hop', but this conjured up people dancing around in smocks rather than the ghettoes of New York. The sun was an orange ball four inches above the horizon; cricketers paced out arcane runic messages on a pitch far below. The church bell rang. It was enough to make you feel patriotic.

I decided that I couldn't get any more tired than I already was so I took a detour to Castle Cary simply because I liked the sound of it. It turned out to be the best piece of serendipity of the trip, a little town as mellow as 30-year old malt and the same pallid tawny colour. The loudest sounds there were my own footsteps and the cooing of pigeons in the trees. A particularly beautiful house behind a high creeper-covered wall made me stop in my tracks; once again, as at Merthyr, I had a bewilderingly strong sense of *déjà vu*. The hairs on the back of my neck stood up. It was almost eerily powerful, the moment pregnant with expectation. *Something's going to happen now*. I glanced up and down the deserted street; nothing moved, and nothing looked familiar except that house. Afraid someone might grow suspicious of me gawping at the house, I broke the moment and went back to the car.

There is no better time to come across the levels towards Glastonbury

Tor than at sunset, especially if, as on this occasion, there is a man in a white robe standing on the top of the silhouetted hill with his arms outstretched to the last rays of the sun. The view across the meadows and orchards to the Tor with its medieval tower is one of the most memorable in Britain, on a par with the first glimpse of Ely over the Fens or the Queen's View down Loch Tummel to Schiehallion. I would have liked to have climbed the Tor but it would have been dark by the time I got up there, and I knew I would return that way so I hurried on to Wells. And, oddly, the most permanent memory of that long evening is not St Michael's Tower at Glastonbury, or the house at Castle Cary or the elegiac valley below the dovecote at Bruton, nor even the magnificent complexity of Wells Cathedral, but the television aerial which stands on the hilltop north of Wells. Against a sky of the most limpid pale blue the mast caught the sun but the guy-ropes were invisible, so that there appeared to be a 400-foot line ruled in the sky, a white ladder to heaven.

I had a rest-day in Bristol, writing up my notes and meeting a nephew for the first time. Bristol is a sprawling, messy, run-down, treacle-coloured city of immense charm. The centre was blown to smithereens in the last war and the stuff they replaced it with is mostly brutal concrete rubbish, but there are too many compensations for this to matter very much. Clifton is a lovely semi-decayed Regency suburb above the Avon gorge and much of the rest of Bristol is redolent of Victorian pride in technology: iron-clad ships, the Great Western Railway, the Clifton Suspension Bridge. The ghost of Isembard Kingdom Brunel is still around, and the evening sun seems to glower through the smoke and fumes of his great machines. I don't know anywhere that can match a Bristol sunset.

On the morning of 26 April I drove south again to Wells, across the curiously unfriendly Mendip Hills and through the village of Green Ore. There have been mines for copper and gold in these hills since prehistoric times. I was facing the prospect of trying to find something to say about Wells with some trepidation, since from my brief view the night before last it seemed, apart from the cathedral, particularly uninteresting. Happily, just before the city I saw a sign to Wookey Hole Caves, and knew that my bacon was saved.

The caves are privately owned and well exploited commercially. There is a cafeteria and a gift shop and a huge carpark and – no! it can't be true! – several coachloads of French schoolchildren. *Nom d'un nom! C'est la persécution!*

I waited for the guided tour to begin in the company of two middle-aged German women, one of whom was obviously having second thoughts about going underground. Her friend spent a long time polysyllabically reassuring her that the caves were unlikely to collapse precisely at this moment, but to no avail. She bottled out and headed back to the gift shop while we troglodytes plunged into the cool subterranean labyrinth. The tour is aided by a sophisticated system of coloured lights and sound effects, partly because although they are impressively large, the caves are not particularly beautiful. There are 12 chambers open to the public, some of them reached by artificial tunnels blasted out of the rock, for naturally they were connected only by 'sumps' – passages below the level of the River Axe which hollowed out the system.

Local legend (according to the guide, anyway) tells of a witch who resided in the caves 'two thousand years ago' and whose evil spells blighted the land for miles around. Fed up with this old ratbag, the residents of Somerset sent for a monk from Glastonbury, one Benedictus (what else?), to exorcise her. This was remarkably clever given that Glastonbury Abbey wasn't founded until several hundred years later and Christ hadn't even been born. Benedictus went in clutching a candle and had the presence of mind to bless the waters of the Axe, scoop some up, and corner the poor old thing in the second chamber, the so-called Witch's Kitchen. A large stalagmite is supposed to be the hag, turned to stone as the holy droplets touched her. If this is true, then the woman weighed 27 stone and suffered from a particularly unpleasant variety of leprosy. A little way off her familiar, a small dog, is also pointed out. This much more closely resembles a fossilised animal that its mistress; but curiously it appears to have been a well-groomed Pekinese.

Until comparatively recently the first chamber was renowned for its spectacular stalactites, which had formed as water dripped through the dolomitic conglomerate (puddingstone to you and me) over millenia. One day the writer Alexander Pope (1688–1744) was brought to see the caves on a tour of the West Country. He took a fancy to the stalactites, engaged a local troop of musketeers, and had them all shot off the roof of the cavern to decorate the summerhouse in his garden at Twickenham. Presumably most of them were smashed as they fell, anyway, unless they piled up mountains of straw on the floor, or persuaded the soldiers to try to catch several hundredweight of stone spike. Poets are such sensitive souls.

The fantastic clarity of the water as it flows through the caves makes the river appear completely motionless and with a depth of no more than three or four feet. In fact it flows very quickly and is in places over 20 feet deep. In times of heavy rainfall several of the chambers fill up in a matter of seconds, including one of those open to the public. The first human explorers of the caves were neolithic hunter-gatherers and before them came hyenas and rhinoceroses. There was a substantial Celtic community within the first cavern; they made offerings to the spirit of the river in the pool of the second chamber. In recent years the system has been explored by that weird variety of person who thinks it is a good idea to get stuck in a pitch black water-filled hole several miles underground. Using specially-developed diving equipment to resist the extreme pressure and cold of the water, more than 20 successive chambers have been discovered in a descending system over ten miles in length. The largest cave yet discovered is 200 feet in height, with over half a mile of rock above it. Beyond the furthest point of current exploration the river emerges from a sump little more than a foot wide which descends vertically for over 300 feet. The man who has led the explorations to date plans to actually crawl down this nightmare tube, but he has to wait until technology produces a suit which will allow him to avoid being killed by the pressure as he does so. Just thinking about it makes me want to run up the nearest hill and scream my lungs out.

Thankfully the French schoolchildren were not on the same tour as myself. The prospect of being trapped underground with a 150 garrulous *jeunes gens* would have been enough to send me down any 300-foot drain-pipe.

So eventually into Wells itself to find the Cathedral under scaffolding as usual. The close is exceptionally large, cut off from the narrow medieval streets and their snarl-up of traffic by a series of gates. The city is minute, or was; it is now ringed by industrial development. I had little time to explore having spent an hour and a half in the caves and then at the exhibition of Victorian funfair amusements which is an optional extra, where I discovered *les petits* screaming with delight in front of the distorting mirrors and frantically turning the handles of the What The Boutellier Saw machines. But one building stood out from all the others, including the cathedral; St Cuthbert's Parish Church has the most beautiful tower I have ever seen, a pale masterpiece of slender neo-Gothic, breathtaking, sublime.

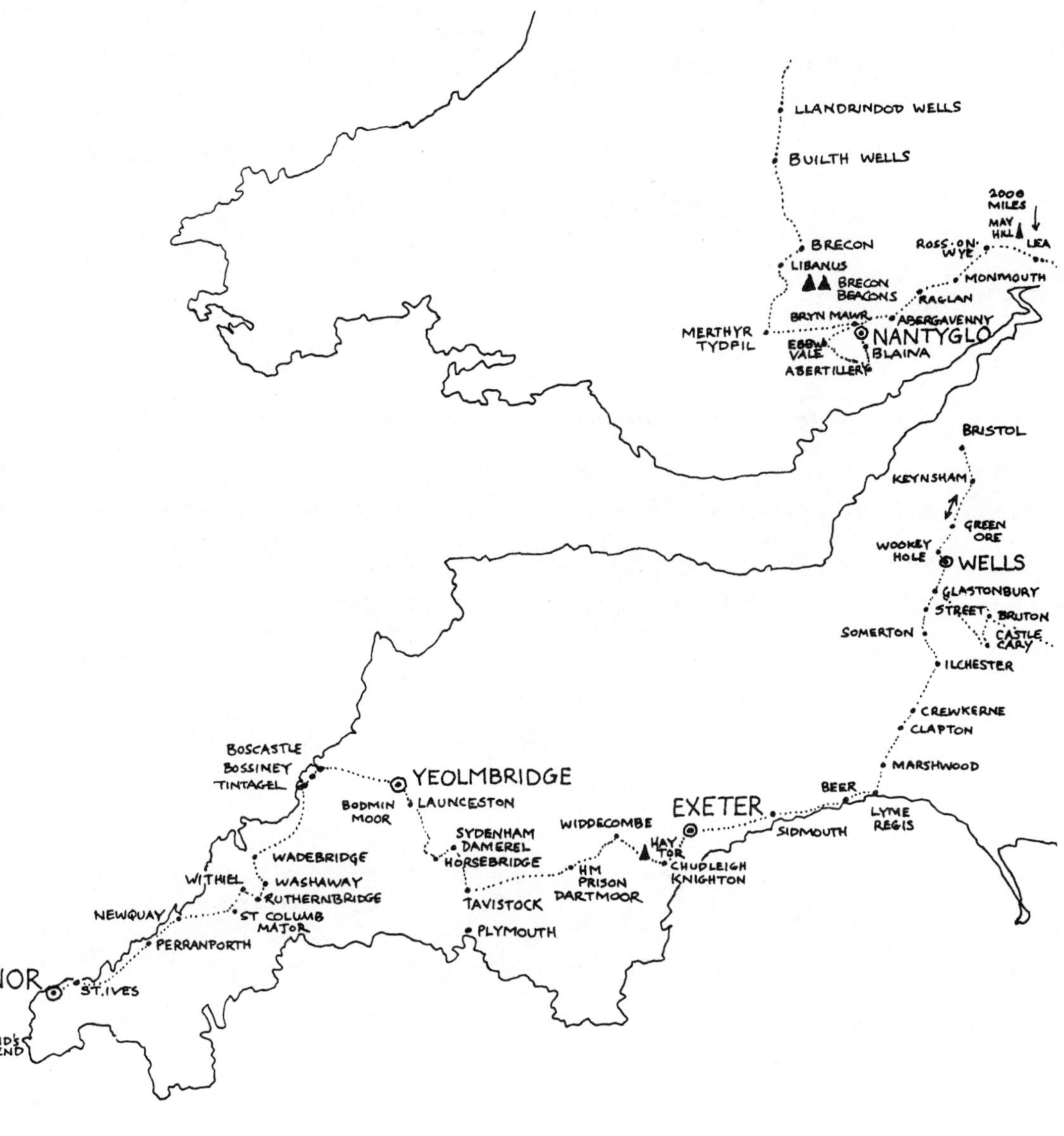

LLANDRINDOD WELLS
BUILTH WELLS
2000 MILES
MAY HILL
LEA
BRECON
ROSS-ON-WYE
LIBANUS
BRECON BEACONS
MONMOUTH
RAGLAN
BRYN MAWR
ABERGAVENNY
MERTHYR TYDFIL
EBBW VALE
NANTYGLO
BLAINA
ABERTILLERY
BRISTOL
KEYNSHAM
GREEN ORE
WOOKEY HOLE
WELLS
GLASTONBURY
STREET
BRUTON
SOMERTON
CASTLE CARY
ILCHESTER
CREWKERNE
CLAPTON
MARSHWOOD
BEER
BOSCASTLE
BOSSINEY
TINTAGEL
YEOLMBRIDGE
LAUNCESTON
BODMIN MOOR
SYDENHAM DAMEREL
WIDDECOMBE
EXETER
HAY TOR
LYME REGIS
SIDMOUTH
HORSEBRIDGE
CHUDLEIGH KNIGHTON
WADEBRIDGE
WITHIEL
WASHAWAY
HM PRISON DARTMOOR
RUTHERNBRIDGE
NEWQUAY
ST COLUMB MAJOR
TAVISTOCK
PERRANPORTH
PLYMOUTH
INOR
S
ST IVES
AND'S END

EXETER

An excellent example of the exquisite exposition of an unexpected expiry

I suppose I had better get it over with: the slightly forced reference above is to a memorial in the aisle of Exeter Cathedral. It commemorates one Sacharissa Hibbert, who died in 1828 at the age of 27. It is a small white marble tablet set into the wall; beneath the simple fact of her existence recorded in lovely neoclassical letters is a miraculously crisp carving of a rose being cut down by a sickle. It made me weep, but then I cry whenever I watch *Dumbo* too.

Before this bout of lachrymosity in the cathedral I had once again come through Glastonbury; this time I had stopped and looked around to find, as I remembered from previous visits, that the town has a singularly unmagical atmosphere, as mystical as Bolton on a wet Sunday in November. The Abbey ruins (you have to pay to get in) and the Tor apart, it is a nasty little place, dirty and crowded. Various ways have been found to exploit the wholly unproven association of the town with King Arthur, varying from the seriously wacky but heartfelt New Age stuff to the extremely tacky souvenirs and garbled 'history' with which tourists are spoon-fed. If the Once and Future King does choose to return to help this island in its hour of peril the first thing he will do will probably be to smash the town of Glastonbury to bits.

It had been a fine, warm morning, but had grown close. Just beyond Glastonbury it grew very dark and a tremendous thunderstorm ensued, forcing me off the road for a time since Blodwen's wipers couldn't cope with the sheer volume of water. There was a strong sulphurous smell in the air and the wind blew up in violent fits, bending the trees spitefully and

236

then mysteriously receding once again into dead calm. The countryside of Somerset in this apocalyptic light took on a haunted, eldritch look, and it was easy to imagine that this had indeed been a land of miracles, portents and heroic deeds.

The fleecing and duping of tourists has a long and proud history in these parts and, indeed, the chief 'evidence' of an Arthurian connection seems to have been an elegant exercise in this branch of economics. The Legends of Arthur and his knights were the smash hit of the Middle Ages, particularly in France, where the courtly tradition the stories exemplified was deeply fashionable. French poetry and chivalry were all the rage in Britain. It seems to have been the French who first associated Glastonbury with Avalon; the oldest sources of the Arthurian cycle are Welsh but may well have originated in the British kingdom of Strathclyde in southern Scotland, whose people migrated to Gwynedd when the Scots arrived from Ireland in the fifth and sixth centuries, or indeed in any of the many other British princedoms and kingdoms of the late Roman and early Dark Age era. It is by no means certain that Arthur was a real person at all; most of the stories were originally told about earlier Celtic heroes, and some are medieval inventions. What is known, however, is that in 1191 the monks of Glastonbury claimed to have discovered the tomb of Arthur and what had formerly been a minor and remote community henceforth became one of the great religious centres, and the Abbey one of the richest in Britain. There are very serious problems in believing the monks' claim, not the least of which is that every shred of archaeological evidence has disappeared. Even the three contemporary accounts we have of the exhumation differ very widely in their descriptions of the tomb and even the inscription found with it. But there are a number of tantalisingly suggestive clues which have persuaded some historians to propose that though the monks may have dressed up the mausoleum they discovered and tinkered with the evidence it may, just may, have actually been Arthur's resting-place. That, as is usual with matters of mystic and spiritual importance, is enough; faith has done the rest for almost a thousand years.*

I do not wish to give the impression that I am fiercely anti-New Age, anti-mystic or even anti-Arthur. Indeed the Arthurian Cycle and the so-called Matter of Britain have been one of my chief obsessions for many years. As with the Anglo-Saxon ship-burial of Sutton Hoo, the archaeology of the Arthurian period a century earlier is one of the most exciting, tantalising and frustrating chapters in British history. I am a firm believer, on no more hard evidence than a gut reaction, that Arthur was a real person, but more importantly the Arthurian legends seem to me to be a seminal influence on British culture; they are to Britain what *The Iliad* and *The Odyssey* are to Europe, and similarly their 'meaning' lies beyond, and

---

* For the best summary of the evidence see Leslie Alcock's *Arthur's Britain*, Penguin, 1971

is far greater than, the incidents related within them. In no small part this is because, as with Homer, the romances overlie and in some places barely conceal an oral tradition which goes back many hundreds of years before the real Arthur could have existed. Stories such as these are thus the only means by which the countless generations of our preliterate ancestors whose artifacts litter our countryside can speak to us. It is small wonder that for some they have come to be crucial to an attempt to make sense of the world in general.

The storm left a landscape shrouded in vapour and smelling like the hot house at Kew. I made my way cautiously through flooded lanes to Ilchester and the Foss Way, here an unlovely dual carriageway. Then I cut south into Dorset, and the green rolling Somerset hills gave way to dry sandy heathland as if the name alone is enough to magic away Arthur and set the scene for *Tess of the D'Urbervilles*. Beyond Crewkerne, on an appalling road, the settlements seemed to die away and for an hour I wrestled the creaking van through countryside as deserted as any I had seen since Redesdale in Northumbria. Later, checking the atlas, I discovered that this was no false impression; between Crewkerne and Lyme Regis, a good 20 miles, are just two hamlets, Clapton and Marshwood, nine miles apart.

Lyme Regis is not a place which was designed with Morris Minors in mind. It is so steep that crampons and ropes are required for a visit to Woolworths, and the streets are coiled like a drunken anaconda. The chief income of the town comes from carpark fees; since there is absolutely nowhere to stop on the roads they feel that they can charge what they like. As I was unwilling to spend the price of a packet of Marlboro Lights for a chance to break both legs falling down the High Street I used the carpark as a turning point and roared back out of town at a steady 8 mph in first gear.

I needed a rest. Beer seemed a promising option. Once in it, however, I consumed only a non-alcoholic Genuine Traditional Recipe Devon ice-cream which had the consistency and taste of putty. Grouped around a little cove at the foot of a steep wooded coombe, it is a spruce little suntrap popular with wrinklies and still engaged in fishing the limpid Channel waters for lobster and crab. Indeed, so crystalline is the sea around this coast that it seems amazing that these crustaceans have not evolved to the extent that they can see an old tub full of potbellied Devon salts coming a mile off. Beer was half-empty, with only a handful of lacquered septuagenarians dozing beneath the yuccas. On the beach a few old sea-dogs sat by the rusting tractors which haul the boats on to the shingle mending nets and pots; they were probably interior designers most of the time. Yet again the public lavatory provided unexpected sociological insight: here the grafitti was uniformly heterosexual – not even so much as a 'Hello, Sailor'. Why should Beer be straight but, for instance, Jedburgh wholly gay? It must be the sea-food, or the hormones in border cattle.

As usual my destination lay slightly too far, given my predilection for byways and the antediluvian nature of my vehicle, to be reached in time for a thorough assessment before darkness and exhaustion overcame me. Seaton and Sidmouth did not delay me; one glance was enough in both cases. Breezeblock, amusements, chipshops . . . go West, young man, and fast.

On arriving in Exeter I felt I at least ought to see the city centre and the cathedral before heading for a B & B, a bath and blissful oblivion. After all, in the morning it might all have fallen down. Actually I was suffering still from a strong feeling of guilt at my hurried and superficial, not to say glib and facetious, assessments of the towns and cities unlucky enough to be on my route. This drove me (quite unnecessarily since it was far too late in the journey to make any difference) to at least go through the motions of investigation even if I was on the verge of collapse, which I usually was. I did it for you, reader.

All that the evening's perambulation told me, however, was that Exeter is as full of winos as Oxford, that no photograph has ever done justice to the cathedral, which is as staggering as the plonkies on the grass all around, and that for a city of its size (pop. 95,621) there are remarkably few places to eat. In the end I settled for Colonel Sanders' Celebration Dinner, which appears to celebrate the invention of hot cardboard.

After a night spent between nylon sheets in a guesthouse near the University where the landlady called me 'me daarrlin'' and a Traditional English Breakfast so full of grease that I didn't dare strike any matches for at least two hours after I set out refreshed into Darkest Exeter. The first impression is that despite its modest size – Norwich for instance is a third as big again – it has a consistently more metropolitan feel than that East Anglian city. Atmospherically it is closer to Bristol, being similarly nautical and industrial and having developed at more or less the same time, between 1800 and 1850. Norwich's heyday was 300 years earlier. But whereas Bristol never lets you forget that it is a major city, neither Exeter nor Norwich let you forget that they are essentially country towns, however sophisticated and complex they have become. The scale of Exeter's great public buildings, being Victorian, is much greater than that of Norwich's, which are earlier, and the medieval centre of Exeter was cleared away at the height of the Victorian era to make way for a series of broad Imperial streets. Hitler did the rest; again, like Bristol, almost the whole town centre was flattened. But whereas Bristol was rebuilt in concrete apparently after the example of a chimpanzee playing with wooden bricks, Exeter wisely opted for a unified scheme of rather subdued neo-Georgian brick. It is dull, but convenient, particularly now that vehicular access is limited to buses only. Around this shopping centre are the remains of a number of medieval churches lost to the bombs, now crumbling crimson sandstone shells planted with flowers.

Many are of great age – one near the Cathedral was consecrated in the same year as Westminster Abbey, 1065.

Inside the cathedral the choir were practising, and very good they were too. What could be more delightful than to sit at the end of the nave in the early morning with the sun streaming through the stained glass and listen to a masterpiece of polyphonic music? Apart from Sacharissa's memorial, I found myself at one point standing on top of Gustav Holst. It always strikes me as rather mean to give someone a memorial stone in the floor. Eventually the ambience started to bring back rather too many memories of my own five years in Choir School, which left me with an abiding love of music and a complete absence of any religious faith. But that is very definitely another story. I lit a couple of candles, the only ritual I can observe without bringing on a feeling of hypocrisy, and made my way back into the sunshine.

It is not only the civic architecture which is on the grand scale in Exeter; they seem to go for very generous houses too. Four or five-storey Victorian houses are not uncommon, particularly in St David's, which is reached from the city centre via a narrow iron bridge over the rooftops of medieval houses below. The sections of the bridge, built in 1834, were cast at Blaina Ironworks, a quarter of a mile along the hillside from Nantyglo. The hilly topography of the city adds the usual something extra, as with Edinburgh and Birmingham, Norwich and Bristol: there is always a view however dispiriting the streets. And the streets of St David's, though not exactly squalid, are by no means as salubrious as their faded grandeur implies they once were. The enormous houses are divided into bedsits and flats or, occasionally, offices. Only at the city end have some been restored and given over to lawyers' and doctors' businesses. As is frequently the case with grand houses of this sort, their very size today makes them difficult to maintain; families want to live further out in the suburbs. The houses have begun to peel and crack; buddleia sprouts from the guttering. In the evening, walking down to my bed-and-breakfast, I was greeted by a number of young and not so young women who were not dressed for a cold April night.

At the top of the most central hill in the city is another sign of the wisdom of its Victorian City Fathers – a long, curving park along the foot of the old fortifications. From here Exeter's modern, sprawling estates can be seen eating into the lush South Devon countryside – sadly, the countryside is almost out of sight. Perhaps the moment when green fields are no longer visible from this point will be the moment which tips the psychological balance of the city from friendly provincial urbanity into something harsher, less relaxed and more claustrophobic. I hope not. For the moment it is a civilised place, scruffy in places, yes, but not overbearing, pretentious or preserved in aspic. There is life at the centre. When the heart of a city empties at five o'clock, look out.

YEOLMBRIDGE

Yeti

The landscape of South Devon seems to me to be the only arrangement of hills, fields and trees which could possibly have produced the rich Devon burr or clotted cream. Nowhere else exemplifies the ideal of English countryside so well; the Marches are too expansive and mysterious, the Midlands too civilised, Norfolk too denuded, Sussex too tame, Yorkshire too gritty and Hampshire too full of *Telegraph* readers. South Devon is steeply rolling, on a scale neither exhaustingly large nor uninterestingly gentle. The lines are sinuous, generous, like those of a fertility goddess, the valleys and clefts pubically wooded. The soil is a rich dark red, in places almost bloody, fading to blush-pink where it is seeded with lime or where a steep sunny hillside dries it out. It is almost all pasture – as is anywhere which now corresponds even vaguely to the 18th-century version of landscape which remains the standard against which the British measure lowland beauty. Modern methods of cultivation have destroyed too many trees and hedges elsewhere; some areas have acquired a new, more austere beauty as a result of this loss, others have the ugliness of a flayed corpse.

I meandered through the deep lanes, which look on the map like the doodlings of a labyrinth designer driven mad in search of the fourth dimension. Heading consistently in one direction is impossible; unless one is willing to stop every 200 yards and consult the map one simply has to follow one's nose, take as many left turns as right and hope that they average out. I only once found myself driving up my own exhaust pipe – a particularly noisome farmyard spilling squelch on to the lane gave the game away. I knew I had passed that way ten minutes earlier because that particular combination of bovine gases is something no one could ever forget.

Thus I found myself at length where I wanted to be – at the foot of Dartmoor. There is no warning to be read from the landscape as you approach. You suddenly realise that it is hanging above you like a thundercloud. Then a large roadsign tells you which roads on the moor are suitable for various types of vehicle: 'black' routes for anything up to coaches and artics, 'brown' for cars and vans and 'blue' for suicidal dwarfs on unicycles. This is not a great deal of help, since most people find that they have only enough time to glimpse the first couple of words before they are past the sign and shifting frantically down through the gears as they shoot upwards towards the rim of the moor at the angle of the Space Shuttle on take-off. The climb is initially through broad-leaved woodland, then the trees seem to shrink almost as you watch, so quickly does the altitude affect their mature height. After only a couple of minutes all that remain are twisted, rickety little thorns and beeches clutching the stones in a desperate attempt to remain terrestrial. The road levels on to a kind of shelf and you realise that what you thought from below was the summit is a cruel deception; once more you have to persuade your weary and overheated steed up the final wall. The top is as remote from the friendly enfolding lands below as Sutherland is from Sussex. Ahead, the horizon is a simple clean line dividing the uniformly tea-leaf coloured ground from the (today) uniformly dove-grey sky.

The first thing which might be described as a feature appeared through the mist like a Henry Moore sculpture: Hay Tor, above the cunningly named village of Haytor. Since the carpark which took up 90 per cent of the village was full and a stream of brightly-anoraked people was visible snaking up the gentle slope to the stones I thought I'd join them; this, I thought, is obviously what people come up here to do. Half an hour later, exhausted by a 'gentle' climb which proved to be of Eiger-like ferocity (except that the Eiger isn't covered by grass as slippery as greased Teflon) I reached the Tor to discover that not only was the view from the summit identical in every respect to that anywhere else on the moor, but the brightly-anoraked snake was composed of French schoolchildren. A minute later even these unprepossessing items were almost obliterated by a fog which descended as quickly and inexplicably as the Sterling/Deutschmark rate. I slid back down to the road, bumping into the odd wild pony en route, to find the carpark mysteriously deserted. Presumably the owners of several hundred vehicles had been inside the café just behind it and had sensibly gone home as soon as the mist came down. I brewed a cup of tea and swore never to venture higher than 300 feet again. Having warmed my insides and got some feeling back into my hands I set off once again.

Although, because it is a National Park, cars are forbidden from stopping except in officially designated areas, all along the road there were cars which had been swung off the tarmac and abandoned as their owners went off for a walk. There was a great deal of litter. Everywhere there were people allowing their dogs to run free despite explicit and frequent signs warning them not to; the dogs merrily worried the sheep and the horses, which at least one family I passed seemed to find hilariously funny. Good old Rover – oh look, Mummy, he's decapitated that sheep. Dartmoor has a unique ecology and is the most beautiful of the three great south-western moors. It is a national scandal that the Army has been permitted to take over almost all the land between Yes Tor in the north and Rough Tor in the centre; there is now such gross agricultural overproduction in many other areas that there can be no question that they could be found adequate accommodation on less valuable land. The decision to route the Oke-hampton bypass over the moor is one of the most fat-headed decisions of a phenomenally fat-headed government and looks very suspiciously as if it was the result of pressure brought to bear by a handful of wealthy land-owners. Worst of all the management of the moor seems to be criminally under-resourced and the signs of over-use are plain to see; in some places the natural vegetation is worn away in great swathes. People play football, ride motorcycles across country, light bonfires and dump old fridges and mattresses.

When a public building is too full it is regarded as unsafe. Nobody would enjoy going to the cinema if, after all the seats were full, another thousand people were let in. Why, if the survival of the moor itself depends on it, should access to it not be limited to the residents and a daily quota of visitors? Why not charge them admission, indeed, to pay for the proper management of wildlife and provide development for the remote communi-ties there? Only two roads cross the moor, so the introduction of tolls and the control of access would be perfectly simple. However, I don't suppose that any government would have the balls to do it. Restricted parking in cities is one thing; restricting access to a national treasure is another. Unless, of course, it is privately owned, in which case Joe Public can be kept out, and the owner can destroy the whole site with impunity. No doubt there would be an outcry from people who would swear by the Magna Carta that it was the God-given right of every Briton to walk the retriever (unleashed) on Dartmoor. But no such right exists. And if it is the duty of the authorities to preserve what has been entrusted to them then they should do whatever is necessary to do so. But then I'm against charging for admission to national monuments, aren't I?

Through Widecombe-in-the-Moor, where Tom Pearce's old mare doth appear ghastly white, a village now partly owned by the National Trust with a lovely 14th-century church, a strangely green little place tucked in a shallow bowl in the high moor. Then on to the main trans-moor road, past the prison. News broadcasts always make out HM Prison Dartmoor to be a grim Victorian fortress set in impenetrable bogs and permanently shrouded in mist. It is, in fact, a collection of rather pleasant-looking buildings in the green, tree-scattered countryside of the gently descending western edge. Any old lag who escapes 'on to the moors' instead of jogging down the hill into Tavistock needs his head examined and ought to be in Broadmoor, not Dartmoor.

Tavistock looks as it sounds: the quintessence of small squirearchical foxhuntin' towns. Compact and elegant, basking in the west-facing nook at the foot of the moor and set along a beautiful river valley, that of the Tavy, the only British river to be named after a mongoose, Tavistock is far enough from the nearest city, Plymouth, to have escaped any overspill development or speculative commuter-clutter. It was 2.30 and I was starving; a hot Cornish pasty (although still in Devon) filled the corners nicely. Why do the objects described as Cornish pasties available in supermarkets look like anaemic armadilloes and taste like their droppings? This one, from a bakery, was full to capacity with steaming veg., also unknown in the mass-produced variety, where a greyish paste is smeared thinly on the interior walls like mould.

The afternoon was hot, cloudless, still: a summer's day lost in a cold spring. I lost myself deliberately in the steep lanes of the Tamar valley, where there was a sign to a village called Chipshop. At least I suppose it was a village, though it's not on the map. A chipshop on its own in countryside 12 miles from anywhere sounds too civilised to be credible. I nosed down a narrow, worryingly vertical lane into a village called Sydenham Damerel, where a cat, asleep on the white line in the middle of the road was woken by what it probably thought was an army of hamsters but proved to be the suspension of a knackered Morris van. The cat stalked to the side of the road in a huff. It appeared to be the only resident. I had visions of a sort of Edgar Allen Poe nightmare in which the aging occupants of a remote village have been eaten by cats. The puss eyed me in a manner which suggested Clement Freud examining a dish of truffles. I moved on.

At the bottom of the hill I came to a hamlet, also not on my map, called Horsebridge where the Tamar is spanned by a beautiful double-arched medieval bridge with triangular recesses in the parapets so that pedestrians can step aside to allow larger traffic to pass. On the other side was Cornwall. The valley was as still as a photograph, and as silent except for the ceaseless extemporisation of skylarks. I leaned for a while over the bridge and watched the weed waving hypnotically in the shallow river. In the meadow above the bridge a huge chestnut tree was putting out its candelabra. It was almost May, I was almost there.

Up the other side was Launceston, as nasty a little town as you could find anywhere in the country, topped by a little red fort like an angry pimple. The centre of the town is a mess of mediocre buildings of various periods, but this is completely overwhelmed by a gigantic new estate of pale grey terraced boxes – there must be close on 500 of them – which has been built on the facing hillside like a filing cabinet bolted on to a Hepplewhite wardrobe. If this is typical of Cornwall, I thought, please grant them independence soon.

The only Y available, Yeolmbridge, lies four miles to the north of this ghastly excrescence. Sadly, for the first time in the trip, the place I had selected as my destination proved to be so utterly dull that I could find no words for it. At least Tilbury had been thoroughly hideous; Yeolmbridge wasn't thoroughly anything. Indeed, it was almost nothing, a line of six or seven houses of vague ugliness along a stream. There, I managed to say something. But wait, what about the Thing Beginning With The Same Letter?

Very well . . . they do say that on cold winter nights the inhabitants of Yeolmbridge huddle together for warmth around the glowing Ferguson Nicam Stereo 28-inch FST satellite TV and watch Cilla with one ear cocked (each). A low bellowing rends the night, audible even above the howling gale, the lashing rain, Cilla's rendition of *Everything Is Beautiful*, and the tittering of the pixies behind the deep-freeze in the garage. Their faces turn as white as that old horse over Widecombe way. Can it be? There – it comes again, the Curse of this Corner of Cornwall, a beast able to smash down a wall of solid B & Q breezeblock with one flick of its clawed paw: the Treboddlecock, or Cornish Yeti. A shaggy, tall shape oft glimpsed 'neath the guttering moon on Bodmin Moor, the harsh snows of winter drive this eight-foot simian down to the peaceful valleys in search of sustenance. It preys, in the absence of pasties, on the weedy commuters who have invaded its primeval domain, eating anything in its path: Volvos, little lawn tractors, gnomes, white patio furniture, estate agents. By morning it has returned to its secret lair leaving only a trail of mangled skateboards and birdbaths. As the blood-red dawn comes up the survivors phone the Norwich Union and prepare for another day of family fun in the DIY stores of Plymouth.

ZENNOR

Zawn

For the last time, I hope, in my life I spent the night in the back of the van, there being no Yeolmbridge Hilton. It was one of the coldest nights of the journey, with a full moon and a hard frost. As soon as I had restored my circulation in the morning and without waiting to eat or to roll up my sleeping bags I set off towards Tintagel, planning to run down to Zennor along the north coast, and deciding that getting the car heater going was more important than breakfast if I wanted to live. Seven o'clock found me in Boscastle, built in a ravine, so that as you come round the hairpin bends you pass the lower windows of the front of a house and the upper windows at the back. It spreads in amazing fashion up what is virtually a cliff, with tall houses built wherever there is half a ledge to support them. Then Trethery, a warning of what was to come, a smattering of bungalows and caravans and hotels along a bleak, windswept headland. Bossiney was as bad, with the addition of signs everywhere for accommodation, gifts, souvenirs and 'Cream By Post'. Souvenirs of what? Grass?

To serious fans of Arthuriana, Tintagel is second only to Glastonbury in romance, and like that town is a disappointment, even on a jewel-clear morning before eight o'clock when there is nobody around but the gulls. The tradition that Arthur was born here appears only late in the cycle, in the French poetry, though perhaps derived from earlier Cornish stories brought over to Brittany by refugees from the Anglo-Saxon invasion. The Cornish, like the Bretons, the Welsh and the Scots, insist that Arthur was one of them, and the Tintagel story is a fixed point of most versions of the romances; the story of Uther Pendragon's rape of Igraine while disguised as her husband by Merlin's magic is too good a bit of saucy sorcery to omit. The village, not to put too fine a point on it, is a dump, but the remains of the great fortress which clung to the almost sea-encircled promontory are worth seeing, even though you have to put up with a shed nearby which advertises Cornish pasties made by 'a real old Cornish Biddy'. What subtle enhancement of the Celtic ambience.

When the castle was excavated it did prove to contain remains from the Arthurian era, alongside others from as far back as the Iron Age. It also housed a community of Irish monks for a time, who lived in stone huts like beehives. Most of what little remains today is late medieval, however. Below it, Merlin's Cave looks distinctly too damp for any baby to survive in for long. The castle is now owned by English Heritage (ironically, since Arthur fought the English tooth and nail) and was therefore closed at that early hour. Nevertheless, I climbed the steep and very treacherous steps to the gate and tried to summon up the Arthurian spirit as I sat on the topmost step. English Heritage's predilection for concrete, barbed wire and Yale locks, however, mitigates against any romantic daydreaming. Besides, it was bitterly cold.

On the way out you pass somewhere selling 'Cornish Rustic Slate' – as opposed, I presume, to Cornish Sophisticated Slate – and also the 'Home of the Pixies and Elves', a gnomery best left to the imagination. I suppose it is interesting that a Celtic legend of wraith-like sinister spirits who stole and sometimes ate children and lured people to the Underworld has been transformed into this array of fat little German dwarfs fishing and sitting on toadstools. Thankfully one cannot imagine Sneezy, Grumpy *et al.* inhabiting the Cornish landscape very successfully. Away from the safety of the begonias they would all too easily fall prey, I suspect, to their nasty Cornish ancestors, and good riddance.

In general the north Cornish coast is about as attractive as Middlesbrough, only less clean. The flattish pallid landscape is peppered with derelict industrial buildings, china-clay pits which spread white dust for miles and gimcrack bungalows and snack-bars. The simplicity of the landscape might once have been beautiful; but its very featurelessness means that the slightest intrusion turns what might be lovely emptiness into a dreary waste. If development had been organised responsibly this might not have happened even given the long industrial exploitation; it is the recent stuff which has done the most damage. But as at Launceston nobody seems to have given a toss. No doubt without it the local economy would be in ruins, but surely no amount of money is worth selling your birthright for a rash of flimsy little shacks called things like 'Pixi-Kot'?

Bored of these villages and the drab main road I abandoned the coast for a loop through the interior, but this was little better. Just after Wadebridge, for instance, is a pub which was probably once called something decent like The Stoatstrangler's Arms but is now Slade's House Country

Inn. If they have to call it a country inn, you can bet that that's exactly what it isn't. It is a roadhouse next to a housing estate.

I fancied that Washaway might live up to its lovely name – it did – and thereafter got happily lost in a maze of steep lanes, narrowly avoiding sundry unsuspecting rabbits, pheasants, a fox and a JCB. Luckily Blodwen has an Advanced Braking System – steering into the hedge. Ruthernbridge was an idyllic little place, only a handful of cottages, none of them called Biddinook, a chapel and an ancient bridge in a densely-wooded valley. Immediately afterwards you pass a collection of 'holiday cottages' (garden sheds with TV aerials), a garden so stuffed with gnomes that it probably contravenes the Health and Safety Act, a pick-up truck with cowhorns attached to the grill and a collection of American Army trucks in full battle order.

This bizarre cultural schizophrenia continues. Withiel is lovely, and then after joining a more major road – one actually wider than the van – you come upon the Frontier City American Theme Park. I'm not sure that the Alamo had slate dry-stone walls, but there you go. I found myself back on the main road after all, bypassed St Columb Major and went to Newquay, a bad mistake. Not me; it. It doesn't appear to have any houses, only hotels. The 'Koh-i-Noor', the 'Alpen Lodge' . . . evidently the place is popular with Swiss diamond merchants. It got worse. Perranporth looks like a Mexican border town. Allegedly it is a Mecca for surfers. I'm glad it's a Mecca for someone, but don't surfers have some pride? Aren't they supposed to care deeply for the natural environment? Apparently not . . . they care about fluorescent shorts, furry dice and Guns 'n' Roses.

Exasperated by 60 miles of unmitigated crap I decided to give the place one more chance before heading non-stop to the end of the alphabet. St Ives at least has something of a reputation among the great and good.

> As I was going to St Ives
> I met a man with seven wives.
> I asked, Why not just one or two?
> He said 'There's sod all else to do.'

The trenchant chauvinism of a hundred variations on this little ditty were belied en route by grafitti sprayed on to several footbridges spanning the dual carriageway. NO GULF WAR – read the first, followed shortly by WAR = MURDER. Hooray! There is civilisation in Cornwall yet.

St Ives seems unlikely to attract a new generation of avant-garde artists following in the footsteps of Nicholson and Hepworth, unless they are seriously into junk food. Nonetheless, it is easy to see what brought them here and keeps a few good and a great many deluded and untalented painters here still. The light is astonishingly brilliant, for a start; opalescent sunshine gives the effect of covering everything in a chalk-white wash. In fact everything is covered in gullshit, which streaks the buildings in a

Jackson Pollock-style frenzy of abstract excretion. If they could devise a way to make these ornaments multicoloured instead of green – the gulls here live on chips and burgers but it still turns green en route – the place could be a haven for chainsmoking people in black polo-necked sweaters. The worst thing about the town apart from the smell is that your shoulders ache from subconsciously walking around waiting for a pint of guano to hit your bald patch.

There are a number of 'galleries' in between the cholesterol parlours. I went into one. There were staid little watercolours of beached yachts and a plethora of quite alarmingly bad oil paintings of Alpine scenery which looked like the illustrations of the Late Jurassic Period you used to get in *Look and Learn*, a sort of dinosaur soup. Many of them were so highly personal that they looked like science-fiction jackets; Space Rangers of the Bernese Oberland. On the whole St Ives looked worse close up than it did from a distance. I couldn't decide whether it was basically attractive but spoiled or basically nasty with compensations. I didn't much care by then and I don't suppose you do either.

Beyond St Ives the scenery finally came good. Unfortunately I only had six miles to go, but they were six miles of gripping stuff. Instead of being bleak and windswept and flat it becomes bleak and windswept and hilly *and* covered in gigantic boulders. Most of Cornwall had been dreary, but not dreary enough to be interesting. The last ten minutes were wonderfully, spectacularly dreary. Young Werther would have felt right at home there. I had expected that Cornish nationalism, like the Welsh and Scottish varieties, was at least partially inspired by a love of the landscape, but this cannot be the case, since anyone who loves the Cornish landscape must be blind or mad, or both.

Zennor runs along a single track which turns off the coast road at the bottom of a steep hill in a wide, green, shallow valley strewn with rocks and filled with the smell and noise of the Atlantic beyond: in fact it is almost exactly like Armadale in Sutherland. The sense of ending where I had begun was powerful, but momentary. Zennor's squat little church tower could never be Scottish, nor could its dedication, to St Senara (who?). There is also a pub, The Tinkers' Arms, which Armadale could definitely use. I celebrated my arrival with a half of bitter and a cigar which had dried out in the glove compartment and tasted like camel dung. Then, diligent to the last, I went in search of the low-down.

I found it in the Zennor Wayside Museum, a delightful collection of odds and sods from the past hundred years or more of Cornish agriculture and mining, all crammed into a small cottage and a couple of sheds and lovingly labelled and explained in biro. Sadly, after 55 years, it is up for sale due to rising costs. I hope whoever buys it doesn't alter a thing; as a last resort it should be publicly funded, but this would doubtless destroy its cheerful amateurism . . . and I mean that as a compliment, because it is easily the most informative local museum, and the least patronising, I have ever seen. I said as much to the proprietor, and asked him, with suitable explanation, if he had anything beginning with Z. He did not, but he fetched an Ordnance Survey map and pointed to a crinkle on the coast: Zennor Zawn. 'You can't miss it,' he said, 'it's a blooming great chasm in the rocks.' And so it proved. A zawn is a very narrow cleft between two slices of rock, or one slice and the cliff it has sheered off from, in which smugglers and other naughty people hid their booty from the prying eyes of the Excise. I walked out on to Zennor Head, struggling to keep my footing in the wind. It was late on the thirty-second day of my journey and I was not in the peak of physical condition. Also the half of bitter on an empty stomach had gone to my head, not to mention the camel dung fumes. Heroically, I scrambled out, mostly on all fours, and peered over the edge of the cliff, remembering just in time to take off my glasses. Down in the zawn the sea muttered like a crabby old man, if you'll forgive the pun. D. H. Lawrence and Virginia Woolf had both wandered over this headland, though not together as far as I know. Being stuck out here with D. H. Lawrence might explain a lot of Ginny's behaviour, come to think of it.

Lawrence wrote *Women in Love* in Zennor; Woolf wrote letters to Vita and revelled in the barbarism of it all. Now the artist Patrick Heron lives there, and someone whose name I forget wrote his Cornish Symphony in the upstairs room of the museum. It is easy to see why these people came; the landscape is a tortured, haunted combination of dream and nightmare, flowers and cottages mingled with twisted rocks and thorns deformed by the shrieking wind.

'When we came over the shoulder of the wild hill above the sea, to Zennor,' wrote Lawrence to Lady Ottoline Morrell in 1916, 'I felt we were coming into the Promised Land. I know there will be a new heaven and a new earth take place now; we have triumphed. I feel like a Columbus who can see a shadowy America before him: only this isn't merely territory, it's a new continent of the soul.'

Later, to Katherine Mansfield, he wrote, 'This is the best place I have been in, I think.'

I walked out towards the end of the headland. I felt as if I had discovered not a new continent but the edge of the flat earth.

At the end of the headland I sat down behind a huge boulder out of the wind, which hooted musically through a hole above my head. Bluebells were flowering around my feet, and gorse like an explosion of custard, and other flowers pink and white. Far below, the sea was slate-blue; the cliffs toward Land's End black. The horizon was lost in pearly mist; the sun shone weakly and despite the wind the water in the cove below was almost unwrinkled. The surface of the sea appeared to be at an odd angle, as if in a badly-taken photograph.

I considered, and quickly rejected, the idea of going on to Land's End.

250

It would only be a disappointment. I had my own Land's End. I waited to see if anything would happen within or outside me. I smoked a cigarette, grew cold. The sun faded and the sea-fog thickened menacingly. Nothing did happen, which was as it should be.

It was an end which was not an end; I had to gather one final reserve of energy for the long haul back to Scotland. Perhaps, I thought, that explains the curious sensation of not yet being at rest, of still wanting to move, despite the rock I am sitting on, the rock I had always intended to sit on and gaze out at nothing. Or perhaps it is my feeling of not having found what I had been looking for, whatever that might have been. It's a dreadful cliché, I know, this vague expectation of revelation. I had done a lot of looking but precious little seeing. America was discovered accidentally, after all, by a man who was looking for something else entirely, and who only had the word of a mad scientist that he wasn't going to fall over the edge into oblivion. I had been looking for something else, too. Equally hackneyed was the obvious answer, that whatever I had been seeking was inside myself. Hackneyed, true, and unsatisfactory.

It had not been the journey I had expected to make, and I was not sure that had I the chance to begin it again I would accept the challenge. It had been anxious, hurried, unsatisfying; fulfilling only in the lesser sense that I had accomplished the physical task I had set myself. The spiritual element had faded and died somewhere along the road, unable to survive the pace. My observations en route seemed skeletal, fleshless – my notes from the last couple of weeks had often been little more than cursory. I felt that the trip in the end had had little more point than driving round and round a racetrack. Three thousand, three hundred and twenty-five miles had left me with an unslaked *wanderlust*, a thirst for a journey of leisure and contemplation and learning. The effect had been exhilarating at times but also stupefying, debilitating . . . still, it was done. Perhaps in retrospect I would see it differently. I sat for a long time listening to the stones sing, then I walked back along the headland and down the village street without stopping until I reached the car, where I made myself a cup of tea, wiped the steam from the windows, and drove home.

Later I realised that in essence I had been looking for an answer to an unspoken question: why do I like this country? Damn, now I'll have to go back and look again.

POSTSCRIPT

This book was written between 2 May and 12 August 1991 directly from my notes on to the typewriter with almost no revisions or re-writing, on days off from work, in the evenings and at weekends. Thus the narrative mirrors the journey itself in that it was made too fast for mature reflection. This haste accounts for its extremely simple structure and, probably, a great many factual errors and ill-considered judgments, for which I apologise.

Far from crystallising in my memory as I had hoped, the journey has faded rapidly, particularly the second half, which was very largely an unenjoyable experience in which perception was dulled by fatigue. But I hope that at least some of the book is valid and worthwhile, not least because if it succeeds in raising even a little money for the British Dyslexia Association, people who might never have read it may as a result be able to make their own judgments upon it.

Blodwen was unfazed by the experience and continued to ferry my family about with equanimity until the beginning of August, when her MOT was due. It was apparent that the damage to her suspension would be too severe for this examination and she is currently garaged. Her future is uncertain, and in the meantime her duties have been taken over by an efficient, quiet, fast, comfortable and very dull Japanese hatchback.

Newburgh, Fife
August 1991